Narrative of the Life of Frederick Douglass, an American Slave, Written by Himself

Frederick Douglass

Narrative of the Life of Frederick Douglass, an American Slave, Written by Himself

Critical Edition

John R. McKivigan
Peter P. Hinks
Heather L. Kaufman
EDITORS

Gerald L. Fulkerson
TEXTUAL EDITOR

Rebecca A. Pattillo
ASSISTANT EDITOR

Kate Burzlaff, Alex Smith, and Andrew Willey
RESEARCH ASSISTANTS

Yale UNIVERSITY PRESS
New Haven and London

Facing the title page: Frontispiece of 1845 edition of *Narrative of the Life of Frederick Douglass, an American Slave, Written by Himself* (Boston: Published at the Anti-Slavery Office, 1845). Wesleyan University Library, Special Collections and Archives.

First edition 2001. Critical edition 2016.

This edition is based on *The Frederick Douglass Papers,* Series Two: *Autobiographical Writings,* Volume 1: *Narrative,* ed. John W. Blassingame, John R. McKivigan, and Peter P. Hinks (New Haven: Yale University Press, 1999), published with assistance from the National Historical Publications and Records Commission.

Yale University Press books may be purchased in quantity for educational, business, or promotional use. For information, please e-mail sales.press@yale.edu (U.S. office) or sales@yaleup.co.uk (U.K. office).

Set in Minion type by Integrated Publishing Solutions. Printed in the United States of America.

Library of Congress Control Number: 2016935415
ISBN 978-0-300-20471-1 (pbk. : alk. paper)

A catalogue record for this book is available from the British Library.

This paper meets the requirements of ANSI/NISO Z39.48–1992 (Permanence of Paper).

10 9 8 7 6 5 4 3 2 1

The text of the *Narrative* in this volume follows an approved CSE edition published by Yale University Press in 1999, which included a complete textual apparatus in accordance with CSE guidelines.

Contents

❁❁❁

Preface

❁❁❁

When approached by Yale University Press to prepare a new paperback edition of the *Narrative of the Life of Frederick Douglass, an American Slave,* we were challenged to prepare a volume superior to the edition the Frederick Douglass Papers project produced in 2001 under the direction of the late John W. Blassingame. That volume has sold well in a highly competitive marketplace containing many other modern editions of this iconic work of African American history and literature. Two editors of this current volume worked with Blassingame on the 2001 edition and, aware of its unique attributes, were determined to retain them while finding other ways to make the volume even more valuable for potential readers. The current edition of Douglass's seminal narrative builds on the strengths of the original edition while making it more accessible to today's students and general readers.

A considerable asset of the 2001 edition is its central text. The staff of the Frederick Douglass Papers painstakingly determined Douglass's words as he had originally constructed them, free of both the intentional "corrections" introduced by copy editors and accidental "corruptions" caused by typesetters in every subsequent printing since Douglass's day. By adhering to the strictest professional editing standards, the Yale edition of the *Narrative* is the only one available to modern readers that carries the prestigious "Approved Text" imprimatur of the Modern Language Association's Committee on Scholarly Editing. The text has been reprinted without change in the new edition.

The new Yale edition retains the original 2001 introduction written by the founding editor of the Frederick Douglass Papers, John W. Blassingame. Blassingame was the preeminent historian of the slave narrative genre at the time of his death in 2000. His posthumously published introduction explicates how Douglass's autobiography became the most historically influential of these slave narratives. His introduction illuminates both the abolitionist ideology and the literary canons that guided Douglass in framing his life story as an antislavery weapon. In particular, Blassingame demonstrates Douglass's attention to the accuracy of every detail to describe the conditions that he and his fellow slaves endured. For the new edition, we decided not to alter this classic essay (other than to make a few minor stylistic variations and update the notes) but instead to supplement it with a new afterword. There we introduce more modern scholarship on the *Narrative* and discuss its enduring popularity and its influence on the modern-day appreciation of the slave experience.

This edition also includes an enhanced selection of documents, to which we supply brief introductions. A set of historical documents presents socioeconomic and intellectual forces that shaped and influenced Douglass's life and provides an overview of the institution of slavery in the Chesapeake Bay region and beyond as the drama over slavery intensified. Several documents describe the establishment and evolution of human bondage in Maryland. Other documents illustrate the growing debate both locally and nationally over the morality of treating human beings as property. Douglass's own growing antagonism toward his slave status may well have been shaped by reading some of the reproduced documents, including a speech excerpt found in Caleb Bingham's famous primer, *The Columbian Orator,* and newspaper accounts of slave rebellions and early abolitionist activities. Also reproduced is a short example of Douglass's oratorical contribution to the New England abolitionist movement in the years before the publication of the *Narrative.*

Another set of documents provides contemporary comments on the accuracy of the *Narrative* and on its reception in the North and the South. No previous slave narrative had generated a critical reception approaching that accorded Douglass's. Blassingame's comprehensive review of this reception demonstrates how Douglass rehabilitated the vital moral force of the slave narrative. Here we reproduce some of the most illuminating of those reviews as well as one of Douglass's replies to his critics.

To help readers comprehend the *Narrative*'s place in African American literature and history, this new edition also includes a final set of documents: excerpts from several key scholarly studies. These are contextualized in the afterword and augmented by a bibliography of modern titles on Douglass, his autobiography, and the testimony of American slaves on the "peculiar institution" of slavery. We have supplied introductory comments for all the selections.

For this edition we kept the historical annotations to the *Narrative* that help modern readers assess Douglass's accuracy in depicting Maryland. These annotations identify the dozens of individuals, black and white, ordinary and famous, whom Douglass names. They also detail most of the events, both well-known and obscure, mentioned in the *Narrative*. They identify the original sources for numerous quotations and allusions in his book. To enhance the accessibility of these annotations, we have shortened and refined some of them, eliminated most source citations, and added new notes to define unfamiliar nineteenth-century terminology. A chronology and a set of genealogies provide further background.

By retaining the best attributes of the original 2001 edition, while reinforcing them with updated scholarship to further the readers' appreciation of Douglass's and the slaves' world, we present our audience with the most broadly useful volume available of Frederick Douglass's classic *Narrative*.

John R. McKivigan
Peter P. Hinks
Heather L. Kaufman

Introduction

John W. Blassingame

Frederick Douglass's antebellum reputation as a writer rests firmly on the autobiography he published when he was twenty-seven years old. At first glance, Douglass's incomparable literary success is inexplicable. During the two decades he spent as a Maryland slave, for example, Douglass displayed few of the talents that would mark his later literary career. Indeed, one observer who knew Douglass during the years he spent in bondage recalled that he was "an unlearned, and rather ordinary negro." However ordinary Douglass appeared as a slave, he had become an extraordinary man by 1845, seven years after his escape from bondage. If not yet learned, Douglass was at least highly literate by 1845.[1]

In typical nineteenth-century fashion, Douglass was fond of referring to his autobiography in self-effacing terms. Speaking of his *Narrative* in 1845, for instance, he asserted that "a person undertaking to write a book without learning will appear rather novel, but such as it was I gave it to the public."[2] Like many authors, Douglass did not often reflect on or clearly elucidate the nature of his "learning" or the various literary influences bearing upon his writing. Nevertheless, it is obvious that when Douglass began writing his autobiography in the winter of 1844–45, he understood the conventions and literary canons that applied to the genre.[3]

The manifold influences bearing upon Douglass's autobiography included antebellum literary criticism, previously published black and white slave narratives, his knowledge of other autobiographical writings, and several events that took place between 1838 and 1845. Many of the conventions followed by Douglass were similar to those of other nineteenth-century American and English autobiographers, black and white. The similarities between black and white autobiographers were most evident in the narratives of those who had been enslaved or captured by Indians in the Americas or of white Europeans and Americans who were shipwrecked and enslaved in Africa.[4]

Because antebellum Americans frowned upon the reading of novels, they avidly read personal accounts of shipwrecks, slavery, and Indian captivities that had all of the characteristics of romanticized adventures. Between 1682 and 1860, for instance, some Indian captivity narratives went through as many as forty-one editions. Among the earliest forms of American literature, these narratives expressed the religious sentiment of the age, employed biblical allusions extensively, exemplified the redemptive power of suffering, and illustrated divine providence. Authors stressed the didactic purposes served by their accounts. Frequently serialized in nineteenth-century newspapers and magazines, the narratives had become stylized, sentimental, melodramatic, and sensational tales containing exaggerated accounts of the barbarities, tortures, and manifold horrors suffered by the captives. Journalists fabricated many nineteenth-century accounts, and true stories had to compete with fiction parading as truth.[5]

Perhaps the clearest indication of the merging of black and white autobiographical traditions at an early point in American literary history is that some of the first black autobiographies were also, in part, Indian captivity narratives. Among the African American autobiographers to detail their captivity by and deliverance from Indians were Briton Hammon and John Marrant in *A Narrative of the Uncommon Sufferings and Surprising Deliverance of Briton Hammon, a Negro Man* (1760) and *A Narrative of the Lord's Wonderful Dealings with John Marrant, a Black, Taken Down from His Own Relation* (1785).

A group of powerful literary critics in the United States and the United Kingdom shaped the nineteenth-century autobiographical convention followed by Douglass and other authors. One of the most influential of these critics was an Englishman, the Reverend John Foster, a prolific and popular essayist. An ardent republican, Foster wrote widely on theological and biographical subjects and contributed 184 articles to the *Eclectic Review* between 1806 and 1839. Among the most frequently reprinted of Foster's works was the 1805 collection of his early essays. The book, appearing in several American editions between 1807 and 1845, contained Foster's twenty-one-page essay "On a Man's Writing Memoirs of Himself," which played a primary role in establishing the conventions of English and American autobiography.[6]

Concerned in most of his numerous essays with the formation and evidence of character, Foster drew a distinction between the exterior and the interior of a person's life. He admired "simple conviction" and despised "the sly deceit of self-love" and the "self-describers who . . . think the publication of their vices necessary to crown their fame." As much as he disliked the "confessions" of courtesans, debauchees, drunkards, and criminals, Foster delighted in accounts tracing the various stages that marked an individual's moral, spiritual, and intellectual progress. Above all, he viewed the end of autobiography to be self-understanding, a way for a person "to acquire a complete knowledge of himself" and the course of his growth. It was, of course, axiomatic that a person's self-history differed significantly according to the stage at which it was written, since "in the course of a long life a man may be several moral persons." Recognition of moral, religious, and intellectual advancement and retrogression was essential, according to Foster, because of the lessons they provided and because they constituted a record to compare "with the standard of perfection." Conscience required that there be explicit admission of delinquencies to cultivate humility and diminish vanity and "self-love."[7]

Realizing how difficult it was for people to parade their errors, Foster returned again and again in his essay to the distinction between inner and outer character. Inner character he considered more important because an attempt to represent it exposed one to the powerful temptation to be dishonest. Without a truthful recounting of this hidden compartment, autobiography would lose much of its power for self-instruction. Foster also felt that dishonesty in this area would make an autobiography less interesting or capable of eliciting sympathy from readers. Truth, history, and divinity met as the autobiographer struggled to reveal his or her inner character:

> Each mind has an interior apartment of its own, into which none but itself and the Divinity can enter. In this secluded place, the passions mingle and fluctuate in unknown agitations. Here all the fantastic and all the tragic shapes of imagination have a haunt, where they can neither be invaded nor descried. . . . Here projects, convictions, vows, are confusedly scattered, and the records of past life are laid. Here in solitary state sits Conscience, surrounded by her own thunders, which sometimes sleep, and sometimes roar, while the world does not know. . . . If, in a man's own account of himself, written on the supposition of being seen by any other person, the substance of the secrets of this apartment be brought forth, he throws open the last asylum of his

character. . . . And if it be not brought forth, where is the integrity or value of the history . . . ?[8]

Although actually offering little advice about how to structure autobiography, his few remarks nevertheless resonated through hundreds of prefaces, reviews, and critical essays for the next century. Again and again the critics upheld his singular directive that "the *style* should be as simple as possible."[9]

The critics who followed Foster exhibited far more interest in the readers than the writers of autobiographies. In contrast to Foster, they stressed the autobiography's power to acquaint the reader with human virtues as well as to furnish relaxation and entertainment. Many critics contended that the chief value of the autobiography was that it was a historical document. Through autobiographies—especially those of public figures—readers could see behind the public facades of great figures and learn in detail from the events and influences that shaped their characters.[10]

Writing for an increasingly literate society, American critics valued autobiographies as instructive books for the education of youth. It was infinitely better, they contended, for youths to read autobiographies than novels. Because autobiographers sketched their lives from childhood to their attainment of eminence and stressed "the cultivation of intellectual and moral power," they could provide lessons, examples, and inspirations to the young.[11]

But what was of special concern to antebellum critics was the credibility of any autobiography. Detailing the factors that limited credibility (senility, egotism, and vanity), the critics tried to develop a series of tests to determine where it existed. As critics became more familiar with the genre, they became more confident of their ability to determine the veracity of autobiographies. By concentrating on the patterns of revelation and concealment in a work, the critics believed that they could uncover an author's true self-portrait. A *New York Review* critic, for instance, writing in October 1838, insisted that by a close reading of an autobiography, one could determine whether it was true because "in autobiography we study character in two modes at once. We have, first, what the individual *says* of himself, and secondly, the *unconscious* revelation which he makes of himself as narrator; the picture in the glass, and the real man seen behind it."[12]

A number of critics drew upon their own experience or sought the proof of the credibility of an autobiography in its narrative technique. Frequently they combined the two tests. A *North American Review* critic, for example, argued in 1844 that the most believable autobiographies were those in which minuteness of detail was a salient feature: "Minuteness of narration, whether in fiction or in real life, has a singular charm for all readers. . . . Now, the *only* truth is the *whole* truth. The complete portrait is the only faithful portrait. The only true history or biography is that which tells all." For most readers the credibility of such accounts would be "attested by our experience, which necessarily comprehends the whole of our own thoughts, motives and actions." The "vast edifice" of a life had to be portrayed because the "piecemeal exhibition of another's life finds no counterpart in our own memories, which embrace every incident in our own career."[13]

Much of what critics thought was likely to be incredible about autobiographies was, they contended, inherent in the genre. Since an autobiography involved revelations about the frequently inaccessible interior of life, it often raised unanswerable questions about credibility. The personal secrets of the autobiographer represented what most critics believed constituted the most instructive aspect of his or her self-portrait—thoughts, feelings, imaginations, motives. Critics longed to see what they described as the autobiographer's "thoughts and feelings in their nakedness . . . his envy, jealousy, malice, and uncharitableness." They wanted to read the works of autobiographers willing to risk notoriety and "lay open to the world the deepest and darkest nooks of their own hearts, however ugly and loathsome may be the things which dwell therein." True histories of the inner person would always be rare, however, the critics argued, because most autobiographers lacked the necessary discrimination, analytical skills, sincerity, and self-knowledge to write them. A *New England Magazine* writer sadly concluded in 1834, we "know our enemies better than ourselves, because we judge them with more severity; we can write better lives of them than memoirs of ourselves."[14]

Yet they also imposed limits on such exposure. Self-revelation must not be a promiscuous exercise intended merely to shock and arouse the audience but must promote a moral life and show an eventual turning away from things bad even as they are described in detail.

Nevertheless, the author must have a proper and unavoidable dose of egotism. Many of the critics argued that egotism naturally determined both the focus and the design of life histories. Reviewing Johann Wolfgang von Goethe's autobiography in October 1838, a *New York Review* critic professed that in autobiography "if the author is himself the central point around which all seems to revolve, this is in conformity with the idea of an autobiography, and is necessary to unity of design . . . egotism is the very thing to be desired in such a work."[15]

Following Foster's injunctions, critics also expressed a desire for a "simple" style in autobiographies. Increasingly, critics translated "simple" into "appropriate," a variable standard dependent on the times, the incidents, and the lives being described. What was, under this standard, misplaced ornamentation in one author would be appropriate in another. Critics expected an autobiographer to demonstrate lucidity, modesty, honesty, and economy. Repeatedly, critics praised those self-portraits that were "plain, unaffected" narratives marked by unity of design and artful symmetry. Especially ornate language suggested that the author was insincere.[16]

Many American critics identified Benjamin Franklin as the model autobiographer because of the clarity and economy of his writing. A *North American Review* evaluation of Benjamin Franklin's autobiographical writings in 1818 varied little from the positive assessments of numerous other critics. In spite of "some trifling blemishes," Franklin's work was "always admirable for its precision and perspicuity. It is as transparent as the atmosphere; and his thoughts lie before us like objects seen in one of our finest and clearest days, when their very brightness and distinctness alone give us pleasure."[17]

In the 1830s Douglass first encountered Franklin indirectly in Caleb Bingham's *Columbian Orator.* In his primer, Bingham reprinted Abbé Fauchet's 1790 eulogy of Benjamin Franklin. Fauchet praised Franklin for having "presented new and sublime ideas, in a style simple as truth, and as pure as light." Further he contended that Franklin "laid the sacred foundations of social morality. . . . This amiable moralist descended, in his writings, to the most artless details; to the most ingenuous familiarities; to the first ideas of a rural, a commercial, and a civil life; to the dialogues of old men and children; full at once of all the verdure and all the maturity of wisdom." Fauchet stamped the essentials of antebellum American autobiography in his paean to Franklin and assuredly made his impress upon the young Douglass as well.[18]

Although *The Columbian Orator* was Douglass's key textbook during the time of his enslavement in Maryland, his central texts once he escaped from slavery were abolitionist newspapers, magazines, books, and pamphlets and slave narratives. Such works greatly expanded his knowledge of autobiographies. In abolition sources alone, Douglass read dozens of narratives of fugitive slaves before he sat down to write his autobiography in 1844.

Between 1838 and 1844 Douglass avidly read such antislavery publications as the *Liberator, National Anti-Slavery Standard, Liberty Bell, Emancipator, Anti-Slavery Almanac,* and *American and Foreign Anti-Slavery Reporter* that contained speeches, interviews, and autobiographies of dozens of fugitive slaves including Lunsford Lane, James Curry, Lewis Clarke, and the *Amistad* rebels. Equally significant, the abolition newspapers and magazines published reviews of the autobiographies of blacks and whites and furnished Douglass with further advice on the elements of the proper autobiography. At a very early period, Douglass also came to know the "slave's biographer," Isaac T. Hopper, who published a long-running popular column of slave narratives in the *National Anti-Slavery Standard* under the heading "Tales of Oppression."[19]

Another source of information about the autobiographical canon that Douglass read repeatedly was Theodore Dwight Weld's *American Slavery as It Is.* Douglass quoted frequently from Weld's work in the speeches he gave between 1841 and 1845. Indeed, *American Slavery as It Is* long represented for Douglass the standard by which to measure all statements about the character of America's "peculiar institution." The book was, Douglass wrote in 1853, the "repository of human horrors."[20]

Douglass relied so extensively on personal narratives in *American Slavery as It Is* that they undoubtedly formed the structure, focus, and style of his *Narrative.* He learned, for instance, that most of the accounts that Weld published followed letters vouching for the author's integrity and veracity. Weld himself repeatedly stressed the importance of a truthful portrayal of slavery, urged witnesses to "'speak what they know, and testify what they have seen,'" and commanded them to demonstrate a "fidelity to truth." Conscious of the incredulity of his northern readers, Weld insisted on making a clear distinction between opinion and fact: "Testimony respects matters of *fact,* not matters of opinion: it is the declaration of a witness as to *facts,* not the giving of an opinion as to the nature or qualities of actions, or the *character* of a course of conduct."[21]

American Slavery as It Is may also have played a crucial role in Douglass's original decision to write and publish his *Narrative.* Significantly, in a prefatory "Note" to his book, Weld announced that the American Anti-Slavery Society intended to publish other "TRACTS, containing well authenticated facts, testimony, personal narratives, etc. fully setting forth the *condition* of American slaves." Each prospective author unknown to the Executive Committee of the Society had to furnish references. Weld specified exactly the kinds of narratives in which the society had an interest:

> Facts and testimony respecting the condition of slaves, in *all respects*, are desired; their food, (kinds, quality, quantity), clothing, lodging, dwellings, hours of labor and rest, kinds of labor, with the mode of exaction, supervision, &c.—the number and times of meals each day, treatment when sick, regulations respecting their social intercourse, marriage and domestic ties, the system of torture to which they are subjected, with its various modes; and *in detail*, their *intellectual* and *moral* condition. Great care should be observed in the statement of facts. Well-weighed testimony and well-authenticated facts, with a responsible name, the Committee earnestly desire and call for.[22]

Given this note, it is probably no accident that the publisher Douglass chose for his first autobiography was the American Anti-Slavery Society and that he found two people, William Lloyd Garrison and Wendell Phillips, "personally known" to its executive committee to write prefatory notes to his *Narrative.*

Although the other autobiographical works Douglass read were probably somewhat less influential than *American Slavery as It Is,* they were no less significant. The most salient features of the slave narratives he read in the abolition press were their brevity, directness, simplicity, and lack of specificity. Often editors prefaced the accounts with declarations that publication had been delayed until the fugitive had reached Canada. Editors of the accounts of fugitives who remained in the United States frequently tried to guarantee their anonymity by giving them fictional names, deleting specific references to their masters and places of enslavement, or citing initials for all personal and place names that might possibly serve as keys to the real identity of the narrator. While helping to insure the safety of the fugitive, such practices, the amanuenses realized, seriously undermined the credibility of the accounts. In many cases, however, the guarantee of anonymity was the sine qua non for obtaining accounts from frightened fugitives.[23]

Significantly, Douglass had some of his first exposures to the narratives of fugitive slaves in oral rather than written form at the home of the most prolific of the slaves' amanuenses, Isaac T. Hopper. Reflecting in 1853 on his introduction to Hopper, Douglass asserted that he first saw him in September 1838 when Hopper was a witness in a fugitive slave case. In a review of Lydia Maria Child's biography of Hopper, Douglass discussed his "intimate acquaintance with the venerable, Quakerly gentleman" and his visits to Hopper's home in the early 1840s, where he "listened to some of the admirable stories and adventures in the matter of rescuing fugitives."[24]

Possessing a nearly photographic memory and being totally fearless, Hopper aided hundreds of fugitive slaves, first in Philadelphia and later in New York. Recording the minutest details from the tales of fugitives, Hopper published about sixty of the stories in his "Tales of Oppression" column in the *Standard.* Occasionally, when introducing these narratives, Hopper explained the techniques he employed and taught Douglass much about the art of autobiography.[25]

What impressed critics were "unvarnished" stories of the slaves' lives filled with "unstudied pathos" and "touching" incidents that only an actual observer could describe. Credibility and plainness were everything.[26]

Thus when the scandal over the narratives of Archy Moore and James Williams broke in the late 1830s, the continuing viability of the slave autobiographies was threatened. Published anonymously in 1836, the *Memoirs of Archy Moore* produced disarray among the abolitionists when southerners protested that it was fictional. Reviewers—uncertain about the work's reliability—wavered between describing it as the factual account of a slave and a fictional work. In 1837, however, a historian and abolitionist, Richard Hildreth, admitted that he had created the narrative and disguised it as genuine autobiography. Deeply embarrassed by this affair, the antislavery societies had to rescue this critical tool in their crusade from the refuse pile to which the slaveholders wanted permanently to consign it.[27]

There could not have been a worse time, then, for another crisis of credibility to arise as it did in 1838 with the *Narrative of James Williams,* published by the Massachusetts Anti-Slavery Society and edited by John Greenleaf Whittier. Abolitionists spent much of 1838 countering the attacks on Williams's story. The most systematic defense came from the pen of "Memento." Reminding *Liberator* readers of the general skepticism of Whittier, "Memento" noted that former slaveholder James Birney of Alabama confirmed Williams's characterization of slave life in that state, praised the account of valuable "documentary evidence," and concluded that it was "incontrovertibly true; and is additionally valuable, because it so powerfully corroborates other evidence and facts which have been published."

Because it was "incontrovertibly true," the publication of Williams's story should be followed, "Memento" contended, by a flood of similar ones: "a few more such personal narratives as the life and experience of James Williams will render the boasted 'Southern domestic institutions' as loathsome, as they are cruelly malignant and criminal." What was most significant in the defense was a clear elaboration of the general credibility problem facing all abolitionist writers:

> Amid the strange characteristics of mankind, no one of their moral features is more unaccountable than their complex credulity in some cases, and in others, their marvelous unbelief. This general position is illustrated in an astonishing manner, upon the subject of slavery. It seems as if our northern citizens had determined to resist all evidence respecting the practical concerns of slaveholding, until they are ocularly convinced; while they have resolved never to witness *Life in the Negro Quarters.* It is yet more perplexing, that many of our anti-slavery friends are incredulous respecting the facts which are stated by professed eye-witnesses, and the few competent narrators of slavery as it exists in our country. Thus the only citizens, who personally know what slavery is from their own observation, and who are sufficiently independent to disclose the truth, are not only disbelieved, but are also suspected of untruth, or reproached with falsehood, by the silly retort—"I will not believe it; it cannot be true."[28]

In spite of the complaints and defense of people like "Memento," the Executive Committee of the Massachusetts Anti-Slavery Society eventually had to consider the possibility that Williams had fabricated his story. The committee checked many of the personal and place names mentioned in Williams's account with knowledgeable southerners who almost universally disputed his claims. After its investigation, the committee published a full retraction in November 1838 in which it came "fully to the conclusion,—that the statements of the narrative . . . are wholly false" and withdrew the book from sale. The Williams debacle forced all abolitionist amanuenses to be more cautious, to state whether they were using real or fictitious personal and place names, and to search systematically for corroborating evidence and authenticating testimony for the oral accounts of fugitive slaves. Williams haunted Theodore Weld; he sought to exorcise fraudulent statements from the eyewitness accounts he published in *American Slavery as It Is*. The import of this crisis could not have been lost on Douglass.[29]

Many of Douglass's views of the purpose and structure of autobiographies were those traditionally expressed by black authors since the eighteenth century. Antebellum black authors were well aware of contemporary autobiographical canons and especially the didactic purposes served by such works. Like their white contemporaries, black autobiographers often reflected on the genre and frequently explained their motives for writing in their prefaces and introductions. For example, Olaudah Equiano began his narrative of 1789 by acknowledging that it was "a little hazardous in a private and obscure individual" to publish his memoirs, establish the credibility of his account, and "escape the imputation of vanity." Significantly, the "preface" to Equiano's narrative consisted of his open letter to the British Parliament petitioning for the abolition of the African slave trade and presenting his narrative as the evidence he hoped would convince the members to answer his prayer.[30]

The sentiments expressed in Equiano's open letter would resonate in all of the autobiographies written by antebellum African Americans. Antebellum black autobiographers consistently asserted that the chief reason for portraying their lives was the need to bear witness against slavery, to wake their fellow Americans to its evil, and to cheer those on who labored in the cause of human freedom. Truth, the antebellum black autobiographers contended, would expose the evil of slavery and contribute to its destruction. Interestingly, American whites formerly enslaved in Africa wrote autobiographies with the same didactic purposes and expectations in mind. Although the experiences of white authors formerly enslaved or held captive were recorded in published reminiscences, the autobiographical writings of black slaves grew out of their own lectures. Once published, the autobiography led to more frequent trips to the lectern as the black's *written* and *spoken* voice moved in easy tandem.[31]

Moses Roper, a former North Carolina slave, illustrated many of the conventions of black autobiographies in his "Introduction" to the successive editions of his *Narrative of the Adventures and Escape of Moses Roper, from American Slavery.* In the first edition, published in the United States in 1838, Roper declared that he wrote his autobiography "with the view of exposing the cruel system of slavery" and with the hope that it would become "the instruments of opening the eyes of the ignorant to this system; of convincing the wicked, cruel, and hardened slave-holder; and of befriending generally the cause of oppressed humanity." His decision to publish his life story, Roper assured his readers, "did not arise from any desire to make myself conspicuous." Roper was conscious not only of the possible imputation of vanity to an autobiographer but also of the conventional rules for determining the credibility of such stories. After Thomas Price, the editor of the volume, had quoted from the letters of introduction written by American abolitionists that Roper brought to England and noted the narrative's "internal evidence of truth," the former slave confronted directly the possibility that many readers might feel that his account was "somewhat at variance with the dictates of humanity." Roper assured his readers that he did not present facts "unsubstantiated by collateral evidence, nor highly colored to the disadvantage of cruel task-masters." Finally, Roper observed that his master and other slaveholders would have an opportunity to read and contradict any aspect of his autobiography.[32]

Usually, autobiographers present their views of the genre in the prefaces of their life stories. Unfortunately, during the antebellum period autobiographers often had friends and acquaintances write prefaces, and Douglass followed this route in 1845. Only later in his speeches did Douglass publicly explain why he had written his autobiography. Essentially, Douglass contended, he wrote the autobiography to authenticate his antislavery speeches—and thus his voice. Douglass delivered a typical exposition of this theme in his speech of 18 May 1846 in London in which he pointed out that after delivering antislavery lectures for four years

> my manner was such as to create a suspicion that I was not a runaway slave, but some educated free negro, whom the abolitionists had sent forth to attract attention to what was called there a faltering cause. They said, he appears to have no fear of white people. How can he ever have been in bondage? But one strong reason for this doubt was, the

> fact that I never made known to the people to whom I spoke where I came from. . . . But it became necessary to set myself right before the public in the United States, and to reveal the whole facts of my case. I did not feel it safe to do so till last spring, when I was solicited to it by a number of anti-slavery friends, who assured me that it would be safe to do so. I then published a narrative of my experience in slavery, in which I detailed the cruelties of it as I had myself felt them.[33]

Douglass knew well that perhaps the central problem he faced was to establish his credibility. To do so, he adopted several strategies. First, he placed a daguerreotype of himself as the book's frontispiece and signed his name below it. Before the reader had even begun the *Narrative,* they had seen a reproduction of the author and of his handwriting, evidence of his literacy. Next he preceded his text with letters from William Lloyd Garrison and Wendell Phillips, who served as witnesses to his veracity. Finally, in the text of the *Narrative* Douglass used real names when referring to people and places and described how he came to know Garrison and Phillips.[34]

The letters of Garrison and Phillips afforded powerful confirmation of Douglass's "many sufferings" and his several attainments. Acknowledging the popular misconception that slavery in Maryland was less severe than in the Deep South, Garrison proclaimed that Douglass's lived experience belied that stereotype and proved that slavery in whatever form still degraded blacks, leaving nothing "undone to cripple their intellects, darken their minds, debase their moral nature, obliterate all traces of their relationship to mankind." Garrison further asserted that he was deeply moved by the way Douglass had emerged from this prison house to "consecrate" his life as an antislavery lecturer with an "intellect richly endowed" and a character filled with "gentleness," "meekness," "manliness." Douglass had passed through all that he claimed. Reiterating some of the points Garrison made, Phillips wrote of his personal acquaintance with Douglass and emphasized his "truth, candor, and sincerity." The *Narrative,* Phillips argued, gave "a fair specimen of the whole truth. No one-sided portrait,—no wholesale complaints,—but strict justice done."[35]

But Douglass did not rest even here in promoting his authenticity. Soon after the publication of the *Narrative,* he took a bold and unprecedented step: he mailed a copy of the *Narrative* to his master Thomas Auld and thereby challenged him publicly to refute it. Auld obviously had the greatest motive and was in the best position to disprove Douglass's *Narrative* if it were untrue. Although Douglass relished this gesture, he also compounded his risk of realizing the fugitive's greatest fear—recapture. At a time when many of his fellow fugitives recounted the story of their lives only on condition that their anonymity be maintained by suppressing their true names, those of their masters, and the places of their enslavement, Douglass's revelations of such details in the face of the obvious threat their publication posed represented the greatest authentication of his text.[36]

The swift acclaim Douglass's work achieved attested to the success of these verifying methods. Of all of the other twenty-seven black autobiographies published before 1846, only six went through four or more editions during the nineteenth century and only three of these were translated into foreign languages. The most successful of them were the narratives of Charles Ball (six English-language editions), James A. Gronnisaw (six English-language and one Swedish edition), Moses Roper (seven English-language and one Celtic edition), and Olaudah Equiano (twelve English-language, one Dutch, and one German edition).

The *Narrative* far outstripped any of its predecessors. Between its appearance in May and September 1845, more than 4,500 copies of the *Narrative* were sold. Three years later it had been translated into French, German, and Dutch. Between 1845 and 1847, two Irish and four English editions were published. According to Douglass, the *Narrative* had "passed through nine editions in England" by January 1848. Nine American editions had been published by 1850. In six years a total of twenty-one editions of the book had been published in the United States, the United Kingdom, and Europe. By 1853, at least 30,000 copies of the book had been sold. The price of the American editions varied between 25 and 35 cents.[37]

The *Narrative* served several extra-literary purposes. Published just as Douglass was leaving the United States for an extended tour of England, Scotland, and Ireland, the *Narrative* promoted his lectures. Sales of the book before and after his appearance in a town helped him meet his expenses. To the extent that readers in the United Kingdom believed the *Narrative,* they were that much more prepared to accept Douglass's lectures castigating America and American slavery. Douglass added further drama to his highly publicized "flight" to Great Britain to avoid the certain recapture assured by the publication of his *Narrative* by constantly alluding to this threat in his speeches.[38]

At the beginning of his tour of the United Kingdom, references to the *Narrative* became stock rhetorical devices in Douglass's speeches. Douglass frequently emphasized the threat of recapture when he began a speech. Typical was his assertion in a speech in Cork, Ireland, in October 1845 that although publication of the *Narrative* removed doubts that he had been a slave, it produced some excitement in the South, endangering his safety: "The excitement at last increased so much that it was thought better for me to get out of the way lest my master might use some stratagems to get me back into his clutches. I am here then in order to avoid the scent of the blood hounds of America, and of spreading light on the subject of her slave system."[39]

The *Narrative* was the most widely reviewed of all antebellum black autobiographies. Dozens of newspapers and magazines published in the United States, the United Kingdom, and Europe praised the book, and reviews exceeding 3,000 words were not unusual. Varying from long summaries containing numerous extracts to thoughtful essays on the nature of black autobiographies, the reviews generally accepted Douglass's self-portrait as true, interesting, and instructive.[40]

Reviewers in the antislavery press flocked to celebrate the *Narrative*. The *Liberator* inaugurated the campaign while the *Narrative* was still being printed. Announcing the forthcoming book in a lead editorial on 9 May 1845, the *Liberator* stressed that Douglass alone wrote the account. The acting editor of the newspaper then reprinted in full Garrison's preface. The reviewer for the *National Anti-Slavery Standard* attested that the book was "illustrated by a remarkably good engraving of the author" and buttressed this authenticating device with an indication of his personal acquaintance with the author. The *Liberator* added that the *Narrative* "was written entirely by Mr. Douglass, and reveals all the facts in regard to his birth-place,—the names of his mother, master, overseer, &c &c."[41]

The May 1845 annual meeting of the New England Anti-Slavery Society was also used to advance the *Narrative*. Attended by Garrison, Phillips, and Douglass, the convention was extensively covered in the press. Quickly taking advantage of free advertising, the first motion of the business committee offered by Wendell Phillips on 27 May welcomed the *Narrative* as "The new Anti-Slavery lecturer" and commended it to "all those who believe the slaves of the South to be either well treated, or happy, or ignorant of their right to freedom, or in need of preparation to make them fit for freedom; and that we urge upon the friends of the cause the duty of circulating it among all classes."[42]

Abolitionist critics contended that the *Narrative* exposed slavery where it was allegedly "mildest" and that it would be an important "auxiliary" in the abolition crusade. The *Liberator* review of 23 May 1845 asserted that the *Narrative* "cannot fail to produce a great sensation wherever it may happen to circulate, especially among the slavocracy. . . . What a lifting of the veil is this, to convince the skeptical that it is impossible to exaggerate the horrors and enormities of that impious system!"[43]

The *Narrative* substantiated the intellectual capacity of African Americans for many critics. The growth of moral sensibilities, acquisition of a rudimentary education, and evidence of courage in the midst of slavery's degradation recounted by Douglass indicated that he was an exceptional man and that all blacks freed of the slave's fetters could improve themselves. The abolitionist editor of the Oberlin *Evangelist* found in Douglass's autobiography an expression of "some of the noblest sentiments of the human heart," a harbinger that "the days of Oppression are numbered," and an example of the potentiality of blacks once emancipated. Abolitionist Mary Howitt in her review of 1847 in London's *People's Journal* described Douglass as "a noble human being" and viewed his *Narrative* as an incomparable catalog of slavery's horrors: "If we were to write ten volumes on the atrocities and miseries of slavery in the abstract, we could say nothing half so impressive and conclusive as is the simple, honest narrative of a real slave, written by himself."[44]

Several critics declared how instructive the book would be to all classes of readers. "This little book taught by examples the cruel workings of the systems of Slavery, in a region where its burden is comparatively light, and the plainness of the narration and the simplicity of the style made it attractive to all classes of readers." One of the most enthusiastic critiques was in the *National Anti-Slavery Standard* of 12 June 1845. Contending that the book would enlighten even slavery's defenders, the reviewer observed: "This book ought to be read by all before whose mental blindness visions of happy slaves continually dance. It is the story of the life of a man of great intellectual power, in the very circumstances of Slavery,—in the Northernmost of the slave states, and under kind masters."[45]

Nonabolitionist journals, especially those published in the United Kingdom, upheld the work's didactic purpose for a European audience distant from American slavery. The Cork *Examiner* on 22 October 1845 asserted that the *Narrative* "gives an insight into the slave system in America, which cannot elsewhere be obtained in so concise and interesting a form." Similarly, *Chamber's Edinburgh Journal* published a review of the *Narrative* on 24 January 1846 in which the author declared that it would "help considerably to disseminate correct ideas respecting slavery and its attendant evils. Some of the passages present a dismal picture of what is endured by the negro race in the slave-holding states of the union." The review in England's Newcastle *Guardian* looked upon the *Narrative* primarily as a revelation about American religion and as a corrective to many previously published accounts of American slavery.[46]

Writers for nonabolitionist journals tended to be more skeptical than the abolitionist reviewers and were anxious to determine the credibility of Douglass's account. Generally assuming "that Frederick Douglass is what he professes," the London *Spectator* reviewer thought it "improbable" that Douglass fought with a slaveholder or learned to read in the manner he described in the *Narrative*. Doubt about Douglass's authorship lingered until the end and the reviewer concluded: "If this narrative is really true in its basis, and untouched by any one save Douglass himself, it is a singular book, and he is a more singular man. Even if it is of the nature of the true stories of De Foe, it is curious as a picture of slavery, and worth reading."[47]

Most critics had fewer doubts about Douglass's credibility than the *Spectator* reviewer. The Boston *Transcript*, for example, contended that the *Narrative* "bears throughout the indelible marks of truth." The Boston *Courier* asserted that the book contained "many descriptions of scenes at the South, which, if true, bear sufficient witness against the 'peculiar institution,' to make every honest man to wish its downfall soon, and by almost any means. And there seems to be no reason for believing that more than the truth is told." In November 1845, the *British Friend* declared that "Truth seems stamped on every page of this narrative."[48]

For a few critics, the prefatory letters enhanced the credibility of Douglass's autobiography. The London *League* referred, for instance, to the book's being "certified by highly respectable persons" as "authentic." William Howitt, reviewing the first Irish edition of the book for the London *Atlas*, commented on Douglass's authenticating prefaces because readers might well ask, "Who is this FREDERICK DOUGLASS? And what guarantee have we that he is what he represents himself to be? In answer to this, we have only to say that his book is prefaced by two admirable letters from the well-known champions of American freedom, WILLIAM LLOYD GARRISON and WENDELL PHILLIPS, bearing the highest testimonies to his character and to his services in the abolition cause."[49]

Other critics distrusted the letters. The most extreme reaction came from the *Religious Spectator* reviewer who felt their endorsement of the book was reason enough not to read it: "We might possibly have laid it aside without reading it, from perceiving that it was published under the patronage of several individuals, whose course on the subject of slavery we have never regarded as either politic or right." The New York *Tribune* found Phillips's letter to be neutral, but Garrison's remarks counterproductive. The *Tribune* was highly critical of the "noble and generous" Garrison and contended that the tone of his comments made Douglass's seem "very just and temperate" in contrast. Beyond this, the *Tribune* argued that the prefatory comments did little to authenticate Douglass's account. Phillips, at least, did not invalidate the account. By contrast, Garrison's comments were, the *Tribune* charged, "in his usual over emphatic style . . . he has indulged in violent invective and denunciation till he has spoiled the temper of his mind. Like a man who has been in the habit of screaming himself hoarse to make the deaf hear, he can no longer pitch his voice on a key agreeable to common ears."[50]

Many commented on Douglass's use of personal and place names. The Bristol *Mercury* asserted that Douglass had done much to remove doubt about his identity in the book by "giving the names of the masters under whom he had lived, and dates and events which would at once prove the correctness of his account." Specificity represented a major part of the *Tribune*'s reason for accepting the validity of the *Narrative:* "He has had the courage to name the persons, times and places, thus exposing himself to obvious danger, and setting the seal on his deep convictions as to the religious need of speaking the whole truth."[51]

But most critics looked beyond specificity for additional evidence to show that Douglass had written his autobiography and that it was a faithful account of his life. Ironically, they found confirmation of Douglass's written words in his spoken words. A thoughtful and very skeptical reviewer for the

Religious Spectator, upon being given a copy of the book, initially cast it aside because it had been published by the American Anti-Slavery Society. With such an imprimatur on the book, he doubted that Douglass had either written it or was a fugitive slave until he learned "upon good authority, that his lectures are characterized by as able reasoning, as genuine wit, and as bold and stirring appeals, as we almost ever find in connexion with the highest intellectual culture."[52]

Skeptical critics in the United Kingdom often delayed the publication of reviews of the *Narrative* until they had an opportunity to hear Douglass speak. In his speeches they found proof that he had written his autobiography. Typical of such critics was the Irish abolitionist Isaac Nelson, who declared in January 1846:

> I looked forward with much interest and some incredulity to a meeting with the author of this unique piece of autobiography, doubting whether any man reared a slave, and so recently escaped from bonds, could, under the circumstances, produce such a work. My meeting with Frederick Douglass dispelled my doubts; he is indeed an extraordinary man—the type of a class—such an intellectual phenomenon as only appears at times in the republic of letters. I have had opportunities of observing his mind in several attitudes, and applied to various subjects during his stay in Belfast, and I take leave to say that not only do I consider him adequate to the task of writing such a book as the one before us, but also of achieving more Herculean feats.[53]

A number of reviewers found it impossible to separate Douglass the antislavery orator from Douglass the autobiographer. Identifying Douglass as an escaped slave and "itinerant lecturer" of the American Anti-Slavery Society, a reviewer for the London *Spectator* declared that Douglass, "having a natural force and fluency of language, and dealing with things within his own experience, . . . appears to have spoken with so much acceptance as to have been stimulated to commit to paper the autobiographical portion of his addresses." The New York *Tribune* reacted in a similar fashion in an 1845 review. Douglass, the *Tribune* reported, "is said to be an excellent speaker—can speak from a thorough personal experience—and has upon the audience, beside, the influence of a strong character and uncommon talents. In the book before us he has put into the story of his life the thoughts, the feelings and the adventures that have been so affecting through the living voice; nor are they less so from the printed page."[54]

Some of the most significant reviews concentrated on Douglass's revelations about the development of his interior character. The *British Friend* in its November 1845 assessment of the style and content of the "plain, but eloquent narrative," declared: "In reading it, one sees before him the fearful tossings and heavings of an immortal soul, herded with beasts, and compelled to grope about, feeling after God among reptiles. The reader feels himself in communion with immortality—sunk to a thing—with the image of God turned into a brute." Similarly, the review in an issue of the Newcastle *Guardian* noted the revelations about Douglass's character contained in "his simple yet spirit-stirring narration" of his life and especially "the risings of noble and generous feelings of his soul, and of the exertions which he made for the acquisition of knowledge, despite the almost insuperable obstacles which were thrown in his way." Abolitionist Ralph Varian, writing in the December 1845 issue of the *British Friend,* asserted that the book was "a revelation of the wondrous power which a highly gifted nature possesses, to triumph over brute force, and circumstances the most disheartening."[55]

The work's plainness of style suggested an absence of guile and thus advanced its credibility for the critics. The Lynn, Massachusetts, *Pioneer* argued that the *Narrative* was "evidently drawn with a nice eye, and the coloring is chaste and subdued, rather than extravagant or overwrought. Thrilling as it is, and full of the most burning eloquence, it is yet simple and unimpassioned. Its eloquence is the eloquence of truth, and so is as simple and touching as the impulses of childhood." In his January 1846 review of the *Narrative,* the Reverend Isaac Nelson of Belfast, Ireland, informed his compatriots: "I regard the narrative of FREDERICK DOUGLASS as a literary wonder. The incidents of his life are of such a kind as to hold the reader spell-bound, while they are related in a style simple, perspicuous, and eloquent." Similarly, while viewing the *Narrative* as a "curiosity" focused too heavily on the "incredible brutality" of some individuals, the London *League*'s reviewer concluded: "But even as a literary production, this book possesses no ordinary claims. The author, though uneducated, or rather self-educated, displays great natural powers: he utters his thoughts always lucidly, and often with a polished and vigorous eloquence." The New York *Tribune* was less reserved in its praise of the style of the book than the *League.* In its long critique, the *Tribune* asserted: "Considered merely as a narrative, we have never read one more simple, true, coherent, and warm with genuine feeling. It is an excellent piece of writing."[56]

The pathos and metaphorical flights in the *Narrative* elicited comments from several reviewers. Douglass's autobiography was, they argued, "affecting," "touching," "unspeakably affecting," and filled with passages demonstrating "simple pathos," "deep pathos," or "pathos and sublimity." Wilson Armistead, reviewing the book in 1848, asserted that "The narrative of Douglass contains many affecting incidents, many passages of great eloquence and power." "A.M.," a *Liberator* correspondent, illustrated most fully the pathetic elements of the *Narrative* when she wrote from Albany, New York: "I have wept over the pages of Dickens' 'Oliver Twist'—I have moistened with my tears whole chapters of Eugene Sue's mysteries of Paris—but Douglass's history of the wrongs of the American Slave, brought, not tears—no, tears refused me their comfort—its horrible truths crowded in such quick succession, and entered so deep into the chambers of my soul, as to entirely close the relief valve. . . . I groaned in the agony of my spirit." According to the critics, the passages demonstrating Douglass's masterful use of pathos included those describing his relationship with his mother, the songs of the slaves, his acquisition of an education, and the treatment of aged slaves. The most frequent comments on the use of metaphors in the *Narrative* centered on Douglass's apostrophe to freedom as he watched ships in the Chesapeake Bay.[57]

The reception accorded the *Narrative* in the South ironically served to verify its details and lend authority to it. The American Anti-Slavery Society apparently exhausted every means to push the book in Maryland and was relatively successful. The early reactions of Marylanders to the *Narrative* boosted sales because they testified to its credibility. For example, the editor of a Philadelphia newspaper, the *Elevator,* while reviewing Douglass's "exceedingly interesting" autobiography, reported that on a trip to Maryland he encountered several blacks who knew Douglass "by his assumed as well as by his real name, and related to us many interesting incidents about their former companion."[58]

More direct testimony validating the *Narrative* came from the pens of white Marylanders personally acquainted with slavery on the Eastern Shore and Douglass's owners. This valuable testimony began when a white resident of Baltimore reported in September 1845 that Douglass's *Narrative* "is now circulating and being read in this city, and five hundred copies are still wanted here. They would be read with avidity, and do much good." Signing his letter "A Citizen of Maryland," the writer then assessed the credibility of Douglass's account: "I have made some inquiry, and have reason to believe his statements are true. Col. Edward Lloyd's relatives are my relatives! Let this suffice for the present." Another white native of Maryland and acquaintance of the Lloyds read Douglass's account in the spring of 1846 and wrote, "[F]rom my knowledge of slavery as it really exists . . . I am fully prepared to bear a decided testimony to the truth of all his assertions, with regard to the discipline upon the plantations of Maryland, as well as his descriptions of cruelty and murder."[59]

Unfavorable southern responses to the *Narrative,* however, far outstripped the favorable ones over the next several years. Whether it was true or false, most southern whites felt the *Narrative* was an incendiary document inciting slaves to rebel. As late as the spring of 1849 a grand jury in Grayson County, Virginia, indicted Jarvis C. Bacon for "feloniously and knowingly circulating" the *Narrative* because the jurors felt the book was "intended to cause slaves to rebel and make insurrection, and denying the right of property of masters in their slaves."[60]

However much Douglass may have sympathized with Jarvis Bacon, he first had to confront the persistent challenge of A. C. C. Thompson of Delaware. Apparently prompted by Douglass's former owner Thomas Auld, Thompson wrote a long review essay of the *Narrative* for the *Delaware Republican.* Describing Douglass's autobiography variously as "dirty," "false," "infamous libel," and a "ridiculous publication," Thompson contended that it was filled with "glaring falsehoods" and declared "the whole to be a budget of falsehoods from beginning to end." While refuting Douglass's claim that slave children were customarily separated from their mothers in Maryland, Thompson concentrated on correcting the *Narrative*'s unflattering characterization of Edward Lloyd, Aaron Anthony, Giles Hicks, Austin Gore, Thomas Lambdin, Edward Covey, and Thomas Auld. From what he knew of these men and Douglass when he was a slave, Thompson concluded that Douglass did not write the book, which, he argued, bore "the glaring impress of falsehood on every page."[61]

This was just the challenge Douglass had been awaiting. Writing to

Thompson from England in 1846, Douglass thanked him profusely for proving that he had been a slave and that the people he wrote about were not fictitious. To Thompson's charge that he had maligned good masters and Christian men with charitable feelings, Douglass restated his complaints concerning his treatment and observed, "The cowskin makes as deep a gash in my flesh, when wielded by a professed saint, as it does when wielded by an open sinner." The chief focus of Douglass's response was, however, on Thompson's "triumphant vindication of the truth" of this *Narrative:* "your testimony is direct and perfect—just what I have long wanted . . . you . . . brush away the miserable insinuation of my northern pro-slavery enemies, that I have used fictitious not real names." Douglass promised to add Thompson's letter as an appendix to the second Irish edition of his *Narrative.*[62]

Thompson launched a second and more systematic attack on Douglass's autobiography after some northern journalists expressed doubts about the *Delaware Republican* review. As the basis for his second attack, Thompson collected letters from Thomas Auld, James Dawson, Dr. A. C. C. Thompson, L. Datsun, and Thomas Graham denying the validity of Douglass's autobiography. The central focus of the letters was the character of Thomas Auld. Auld's neighbors and acquaintances contended that Douglass's portrayal of Auld was "a base and villainous fabrication," "basely false," and "palpably untrue." A number of Thompson's witnesses claimed that Auld's "conduct to his servants was more like an indulgent father than a master." Auld himself denied that he had ever flogged Douglass and claimed that Douglass had suppressed information about his promise that "when he was 25 years old I would emancipate him; . . . He does not say one word about this in his Narrative, as it would not have answered to have mentioned so much truth." Thompson argued that the testimony of Auld and his neighbors demonstrated that "the assertions of this negro Douglass are nothing more than gross misrepresentations."[63]

On 6 February 1846, when Douglass wrote the preface to the second Irish edition of his autobiography, he kept his promise to Thompson. In spite of the confident tone of his earlier response to Thompson, Douglass nevertheless repeated in his preface sections of the report of his farewell meeting in Lynn, Massachusetts, and the resolutions passed at that meeting testifying to his fugitive status. He also reprinted the declaration of a committee of the Hibernian Anti-Slavery Society that Douglass "has long been known to us by reputation, and is now introduced to us by letters from some of the most distinguished and faithful friends of the Anti-Slavery cause in the United States."

Douglass's central focus in the four-page preface, however, was Thompson. Conceding that the two naturally "differ in our details," Douglass began his references to Thompson by declaring: "He agrees with me at least in the important fact, that I am what I proclaim myself to be, an ungrateful fugitive from the 'patriarchal institutions' of the Slave States; and he certifies that many of the heroes of my Narrative are still living and doing well, as 'honored and worthy members of the Methodist Episcopal Church.'" The Thompson-Douglass exchange maintained interest in the *Narrative* for years after its publication. Douglass fueled the fires by repeatedly referring to it in his speeches, letters, and editorials.[64]

What concerned Douglass most, however, about Thompson's charges was the allegation that he had misrepresented the character of his master Thomas Auld. Since Auld had specifically denied that Douglass's portrayal of him was accurate, Douglass concentrated more and more on Auld in his speeches and writings. With consummate skill, Douglass transformed Auld, in the public mind, into the archetypal vindictive slaveholder desperate to recapture and punish his former slave. Speaking in London in May 1846, Douglass gave a characteristic presentation when he said that his master, after trying unsuccessfully to refute the *Narrative,* had transferred title in him to his brother, who "resolves that if ever I touch American soil, I shall be instantly reduced to a state of slavery. However, it is not to a state of slavery that they wish now to have me reduced. They have a feeling of revenge to gratify."[65]

Thomas Auld's actions after Douglass arrived in England highlighted and exaggerated the danger the fugitive slave faced. By giving the impression that Douglass would be immediately reenslaved if he returned to the United States, Auld created greater sympathy for Douglass in the United Kingdom that eventually led abolitionists there to raise money to purchase the fugitive so they could manumit him. Long before the inauguration of this manumission effort, however, Douglass began a literary and oratorical campaign to neutralize Thomas Auld's assault on the credibility of his *Narrative.* Even in responding to attacks from third parties, Douglass tried, whenever possible, to allude to Auld's letter to Thompson. The earliest opportunity Douglass had for a full response to Auld came in 1846, when an American in the United Kingdom declared that Douglass lied about slavery in his speeches. Writing a response from Glasgow in April 1846, Douglass concentrated on Auld and contended that Auld felt so keenly Douglass's "exposures" and "severe goadings" that his "old master is in a state of mind quite favorable to an attempt at re-capture . . . to feed his revenge." According to Douglass, Auld told "a positive lie," when he swore "he never struck me, or told any one else to do so." Recalling an occasion when Auld beat him "until he wearied himself," Douglass declared: "My memory in such matters, is better than his."[66]

Two years later Douglass began using Auld's denial of the validity of the *Narrative* in an attempt to goad his former master into a public debate. He inaugurated the campaign by writing his first public letter to his master on 3 September 1848, the anniversary of his escape from slavery. Receiving no reply from Auld, Douglass then reprinted his response of 1846 to A. C. C. Thompson in the 13 October 1848 issue of the *North Star*. Then, on 3 September 1849, Douglass wrote his second letter to Auld. Although other fugitive slaves wrote public letters to their masters, few of them tried to use their correspondence as Douglass did to shore up the credibility of their autobiographies. Douglass, for example, began his second "friendly epistle" to Auld by denying that he would "wilfully malign the character even of a slaveholder" and asserted: "I can say, with a clear conscience, in all that I have ever written or spoken respecting yourself, I have tried to remember that, though I am beyond your power and control, I am still accountable to our common Father and Judge,—in the sight of whom I believe that I stand acquitted of all intentional misrepresentation against you. Of course, I have said many hard things respecting yourself; but all has been based upon what I knew of you at the time I was a slave in your family."[67]

Three other critics agreed, in part, with the claims of Thomas Auld and A. C. C. Thompson. The most important of such reviews of the *Narrative* appeared in July 1849 when the Reverend Ephraim Peabody included it in his thirty-two-page *Christian Examiner* essay, "Narratives of Fugitive Slaves." Peabody's review of the autobiographies of Henry Watson, Lewis and Milton Clarke, William Wells Brown, Josiah Henson, and Douglass was important for two reasons. First, Peabody was one of the few antebellum critics to concentrate on black autobiographies as literature. Second, Frederick Douglass published a response to Peabody's essay. In his oft-quoted opening paragraph, Peabody declared: "AMERICA has the mournful honor of adding a new department to the literature of civilization,—the autobiographies of escaped slaves." Viewing such works as "remarkable as being pictures of slavery by the slave" revealing the black's "native love of freedom" and sense of poetry and romance, they contained, Peabody asserted, adventures comparable to the *Iliad* and the *Odyssey.*[68]

Peabody was most impressed with the autobiography of Josiah Henson and spent fourteen pages summarizing it because, he asserted, his readers would "be interested in the efforts of one who, without noise or pretension, without bitterness towards the whites, without extravagant claims in behalf of the blacks, has patiently, wisely, and devotedly given himself to the improvement of the large body of his wretched countrymen amongst whom his lot has been cast." Writing approvingly of Henson's attempt to purchase his freedom, his religious convictions, his "fidelity," "freedom from exaggeration," "absence of personal bitterness," and "commiseration for all classes," Peabody declared that Henson's narrative presented "the best picture of the evils incident to slave life on the plantations which can be found."[69]

All of the other autobiographies, and especially Douglass's, suffered in comparison to Henson's. Indeed, from Peabody's perspective, beside Henson's account, the other autobiographies

> possess no especial interest beyond what must belong to the life of almost any fugitive slave. They are records of degradation on the part of both blacks and whites,—of suffering and wrong and moral corruption. They give, doubtless, a just idea of what slavery is to the slave. But, on the other hand, while we have no reason to question the truth of particular facts representing individuals, we have no doubt that they convey an altogether erroneous idea of the general character of the masters. The best qualities of the master are likely to appear anywhere rather than in his connection with the slave. And except it be an easy kindness, the slave is in no position to estimate aright the virtues of one who, towards himself, appears simply as a power whom he cannot resist. They stand in such utterly false relations to each other, that their whole intercourse must necessarily be vitiated, and the worst qualities of each, and these almost exclusively, must be perpetually forced on the attention of the other. But human society could not long

> exist were the great body of slaveholders like those whom these narratives describe.[70]

Peabody admitted that he was personally acquainted with Douglass and that his narrative "contains the life of a superior man." He then shifted to a critique of Douglass's speaking style. Peabody took special umbrage at Douglass's "severity of judgement and a one-sidedness of view," his "seeing only the evils of slavery" and his "violence and extravagance of expression." Although Peabody acknowledged "the sympathy which his narrative excites, and our respect for the force of character he has shown in rising from the depths of bondage," he let his critical remarks stand in hopes they would lead Douglass to follow a wiser course.[71]

Douglass responded to Peabody in an editorial in the *North Star* on 3 August 1849. Contending that because Peabody was a northern minister he was "ill qualified" to write his essay, Douglass argued that, contrary to Peabody's claims, there were few truly antislavery masters. Northerners had, for too long, been deceived by southern words. Douglass conceded that "slaveholders frequently speak of slavery as an evil . . . in the presence of persons from the North," but rarely in front of slaves, and concluded that "if we judge the slaveholder by his words, it will be difficult to convict him of unkindness to his slaves, or to charge him with the desire to continue the relation of slavery; but the unmistakable language of conduct leaves no doubt of his guilt in both these points. To detest slavery in words, and to cling to it in practice, is a display of hypocrisy that should deceive no one." Rejecting Peabody's advice about the style and content of his lectures, Douglass then turned to his criticisms of the slave autobiographies. In the process he defended the honesty of his portrait of slaveholders:

> Speaking of the Narratives, Mr. Peabody admits, "they give a just idea of what slavery is to the slave," but adds, "they convey an altogether erroneous idea of the character of the masters." Here we think Mr. Peabody's logic at fault. What slavery is to the slave, the slaveholder is to the slave; and the character of the slaveholder may be fairly inferred from his treatment of the slave. It is not by the courtesy and hospitality which slaveholders extend to Northern clergymen and travellers, whose good opinions they think desirable, that we are to learn their true characters. Here they have an end to attain. But it is

> their conduct towards those over whom they have unlimited power, by which they are to be tried and adjudged. In this relation they act freely and without restraint; in the other case they act from necessity.[72]

Support for, and popularization of, the views Douglass expressed in his *Narrative* and responses to Thompson and Peabody came from Harriet Beecher Stowe. The publication of Stowe's *Uncle Tom's Cabin* in 1852 led to renewed interest in all slave autobiographies, and especially those of Josiah Henson, Lewis Clarke, and Douglass. When reviewers questioned "whether the representations of 'Uncle Tom's Cabin' are a fair representation of slavery as it at present exists," Stowe published in 1853 *A Key to Uncle Tom's Cabin*, which, she claimed, was the factual base for the novel. The *Key* contained a collection of "real incidents,—of actions really performed, of words and expressions really uttered." To prove that George Harris, the intelligent mulatto character, was not overdrawn in her novel, Stowe quoted extracts from the autobiographies of Lewis and Milton Clarke, Josiah Henson, and Frederick Douglass because their accounts, she contended, were "related by those who know slavery by the best of all tests—experience; and they are given by men who have earned a character in freedom which makes their word as good as the word of any man living." The central incident that Stowe focused on in Douglass's *Narrative* was his description of his acquisition of an education, which she argued was "a most interesting and affecting parallel" to George's teaching himself to read and write.[73]

Stowe's defense and use of Douglass's *Narrative* and other black autobiographies prompted the *Key*'s critics to comment specifically on the slave testimony section and to publish their reflections on slave autobiographies and Douglass's account. For reviewers in southern newspapers and magazines, the *Key* sometimes led to extended criticism of a body of literature they had previously ignored. The critic in the July 1853 issue of the *Southern Quarterly Review*, for example, found little that was credible in slave autobiographies:

> The runaway narratives are, no doubt, pure inventions of the cunning fugitives, to work upon the charities and sympathies of those who are simple enough to receive their statements as truthful. . . . Such tales of torture of the whites, such pictures of sorrow by the meek and sensitive blacks, would draw tears from eyes of stone. . . . These narratives are now pretty much stereotyped. The runaways have learned their part,

> and they go through it, on the one key, with great dexterity, and with daily improvement on the music; so that the horrors of poor Frederick Douglass, himself, have been greatly surpassed by later sufferers, who have set up as rivals for Northern favour.[74]

Although there is no evidence that Douglass responded to the essay in the *Southern Quarterly Review,* he did react to similar criticisms of Harriet Beecher Stowe's works in *Graham's Magazine.* The dispute arose over some general comments made by the editor in the course of reviewing *Uncle Tom's Cabin.* He included his severe criticisms of recent writings on slavery in an essay entitled "Black Letters; or Uncle Tom-Foolery in Literature." George Graham complained that the bookshelves "groan under the weight of Sambo's woes, done up in covers! . . . We hate this niggerism, and hope it may be done away with." Graham admonished writers to "turn to something worthier than these negro subjects" and expressed his displeasure over the literary "incursion of blacks." After a scathing attack on *Uncle Tom's Cabin,* Graham refused to review "the other black books—those literary nigritudes—those little tadpoles of the press—sable bodies and stirring tales."[75]

Douglass replied by classing Graham among the "Northern cringers to the slave power" and arguing that it was an "ungenerous and ungentlemanly attack (*'miscalled a Review'*)." Graham's attack on Stowe was, however, understandable: "Recrimination is the favorite artillery of the defenders and abettors of the slave system." Graham accepted Douglass's challenge by attacking him specifically in the March issue of his magazine. Graham contended that although he respected Douglass, "we hate the present negro literature—especially that of Fred.'s, which by abusing the white, is intended to elevate the black man." Arguing that Graham indicted himself, Douglass reprinted Graham's March editorial without comment.[76]

Among antebellum critics of Douglass's *Narrative,* George Graham was in a distinct minority of those claiming that the book had little literary merit. Along with A. C. C. Thompson, Ephraim Peabody, Thomas Auld, and the *Southern Quarterly Review,* Graham felt the book exaggerated the faults of southern whites, contained more invention than truth, or had not been written by Douglass. Contrary to these views, the overwhelming majority of antebellum critics found much to praise in the *Narrative.*

Blazoned, scrutinized, celebrated, excoriated, Frederick Douglass by the early 1850s was fixed in the American public's mind as a real person who had earlier passed through the mill of slavery on the Eastern Shore of Maryland. Subjected to the tough test of credibility leveled against nineteenth-century autobiographers, he had almost singlehandedly restored vigor to the slave narratives as key weapons in the antislavery crusade. But Douglass also established that his tremendous gift as a writer was not limited to political instruments. Douglass proved himself a master of one of the most American of literary genres—the salvational autobiography.

Embracing the tradition of Puritan conversion narratives, Indian captivity narratives, and especially the secularized yet deeply moral autobiographies best represented by Benjamin Franklin's, Douglass so crafted his work that his positive relationship with them all was unmistakable as he, too, encountered and renounced the snares of the world and stayed to an ever clearer pursuit of moral responsibility, wisdom, and freedom. However black, enslaved, and seemingly other, his affecting and lucid prose argued for oneness with Franklin and his racial brethren. By jeopardizing his very security as a fugitive in order to rebuild the credibility of the American slave narrative, none so dramatically as Douglass integrated both the horror and the great quest of the African American experience into this deep stream of American autobiography. He advanced and extended that tradition and is rightfully designated one of its greatest practitioners.

Wye House, plantation home of the Lloyd family, employer of Douglass's first owner, Aaron Anthony. Courtesy of the Maryland Historical Society, Z24.565VF.

"Captain's House" on the Wye House plantation. Courtesy of the Maryland Historical Society, Z24.562VF. Photograph by H. Robins Hollyday.

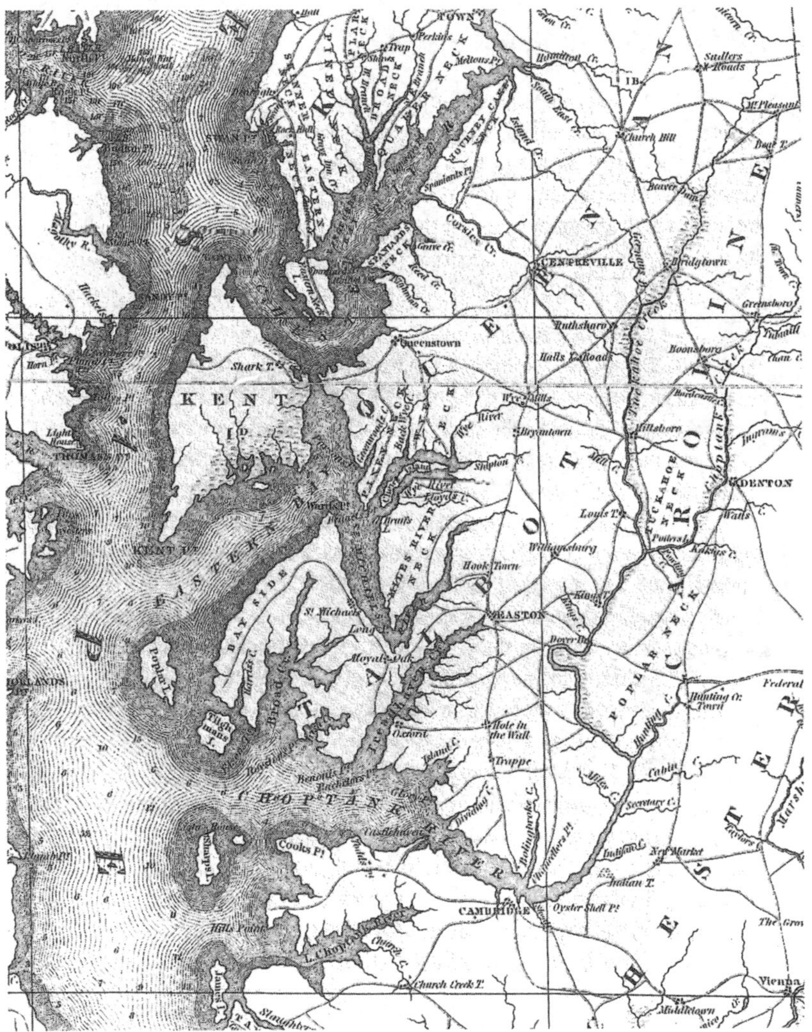

The Maryland Eastern Shore at the time of Douglass's boyhood. Lucas Fielding, Jr., *The State of Maryland. Detail of the Eastern Shore* (Baltimore, 1840). Courtesy of the Library of Congress, Geography and Map Division, LC-g3844b-wd000016.

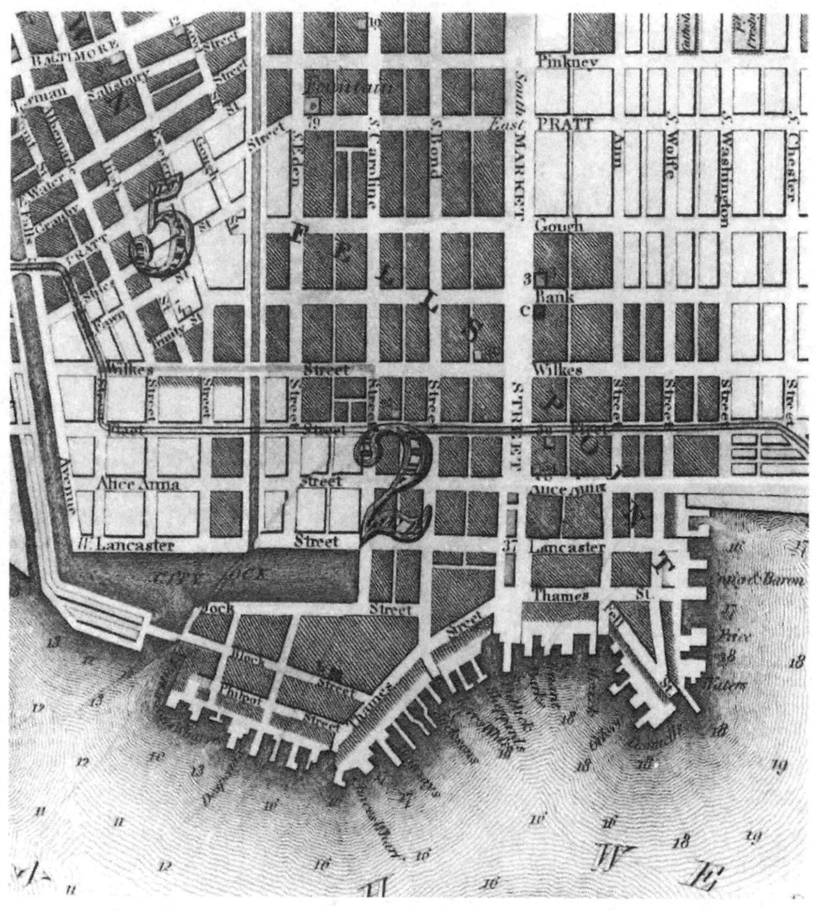

Baltimore's Fells Point neighborhood at the time of Douglass's residence in the 1820s and 1830s. Lucas Fielding, Jr., *Plan of the City of Baltimore* (detail) (Baltimore, 1836). Courtesy of the Library of Congress, Geography and Map Division, LC-g3840-ct000793.

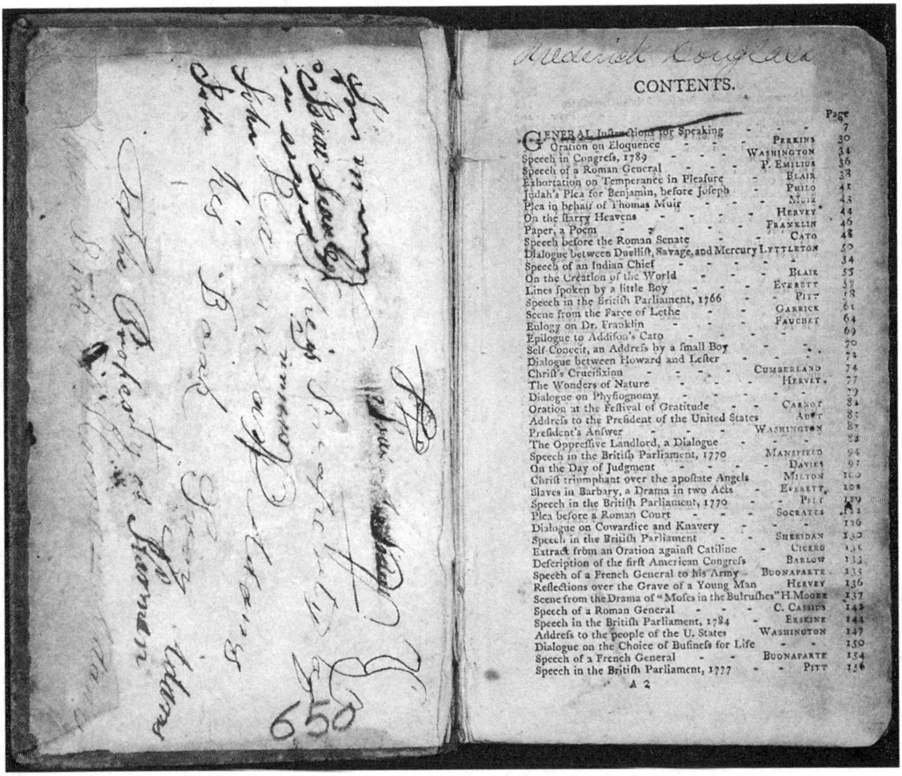

Annotations by Douglass in his copy of *The Columbian Orator* by Caleb Bingham, first published in 1797. Courtesy of the National Park Service, Frederick Douglass National Historic Site, Washington, D.C., FRDO 000650.

NARRATIVE

OF THE

LIFE

OF

FREDERICK DOUGLASS,

AN

AMERICAN SLAVE.

WRITTEN BY HIMSELF.

BOSTON:

PUBLISHED AT THE ANTI-SLAVERY OFFICE,

No. 25 Cornhill

1845.

Title page of the *Narrative*. Wesleyan University Library, Special Collections and Archives.

NARRATIVE

OF THE

LIFE

OF

FREDERICK DOUGLASS,

AN

AMERICAN SLAVE.

WRITTEN BY HIMSELF.

BOSTON:
PUBLISHED AT THE ANTI-SLAVERY OFFICE,
No. 25 Cornhill
1845.

PREFACE.

In the month of August, 1841, I attended an anti-slavery convention in Nantucket, at which it was my happiness to become acquainted with Frederick Douglass, the writer of the following Narrative. He was a stranger to nearly every member of that body; but, having recently made his escape from the southern prison-house of bondage, and feeling his curiosity excited to ascertain the principles and measures of the abolitionists,—of whom he had heard a somewhat vague description while he was a slave,—he was induced to give his attendance, on the occasion alluded to, though at that time a resident in New Bedford.

Fortunate, most fortunate occurrence!—fortunate for the millions of his manacled brethren, yet panting for deliverance from their awful thraldom!—fortunate for the cause of negro emancipation, and of universal liberty!—fortunate for the land of his birth, which he has already done so much to save and bless!—fortunate for a large circle of friends and acquaintances, whose sympathy and affection he has strongly secured by the many sufferings he has endured, by his virtuous traits of character, by his ever-abiding remembrance of those who are in bonds, as being bound with them!—fortunate for the multitudes, in various parts of our republic, whose minds he has enlightened on the subject of slavery, and who have been melted to tears by his pathos, or roused to virtuous indignation by his stirring eloquence against the enslavers of men!—fortunate for himself, as it at once brought him into the field of public usefulness, "gave the world assurance of a MAN," quickened the slumbering energies of his soul, and consecrated him to the great work of breaking the rod of the oppressor, and letting the oppressed go free!

I shall never forget his first speech at the convention—the extraordinary emotion it excited in my own mind—the powerful impression it created upon a crowded auditory, completely taken by surprise—the applause which followed from the beginning to the end of his felicitous remarks. I think I never hated slavery so intensely as at that moment; certainly, my perception of the enormous outrage which is inflicted by it, on the godlike nature of its victims, was rendered far more clear than ever. There stood one, in physical proportion and stature commanding and exact—in intellect richly endowed—in natural eloquence a prodigy—in soul manifestly "created but a little lower than the angels"—yet a slave, ay, a fugitive slave,—trembling for his safety, hardly daring to believe that on the American soil, a single white person could be found who would befriend him at all hazards, for the love of God and humanity! Capable of high attainments as an intellectual and moral being—needing nothing but a comparatively small amount of cultivation to make him an ornament to society and a blessing to his race—by the law of the land, by the voice of the people, by the terms of the slave code, he was only a piece of property, a beast of burden, a chattel personal, nevertheless!

A beloved friend from New Bedford prevailed on Mr. DOUGLASS to address the convention. He came forward to the platform with a hesitancy and embarrassment, necessarily the attendants of a sensitive mind in such a novel position. After apologizing for his ignorance, and reminding the audience that slavery was a poor school for the human intellect and heart, he proceeded to narrate some of the facts in his own history as a slave, and in the course of his speech gave utterance to many noble thoughts and thrilling reflections. As soon as he had taken his seat, filled with hope and admiration, I rose, and declared that PATRICK HENRY, of revolutionary fame, never made a speech more eloquent in the cause of liberty, than the one we had just listened to from the lips of that hunted fugitive. So I believed at that time—such is my belief now. I reminded the audience of the peril which surrounded this self-emancipated young man at the North,—even in Massachusetts, on the soil of the Pilgrim Fathers, among the descendants of revolutionary sires; and I appealed to them, whether they would ever allow him to be carried back into slavery,—law or no law, constitution or no constitution. The response was unanimous and in thunder-tones—"NO!" "Will you succor and protect him as a brother-man—a resident of the old Bay State?" "YES!" shouted the whole mass, with an energy so startling, that the ruthless tyrants south of Mason and Dixon's line might almost have heard the mighty burst of feeling, and recognized it as the pledge of an invincible determination, on the part of those who gave it, never to betray him that wanders, but to hide the outcast, and firmly to abide the consequences.

It was at once deeply impressed upon my mind, that, if Mr. DOUGLASS could be persuaded to consecrate his time and talents to the promotion of the anti-slavery enterprise, a powerful impetus would be given to it, and a stunning blow at the same time inflicted on northern prejudice against a colored complexion. I therefore endeavored to instil hope and courage into his mind, in order that he might dare to engage in a vocation so anomalous and responsible for a person in his situation; and I was seconded in this effort by warm-hearted friends, especially by the late General Agent of the Massachusetts Anti-Slavery Society, Mr. John A. Collins, whose judgment in this instance entirely coincided with my own. At first, he could give no encouragement; with unfeigned diffidence, he expressed his conviction that he was not adequate to the performance of so great a task; the path marked out was wholly an untrodden one; he was sincerely apprehensive that he should do more harm than good. After much deliberation, however, he consented to make a trial; and ever since that period, he has acted as a lecturing agent, under the auspices either of the American or the Massachusetts Anti-Slavery Society. In labors he has been most abundant; and his success in combating prejudice, in gaining proselytes, in agitating the public mind, has far surpassed the most sanguine expectations that were raised at the commencement of his brilliant career. He has borne himself with gentleness and meekness, yet with true manliness of character. As a public speaker, he excels in pathos, wit, comparison, imitation, strength of reasoning, and fluency of language. There is in him that union of head and heart, which is indispensable to an enlightenment of the heads and a winning of the hearts of others. May his strength continue to be equal to his day! May he continue to "grow in grace, and in the knowledge of God," that he may be increasingly serviceable in the cause of bleeding humanity, whether at home or abroad!

It is certainly a very remarkable fact, that one of the most efficient advocates of the slave population, now before the public, is a fugitive slave, in the person of Frederick Douglass; and that the free colored population of the United States are as ably represented by one of their own number, in the person of Charles Lenox Remond, whose eloquent appeals have extorted the highest applause of multitudes on both sides of the Atlantic. Let the calumniators of the colored race despise themselves for their baseness and illiberality of spirit, and henceforth cease to talk of the natural inferiority of those who require nothing but time and opportunity to attain to the highest point of human excellence.

It may, perhaps, be fairly questioned, whether any other portion of the population of the earth could have endured the privations, sufferings and horrors of slavery, without having become more degraded in the scale of humanity than the slaves of African descent. Nothing has been left undone to cripple their intellects, darken their minds, debase their moral nature, obliterate all traces of their relationship to mankind; and yet how wonderfully they have sustained the mighty load of a most frightful bondage, under which they have been groaning for centuries! To illustrate the effect of slavery on the white man,—to show that he has no powers of endurance, in such a condition, superior to those of his black brother,—DANIEL O'CONNELL, the distinguished advocate of universal emancipation, and the mightiest champion of prostrate but not conquered Ireland, relates the following anecdote in a speech delivered by him in the Conciliation Hall, Dublin, before the Loyal National Repeal Association, March 31, 1845. "No matter," said Mr. O'CONNELL, "under what specious term it may disguise itself, slavery is still hideous. *It has a natural, an inevitable tendency to brutalize every noble faculty of man.* An American sailor, who was cast away on the shore of Africa, where he was kept in slavery for three years, was, at the expiration of that period, found to be imbruted and stultified—he had lost all reasoning power; and having forgotten his native language, could only utter some savage gibberish between Arabic and English, which nobody could understand, and which even he himself found difficulty in pronouncing. So much for the humanizing influence of THE DOMESTIC INSTITUTION!" Admitting this to have been an extraordinary case of mental deterioration, it proves at least that the white slave can sink as low in the scale of humanity as the black one.

Mr. DOUGLASS has very properly chosen to write his own Narrative, in his own style, and according to the best of his ability, rather than to employ some one else. It is, therefore, entirely his own production; and, considering how long and dark was the career he had to run as a slave,—how few have been his opportunities to improve his mind since he broke his iron fetters,—it is, in my judgment, highly creditable to his head and heart. He who can peruse it without a tearful eye, a heaving breast, an afflicted spirit,—without being filled with an unutterable abhorrence of slavery and all its abettors, and animated with a determination to seek the immediate overthrow of that execrable system,—without trembling for the fate of this country in the hands of a righteous God, who is ever on the side of the oppressed, and whose arm is not shortened that it cannot save,—must have a flinty heart, and be qualified to act the part of a trafficker "in slaves and the souls of men." I am confident that it is essentially true in all its statements; that nothing has been set down in malice, nothing exaggerated, nothing drawn from the imagination; that it comes short of the reality, rather than overstates a single fact in regard to SLAVERY AS IT IS. The experience of FREDERICK DOUGLASS, as a slave, was not a peculiar one; his lot was not especially a hard one; his case may be regarded as a very fair specimen of the treatment of slaves in Maryland, in which State it is conceded that they are better fed and less cruelly treated than in Georgia, Alabama, or Louisiana. Many have suffered incomparably more, while very few on the plantations have suffered less, than himself. Yet how deplorable was his situation! what terrible chastisements were inflicted upon his person! what still more shocking outrages were perpetrated upon his mind! with all his noble powers and sublime aspirations, how like a brute was he treated, even by those professing to have the same mind in them that was in Christ Jesus! to what dreadful liabilities was he continually subjected! how destitute of friendly counsel and aid, even in his greatest extremities! how heavy was the midnight of woe which shrouded in blackness the last ray of hope, and filled the future with terror and gloom! what longings after freedom took possession of his breast, and how his misery augmented, in proportion as he grew reflective and intelligent,—thus demonstrating that a happy slave is an extinct man! how he thought, reasoned, felt, under the lash of the driver, with the chains upon his limbs! what perils he encountered in his endeavors to escape from his horrible doom! and how signal have been his deliverance and preservation in the midst of a nation of pitiless enemies!

This Narrative contains many affecting incidents, many passages of great eloquence and power; but I think the most thrilling one of them all is the description DOUGLASS gives of his feelings, as he stood soliloquizing respecting his fate, and the chances of his one day being a freeman, on the banks of the Chesapeake Bay—viewing the receding vessels as they flew with their white wings before the breeze, and apostrophizing them as animated by the living spirit of freedom. Who can read that passage, and be insensible to its pathos and sublimity? Compressed into it is a whole Alexandrian library of thought, feeling, and sentiment—all that can, all that need be urged, in the form of expostulation, entreaty, rebuke, against that crime of crimes,—making man the property of his fellow-man! O, how accursed is that system, which entombs the godlike mind of man, defaces the divine image, reduces those who by creation were crowned with glory and honor to a level with four-footed beasts, and exalts the dealer in human flesh above all that is called God! Why should its existence be prolonged one hour? Is it not evil, only evil, and that continually? What does its presence imply but the absence of all fear of God, all regard for man, on the part of the people of the United States? Heaven speed its eternal overthrow!

So profoundly ignorant of the nature of slavery are many persons, that they are stubbornly incredulous whenever they read or listen to any recital of the cruelties which are daily inflicted on its victims. They do not deny that the slaves are held as property; but that terrible fact seems to convey to their minds no idea of injustice, exposure to outrage, or savage barbarity. Tell them of cruel scourgings, of mutilations and brandings, of scenes of pollution and blood, of the banishment of all light and knowledge, and they affect to be greatly indignant at such enormous exaggerations, such wholesale misstatements, such abominable libels on the character of the southern planters! As if all these direful outrages were not the natural results of slavery! As if it were less cruel to reduce a human being to the condition of a thing, than to give him a severe flagellation, or to deprive him of necessary food and clothing! As if whips, chains, thumb-screws, paddles, bloodhounds, overseers, drivers, patrols, were not all indispensable to keep the slaves down, and to give protection to their ruthless oppressors! As if, when the marriage institution is abolished, concubinage, adultery, and incest, must not necessarily abound; when all the rights of humanity are annihilated, any barrier remains to protect the victim from the fury of the spoiler; when absolute power is assumed over life and liberty, it will not be wielded with destructive sway! Skeptics of this character abound in society. In some few instances, their incredulity arises from a want of reflection; but, generally, it indicates a hatred of the light, a desire to shield slavery from the assaults of its foes, a contempt of the colored race, whether bond or free. Such will try to discredit the shocking tales of slaveholding cruelty which are recorded in this truthful Narrative; but they will labor in vain. Mr. DOUGLASS has frankly disclosed the place of his birth, the names of those who claimed ownership in his body and soul, and the names also of those who committed the crimes which he has alleged against them. His statements, therefore, may easily be disproved, if they are untrue.

In the course of his Narrative, he relates two instances of murderous cruelty,—in one of which a planter deliberately shot a slave belonging to a neighboring plantation, who had unintentionally gotten within his lordly domain in quest of fish; and in the other, an overseer blew out the brains of a slave who had fled to a stream of water to escape a bloody scourging. Mr. DOUGLASS states that in neither of these instances was any thing done by way of legal arrest or judicial investigation. The Baltimore American, of March 17, 1845, relates a similar case of atrocity, perpetrated with similar impunity—as follows:—"*Shooting a Slave.*—We learn, upon the authority of a letter from Charles county, Maryland, received by a gentleman of this city, that a young man, named Matthews, a nephew of General Matthews, and whose father, it is believed, holds an office at Washington, killed one of the slaves upon his father's farm by shooting him. The letter states that young Matthews had been left in charge of the farm; that he gave an order to the servant, which was disobeyed, when he proceeded to the house, *obtained a gun, and, returning, shot the servant.* He immediately, the letter continues, fled to his father's residence, where he still remains unmolested."—Let it never be forgotten, that no slaveholder or overseer can be convicted of any outrage perpetrated on the person of a slave, however diabolical it may be, on the testimony of colored witnesses, whether bond or free. By the slave code, they are adjudged to be as incompetent to testify against a white man, as though they were indeed a part of the brute creation. Hence, there is no legal protection in fact, whatever there may be in form, for the slave population; and any amount of cruelty may be inflicted on them with impunity. Is it possible for the human mind to conceive of a more horrible state of society?

The effect of a religious profession on the conduct of southern masters is vividly described in the following Narrative, and shown to be any thing but salutary. In the nature of the case, it must be in the highest degree pernicious. The testimony of Mr. DOUGLASS, on this point, is sustained by a cloud of witnesses, whose veracity is unimpeachable. "A slaveholder's profession of Christianity is a palpable imposture. He is a felon of the highest grade. He is a man-stealer. It is of no importance what you put in the other scale."

Reader! are you with the man-stealers in sympathy and purpose, or on the side of their down-trodden victims? If with the former, then are you the foe of God and man. If with the latter, what are you prepared to do and dare in their behalf? Be faithful, be vigilant, be untiring in your efforts to break every yoke, and let the oppressed go free. Come what may—cost what it may—inscribe on the banner which you unfurl to the breeze, as your religious and political motto—"NO COMPROMISE WITH SLAVERY! NO UNION WITH SLAVEHOLDERS!"

WM. LLOYD GARRISON.

BOSTON, *May* 1, 1845.

LETTER
FROM WENDELL PHILLIPS, ESQ.

BOSTON, *April* 22, 1845.

My Dear Friend:

YOU remember the old fable of "The Man and the Lion," where the lion complained that he should not be so misrepresented "when the lions wrote history."

I am glad the time has come when the "lions write history." We have been left long enough to gather the character of slavery from the involuntary evidence of the masters. One might, indeed, rest sufficiently satisfied with what, it is evident, must be, in general, the results of such a relation, without seeking farther to find whether they have followed in every instance. Indeed, those who stare at the half-peck of corn a week, and love to count the lashes on the slave's back, are seldom the "stuff" out of which reformers and abolitionists are to be made. I remember that, in 1838, many were waiting for the results of the West India experiment, before they could come into our ranks. Those "results" have come long ago; but, alas! few of that number have come with them, as converts. A man must be disposed to judge of emancipation by other tests than whether it has increased the produce of sugar,—and to hate slavery for other reasons than because it starves men and whips women,—before he is ready to lay the first stone of his anti-slavery life.

I was glad to learn, in your story, how early the most neglected of God's children waken to a sense of their rights, and of the injustice done them. Experience is a keen teacher; and long before you had mastered your A B C, or knew where the "white sails" of the Chesapeake were bound, you began, I see, to gauge the wretchedness of the slave, not by his hunger and want, not by his lashes and toil, but by the cruel and blighting death which gathers over his soul.

In connection with this, there is one circumstance which makes your recollections peculiarly valuable, and renders your early insight the more remarkable. You come from that part of the country where we are told slavery appears with its fairest features. Let us hear, then, what it is at its best estate—gaze on its bright side, if it has one; and then imagination may task her powers to add dark lines to the picture, as she travels southward to that (for the colored man) Valley of the Shadow of Death, where the Mississippi sweeps along.

Again, we have known you long, and can put the most entire confidence in your truth, candor, and sincerity. Every one who has heard you speak has felt, and, I am confident, every one who reads your book will feel, persuaded that you give them a fair specimen of the whole truth. No one-sided portrait,—no wholesale complaints,—but strict justice done, whenever individual kindliness has neutralized, for a moment, the deadly system with which it was strangely allied. You have been with us, too, some years, and can fairly compare the twilight of rights, which your race enjoy at the North, with that "noon of night" under which they labor south of Mason and Dixon's line. Tell us whether, after all, the half-free colored man of Massachusetts is worse off than the pampered slave of the rice swamps!

In reading your life, no one can say that we have unfairly picked out some rare specimens of cruelty. We know that the bitter drops, which even you have drained from the cup, are no incidental aggravations, no individual ills, but such as must mingle always and necessarily in the lot of every slave. They are the essential ingredients, not the occasional results, of the system.

After all, I shall read your book with trembling for you. Some years ago, when you were beginning to tell me your real name and birthplace, you may remember I stopped you, and preferred to remain ignorant of all. With the exception of a vague description, so I continued, till the other day, when you read me your memoirs. I hardly knew, at the time, whether to thank you or not for the sight of them, when I reflected that it was still dangerous, in Massachusetts, for honest men to tell their names! They say the fathers, in 1776, signed the Declaration of Independence with the halter about their necks. You, too, publish your declaration of freedom with danger compassing you around. In all the broad lands which the Constitution of the United States overshadows, there is no single spot,—however narrow or desolate,—where a fugitive slave can plant himself and say, "I am safe." The whole armory of Northern Law has no shield for you. I am free to say that, in your place, I should throw the MS. into the fire.

You, perhaps, may tell your story in safety, endeared as you are to so many warm hearts by rare gifts, and a still rarer devotion of them to the service of others. But it will be owing only to your labors, and the fearless efforts of those who, trampling the laws and Constitution of the country under their feet, are determined that they will "hide the outcast," and that their hearths shall be, spite of the law, an asylum for the oppressed, if, some time or other, the humblest may stand in our streets, and bear witness in safety against the cruelties of which he has been the victim.

Yet it is sad to think, that these very throbbing hearts which welcome your story, and form your best safeguard in telling it, are all beating contrary to the "statute in such case made and provided." Go on, my dear friend, till you, and those who, like you, have been saved, so as by fire, from the dark prison-house, shall stereotype these free, illegal pulses into statutes; and New England, cutting loose from a blood-stained Union, shall glory in being the house of refuge for the oppressed;—till we no longer merely "*hide* the outcast," or make a merit of standing idly by while he is hunted in our midst; but, consecrating anew the soil of the Pilgrims as an asylum for the oppressed, proclaim our *welcome* to the slave so loudly, that the tones shall reach every hut in the Carolinas, and make the broken-hearted bondman leap up at the thought of old Massachusetts.

God speed the day!

Till then, and ever,

Yours truly,

WENDELL PHILLIPS.

FREDERICK DOUGLASS.

NARRATIVE

OF THE

LIFE OF FREDERICK DOUGLASS.

CHAPTER I.

I WAS born in Tuckahoe, near Hillsborough, and about twelve miles from Easton, in Talbot county, Maryland. I have no accurate knowledge of my age, never having seen any authentic record containing it. By far the larger part of the slaves know as little of their ages as horses know of theirs, and it is the wish of most masters within my knowledge to keep their slaves thus ignorant. I do not remember to have ever met a slave who could tell his birthday. They seldom come nearer to it than planting-time, harvest-time, cherry-time, spring-time, or fall-time. A want of information concerning my own was a source of unhappiness to me even during childhood. The white children could tell their ages. I could not tell why I ought to be deprived of the same privilege. I was not allowed to make any inquiries of my master concerning it. He deemed all such inquiries on the part of a slave improper and impertinent, and evidence of a restless spirit. The nearest estimate I can give makes me now between twenty-seven and twenty-eight years of age. I come to this, from hearing my master say, some time during 1835, I was about seventeen years old.

My mother was named Harriet Bailey. She was the daughter of Isaac and Betsey Bailey, both colored, and quite dark. My mother was of a darker complexion than either my grandmother or grandfather.

My father was a white man. He was admitted to be such by all I ever heard speak of my parentage. The opinion was also whispered that my master was my father; but of the correctness of this opinion, I know nothing; the means of knowing was withheld from me. My mother and I were separated when I was but an infant—before I knew her as my mother. It is a common custom, in the part of Maryland from which I ran away, to part children from their mothers at a very early age. Frequently, before the child has reached its twelfth month, its mother is taken from it, and hired out on some farm a considerable distance off, and the child is placed under the care of an old woman, too old for field labor. For what this separation is done, I do not know, unless it be to hinder the development of the child's affection toward its mother, and to blunt and destroy the natural affection of the mother for the child. This is the inevitable result.

I never saw my mother, to know her as such, more than four or five times in my life; and each of these times was very short in duration, and at night. She was hired by a Mr. Stewart, who lived about twelve miles from my home. She made her journeys to see me in the night, travelling the whole distance on foot, after the performance of her day's work. She was a field hand, and a whipping is the penalty of not being in the field at sunrise, unless a slave has special permission from his or her master to the contrary—a permission which they seldom get, and one that gives to him that gives it the proud name of being a kind master. I do not recollect ever seeing my mother by the light of day. She was with me in the night. She would lie down with me, and get me to sleep, but long before I waked she was gone. Very little communication ever took place between us. Death soon ended what little we could have while she lived, and with it her hardships and suffering. She died when I was about seven years old, on one of my master's farms, near Lee's Mill. I was not allowed to be present during her illness, at her death, or burial. She was gone long before I knew any thing about it. Never having enjoyed, to any considerable extent, her soothing presence, her tender and watchful care, I received the tidings of her death with much the same emotions I should have probably felt at the death of a stranger.

Called thus suddenly away, she left me without the slightest intimation of who my father was. The whisper that my master was my father, may or may not be true; and, true or false, it is of but little consequence to my purpose whilst the fact remains, in all its glaring odiousness, that slaveholders have ordained, and by law established, that the children of slave women shall in all cases follow the condition of their mothers; and this is done too obviously to administer to their own lusts, and make a gratification of their wicked desires profitable as well as pleasurable; for by this cunning arrangement, the slaveholder, in cases not a few, sustains to his slaves the double relation of master and father.

I know of such cases; and it is worthy of remark that such slaves invariably suffer greater hardships, and have more to contend with, than others. They are, in the first place, a constant offence to their mistress. She is ever disposed to find fault with them; they can seldom do any thing to please her; she is never better pleased than when she sees them under the lash, especially when she suspects her husband of showing to his mulatto children favors which he withholds from his black slaves. The master is frequently compelled to sell this class of his slaves, out of deference to the feelings of his white wife; and, cruel as the deed may strike any one to be, for a man to sell his own children to human flesh-mongers, it is often the dictate of humanity for him to do so; for, unless he does this, he must not only whip them himself, but must stand by and see one white son tie up his brother, of but few shades darker complexion than himself, and ply the gory lash to his naked back; and if he lisp one word of disapproval, it is set down to his parental partiality, and only makes a bad matter worse, both for himself and the slave whom he would protect and defend.

Every year brings with it multitudes of this class of slaves. It was doubtless in consequence of a knowledge of this fact, that one great statesman of the south predicted the downfall of slavery by the inevitable laws of population. Whether this prophecy is ever fulfilled or not, it is nevertheless plain that a very different-looking class of people are springing up at the south, and are now held in slavery, from those originally brought to this country from Africa; and if their increase will do no other good, it will do away the force of the argument, that God cursed Ham, and therefore American slavery is right. If the lineal descendants of Ham are alone to be scripturally enslaved, it is certain that slavery at the south must soon become unscriptural; for thousands are ushered into the world, annually, who, like myself, owe their existence to white fathers, and those fathers most frequently their own masters.

I have had two masters. My first master's name was Anthony. I do not remember his first name. He was generally called Captain Anthony—a title which, I presume, he acquired by sailing a craft on the Chesapeake Bay. He was not considered a rich slaveholder. He owned two or three farms, and about thirty slaves. His farms and slaves were under the care of an overseer. The overseer's name was Plummer. Mr. Plummer was a miserable drunkard, a profane swearer, and a savage monster. He always went armed with a cowskin and a heavy cudgel. I have known him to cut and slash the women's heads so horribly, that even master would be enraged at his cruelty, and would threaten to whip him if he did not mind himself. Master, however, was not a humane slaveholder. It required extraordinary barbarity on the part of an overseer to affect him. He was a cruel man, hardened by a long life of slaveholding. He would at times seem to take great pleasure in whipping a slave. I have often been awakened at the dawn of day by the most heart-rending shrieks of an own aunt of mine, whom he used to tie up to a joist, and whip upon her naked back till she was literally covered with blood. No words, no tears, no prayers, from his gory victim, seemed to move his iron heart from its bloody purpose. The louder she screamed, the harder he whipped; and where the blood ran fastest, there he whipped longest. He would whip her to make her scream, and whip her to make her hush; and not until overcome by fatigue, would he cease to swing the blood-clotted cowskin. I remember the first time I ever witnessed this horrible exhibition. I was quite a child, but I well remember it. I never shall forget it whilst I remember any thing. It was the first of a long series of such outrages, of which I was doomed to be a witness and a participant. It struck me with awful force. It was the blood-stained gate, the entrance to the hell of slavery, through which I was about to pass. It was a most terrible spectacle. I wish I could commit to paper the feelings with which I beheld it.

This occurrence took place very soon after I went to live with my old master, and under the following circumstances. Aunt Hester went out one night,—where or for what I do not know,—and happened to be absent when my master desired her presence. He had ordered her not to go out evenings, and warned her that she must never let him catch her in company with a young man, who was paying attention to her belonging to Colonel Lloyd. The young man's name was Ned Roberts, generally called Lloyd's Ned. Why master was so careful of her, may be safely left to conjecture. She was a woman of noble form, and of graceful proportions, having very few equals, and fewer superiors, in personal appearance, among the colored or white women of our neighborhood.

Aunt Hester had not only disobeyed his orders in going out, but had been found in company with Lloyd's Ned; which circumstance, I found, from what he said while whipping her, was the chief offence. Had he been a man of pure morals himself, he might have been thought interested in protecting the innocence of my aunt; but those who knew him will not suspect him of any such virtue. Before he commenced whipping Aunt Hester, he took her into the kitchen, and stripped her from neck to waist, leaving her neck, shoulders, and back, entirely naked. He then told her to cross her hands, calling her at the same time a d——d b——h. After crossing her hands, he tied them with a strong rope, and led her to a stool under a large hook in the joist, put in for the purpose. He made her get upon the stool, and tied her hands to the hook. She now stood fair for his infernal purpose. Her arms were stretched up at their full length, so that she stood upon the ends of her toes. He then said to her, "Now, you d——d b——h, I'll learn you how to disobey my orders!" and after rolling up his sleeves, he commenced to lay on the heavy cowskin, and soon the warm, red blood (amid heart-rending shrieks from her, and horrid oaths from him) came dripping to the floor. I was so terrified and horror-stricken at the sight, that I hid myself in a closet, and dared not venture out till long after the bloody transaction was over. I expected it would be my turn next. It was all new to me. I had never seen any thing like it before. I had always lived with my grandmother on the outskirts of the plantation, where she was put to raise the children of the younger women. I had therefore been, until now, out of the way of the bloody scenes that often occurred on the plantation.

CHAPTER II.

My master's family consisted of two sons, Andrew and Richard; one daughter, Lucretia, and her husband, Captain Thomas Auld. They lived in one house, upon the home plantation of Colonel Edward Lloyd. My master was Colonel Lloyd's clerk and superintendent. He was what might be called the overseer of the overseers. I spent two years of childhood on this plantation in my old master's family. It was here that I witnessed the bloody transaction recorded in the first chapter; and as I received my first impressions of slavery on this plantation, I will give some description of it, and of slavery as it there existed. The plantation is about twelve miles north of Easton, in Talbot county, and is situated on the border of Miles River. The principal products raised upon it were tobacco, corn, and wheat. These were raised in great abundance; so that, with the products of this and the other farms belonging to him, he was able to keep in almost constant employment a large sloop, in carrying them to market at Baltimore. This sloop was named Sally Lloyd, in honor of one of the colonel's daughters. My master's son-in-law, Captain Auld, was master of the vessel; she was otherwise manned by the colonel's own slaves. Their names were Peter, Isaac, Rich, and Jake. These were esteemed very highly by the other slaves, and looked upon as the privileged ones of the plantation; for it was no small affair, in the eyes of the slaves, to be allowed to see Baltimore.

Colonel Lloyd kept from three to four hundred slaves on his home plantation, and owned a large number more on the neighboring farms belonging to him. The names of the farms nearest to the home plantation were Wye Town and New Design. "Wye Town" was under the overseership of a man named Noah Willis. New Design was under the overseership of a Mr. Townsend. The overseers of these, and all the rest of the farms, numbering over twenty, received advice and direction from the managers of the home plantation. This was the great business place. It was the seat of government for the whole twenty farms. All disputes among the overseers were settled here. If a slave was convicted of any high misdemeanor, became unmanageable, or evinced a determination to run away, he was brought immediately here, severely whipped, put on board the sloop, carried to Baltimore, and sold to Austin Woolfolk, or some other slave-trader, as a warning to the slaves remaining.

Here, too, the slaves of all the other farms received their monthly allowance of food, and their yearly clothing. The men and women slaves received, as their monthly allowance of food, eight pounds of pork, or its equivalent in fish, and one bushel of corn meal. Their yearly clothing consisted of two coarse linen shirts, one pair of linen trousers, like the shirts, one jacket, one pair of trousers for winter, made of coarse negro cloth, one pair of stockings, and one pair of shoes; the whole of which could not have cost more than seven dollars. The allowance of the slave children was given to their mothers, or the old women having the care of them. The children unable to work in the field had neither shoes, stockings, jackets, nor trousers, given to them; their clothing consisted of two coarse linen shirts per year. When these failed them, they went naked until the next allowance-day. Children from seven to ten years old, of both sexes, almost naked, might be seen at all seasons of the year.

There were no beds given the slaves, unless one coarse blanket be considered such, and none but the men and women had these. This, however, is not considered a very great privation. They find less difficulty from the want of beds, than from the want of time to sleep; for when their day's work in the field is done, the most of them having their washing, mending, and cooking to do, and having few or none of the ordinary facilities for doing either of these, very many of their sleeping hours are consumed in preparing for the field the coming day; and when this is done, old and young, male and female, married and single, drop down side by side, on one common bed,—

the cold, damp floor,—each covering himself or herself with their miserable blankets; and here they sleep till they are summoned to the field by the driver's horn. At the sound of this, all must rise, and be off to the field. There must be no halting; every one must be at his or her post; and woe betides them who hear not this morning summons to the field; for if they are not awakened by the sense of hearing, they are by the sense of feeling: no age nor sex finds any favor. Mr. Severe, the overseer, used to stand by the door of the quarter, armed with a large hickory stick and heavy cowskin, ready to whip any one who was so unfortunate as not to hear, or, from any other cause, was prevented from being ready to start for the field at the sound of the horn.

Mr. Severe was rightly named: he was a cruel man. I have seen him whip a woman, causing the blood to run half an hour at the time; and this, too, in the midst of her crying children, pleading for their mother's release. He seemed to take pleasure in manifesting his fiendish barbarity. Added to his cruelty, he was a profane swearer. It was enough to chill the blood and stiffen the hair of an ordinary man to hear him talk. Scarce a sentence escaped him but what was commenced or concluded by some horrid oath. The field was the place to witness his cruelty and profanity. His presence made it both the field of blood and blasphemy. From the rising till the going down of the sun, he was cursing, raving, cutting, and slashing among the slaves of the field, in the most frightful manner. His career was short. He died very soon after I went to Colonel Lloyd's; and he died as he lived, uttering, with his dying groans, bitter curses and horrid oaths. His death was regarded by the slaves as the result of a merciful Providence.

Mr. Severe's place was filled by a Mr. Hopkins. He was a very different man. He was less cruel, less profane, and made less noise, than Mr. Severe. His course was characterized by no extraordinary demonstrations of cruelty. He whipped, but seemed to take no pleasure in it. He was called by the slaves a good overseer.

The home plantation of Colonel Lloyd wore the appearance of a country village. All the mechanical operations for all the farms were performed here. The shoemaking and mending, the blacksmithing, cartwrighting, coopering, weaving, and grain-grinding, were all performed by the slaves on the home plantation. The whole place wore a business-like aspect very unlike the neighboring farms. The number of houses, too, conspired to give it advantage over the neighboring farms. It was called by the slaves the *Great*

House Farm. Few privileges were esteemed higher, by the slaves of the out-farms, than that of being selected to do errands at the Great House Farm. It was associated in their minds with greatness. A representative could not be prouder of his election to a seat in the American Congress, than a slave on one of the out-farms would be of his election to do errands at the Great House Farm. They regarded it as evidence of great confidence reposed in them by their overseers; and it was on this account, as well as a constant desire to be out of the field from under the driver's lash, that they esteemed it a high privilege, one worth careful living for. He was called the smartest and most trusty fellow, who had this honor conferred upon him the most frequently. The competitors for this office sought as diligently to please their overseers, as the office-seekers in the political parties seek to please and deceive the people. The same traits of character might be seen in Colonel Lloyd's slaves, as are seen in the slaves of the political parties.

The slaves selected to go to the Great House Farm, for the monthly allowance for themselves and their fellow-slaves, were peculiarly enthusiastic. While on their way, they would make the dense old woods, for miles around, reverberate with their wild songs, revealing at once the highest joy and the deepest sadness. They would compose and sing as they went along, consulting neither time nor tune. The thought that came up, came out—if not in the word, in the sound;—and as frequently in the one as in the other. They would sometimes sing the most pathetic sentiment in the most rapturous tone, and the most rapturous sentiment in the most pathetic tone. Into all of their songs they would manage to weave something of the Great House Farm. Especially would they do this, when leaving home. They would then sing most exultingly the following words:—

"I am going away to the Great House Farm!
O, yea! O, yea! O!"

This they would sing, as a chorus, to words which to many would seem unmeaning jargon, but which, nevertheless, were full of meaning to themselves. I have sometimes thought that the mere hearing of those songs would do more to impress some minds with the horrible character of slavery, than the reading of whole volumes of philosophy on the subject could do.

I did not, when a slave, understand the deep meaning of those rude and apparently incoherent songs. I was myself within the circle; so that I neither saw nor heard as those without might see and hear. They told a tale of woe which was then altogether beyond my feeble comprehension; they were tones loud, long, and deep; they breathed the prayer and complaint of souls boiling over with the bitterest anguish. Every tone was a testimony against slavery, and a prayer to God for deliverance from chains. The hearing of those wild notes always depressed my spirit, and filled me with ineffable sadness. I have frequently found myself in tears while hearing them. The mere recurrence to those songs, even now, afflicts me; and while I am writing these lines, an expression of feeling has already found its way down my cheek. To those songs I trace my first glimmering conception of the dehumanizing character of slavery. I can never get rid of that conception. Those songs still follow me, to deepen my hatred of slavery, and quicken my sympathies for my brethren in bonds. If any one wishes to be impressed with the soul-killing effects of slavery, let him go to Colonel Lloyd's plantation, and, on allowance-day, place himself in the deep pine woods, and there let him, in silence, analyze the sounds that shall pass through the chambers of his soul,—and if he is not thus impressed, it will only be because "there is no flesh in his obdurate heart."

I have often been utterly astonished, since I came to the north, to find persons who could speak of the singing, among slaves, as evidence of their contentment and happiness. It is impossible to conceive of a greater mistake. Slaves sing most when they are most unhappy. The songs of the slave represent the sorrows of his heart; and he is relieved by them, only as an aching heart is relieved by its tears. At least, such is my experience. I have often sung to drown my sorrow, but seldom to express my happiness. Crying for joy, and singing for joy, were alike uncommon to me while in the jaws of slavery. The singing of a man cast away upon a desolate island might be as appropriately considered as evidence of contentment and happiness, as the singing of a slave; the songs of the one and of the other are prompted by the same emotion.

CHAPTER III.

Colonel Lloyd kept a large and finely cultivated garden, which afforded almost constant employment for four men, besides the chief gardener, (Mr. M'Durmond.) This garden was probably the greatest attraction of the place. During the summer months, people came from far and near—from

Baltimore, Easton, and Annapolis—to see it. It abounded in fruits of almost every description, from the hardy apple of the north to the delicate orange of the south. This garden was not the least source of trouble on the plantation. Its excellent fruit was quite a temptation to the hungry swarms of boys, as well as the older slaves, belonging to the colonel, few of whom had the virtue to resist it. Scarcely a day passed, during the summer, but that some slave had to take the lash for stealing fruit. The colonel had to resort to all kinds of stratagems to keep his slaves out of the garden. The last and most successful one was that of tarring his fence all around; after which, if a slave was caught with any tar upon his person, it was deemed sufficient proof that he had either been into the garden, or had tried to get in. In either case, he was severely whipped by the chief gardener. This plan worked well; the slaves became as fearful of tar as of the lash. They seemed to realize the impossibility of touching *tar* without being defiled.

The colonel also kept a splendid riding equipage. His stable and carriage-house presented the appearance of some of our large city livery establishments. His horses were of the finest form and noblest blood. His carriage-house contained three splendid coaches, three or four gigs, besides dearborns and barouches of the most fashionable style.

This establishment was under the care of two slaves—Old Barney and Young Barney—father and son. To attend to this establishment was their sole work. But it was by no means an easy employment; for in nothing was Colonel Lloyd more particular than in the management of his horses. The slightest inattention to these was unpardonable, and was visited upon those, under whose care they were placed, with the severest punishment; no excuse could shield them, if the colonel only suspected any want of attention to his horses—a supposition which he frequently indulged, and one which, of course, made the office of Old and Young Barney a very trying one. They never knew when they were safe from punishment. They were frequently whipped when least deserving, and escaped whipping when most deserving it. Every thing depended upon the looks of the horses, and the state of Colonel Lloyd's own mind when his horses were brought to him for use. If a horse did not move fast enough, or hold his head high enough, it was owing to some fault of his keepers. It was painful to stand near the stable-door, and hear the various complaints against the keepers when a horse was taken out for use. "This horse has not had proper attention. He has not been sufficiently rubbed and curried, or he has not been properly fed; his food was too wet or too dry; he got it too soon or too late; he was too hot or too cold; he had too much hay, and not enough of grain; or he had too much grain, and not enough of hay; instead of Old Barney's attending to the horse, he had very improperly left it to his son." To all these complaints, no matter how unjust, the slave must answer never a word. Colonel Lloyd could not brook any contradiction from a slave. When he spoke, a slave must stand, listen, and tremble; and such was literally the case. I have seen Colonel Lloyd make Old Barney, a man between fifty and sixty years of age, uncover his bald head, kneel down upon the cold, damp ground, and receive upon his naked and toil-worn shoulders more than thirty lashes at the time. Colonel Lloyd had three sons—Edward, Murray, and Daniel,—and three sons-in-law, Mr. Winder, Mr. Nicholson, and Mr. Lowndes. All of these lived at the Great House Farm, and enjoyed the luxury of whipping the servants when they pleased, from Old Barney down to William Wilkes, the coach-driver. I have seen Winder make one of the house-servants stand off from him a suitable distance to be touched with the end of his whip, and at every stroke raise great ridges upon his back.

To describe the wealth of Colonel Lloyd would be almost equal to describing the riches of Job. He kept from ten to fifteen house-servants. He was said to own a thousand slaves, and I think this estimate quite within the truth. Colonel Lloyd owned so many that he did not know them when he saw them; nor did all the slaves of the out-farms know him. It is reported of him, that, while riding along the road one day, he met a colored man, and addressed him in the usual manner of speaking to colored people on the public highways of the south: "Well, boy, whom do you belong to?" "To Colonel Lloyd," replied the slave. "Well, does the colonel treat you well?" "No, sir," was the ready reply. "What, does he work you too hard?" "Yes, sir." "Well, don't he give you enough to eat?" "Yes, sir, he gives me enough, such as it is."

The colonel, after ascertaining whom the slave belonged to, rode on; the man also went on about his business, not dreaming that he had been conversing with his master. He thought, said, and heard nothing more of the matter, until two or three weeks afterwards. The poor man was then informed by his overseer that, for having found fault with his master, he was now to be sold to a Georgia trader. He was immediately chained and handcuffed; and thus, without a moment's warning, he was snatched away, and forever sundered, from his family and friends, by a hand more unrelenting than death. This is the penalty of telling the truth, of telling the simple truth, in answer to a series of plain questions.

It is partly in consequence of such facts, that slaves, when inquired of as to their condition and the character of their masters, almost universally say they are contented, and that their masters are kind. The slaveholders have been known to send in spies among their slaves, to ascertain their views and feelings in regard to their condition. The frequency of this has had the effect to establish among the slaves the maxim, that a still tongue makes a wise head. They suppress the truth rather than take the consequences of telling it, and in so doing prove themselves a part of the human family. If they have any thing to say of their masters, it is generally in their masters' favor, especially when speaking to an untried man. I have been frequently asked, when a slave, if I had a kind master, and do not remember ever to have given a negative answer; nor did I, in pursuing this course, consider myself as uttering what was absolutely false; for I always measured the kindness of my master by the standard of kindness set up among slaveholders around us. Moreover, slaves are like other people, and imbibe prejudices quite common to others. They think their own better than that of others. Many, under the influence of this prejudice, think their own masters are better than the masters of other slaves; and this, too, in some cases, when the very reverse is true. Indeed, it is not uncommon for slaves even to fall out and quarrel among themselves about the relative goodness of their masters, each contending for the superior goodness of his own over that of the others. At the very same time, they mutually execrate their masters when viewed separately. It was so on our plantation. When Colonel Lloyd's slaves met the slaves of Jacob Jepson, they seldom parted without a quarrel about their masters; Colonel Lloyd's slaves contending that he was the richest, and Mr. Jepson's slaves that he was the smartest, and most of a man. Colonel Lloyd's slaves would boast his ability to buy and sell Jacob Jepson. Mr. Jepson's slaves would boast his ability to whip Colonel Lloyd. These quarrels would almost always end in a fight between the parties, and those that whipped were supposed to have gained the point at issue. They seemed to think that the greatness of their masters was transferable to themselves. It was considered as being bad enough to be a slave; but to be a poor man's slave was deemed a disgrace indeed!

CHAPTER IV.

Mr. Hopkins remained but a short time in the office of overseer. Why his career was so short, I do not know, but suppose he lacked the necessary severity to suit Colonel Lloyd. Mr. Hopkins was succeeded by Mr. Austin Gore, a man possessing, in an eminent degree, all those traits of character indispensable to what is called a first-rate overseer. Mr. Gore had served Colonel Lloyd, in the capacity of overseer, upon one of the out-farms, and had shown himself worthy of the high station of overseer upon the home or Great House Farm.

Mr. Gore was proud, ambitious, and persevering. He was artful, cruel, and obdurate. He was just the man for such a place, and it was just the place for such a man. It afforded scope for the full exercise of all his powers, and he seemed to be perfectly at home in it. He was one of those who could torture the slightest look, word, or gesture, on the part of the slave, into impudence, and would treat it accordingly. There must be no answering back to him; no explanation was allowed a slave, showing himself to have been wrongfully accused. Mr. Gore acted fully up to the maxim laid down by slaveholders,—"It is better that a dozen slaves suffer under the lash, than that the overseer should be convicted, in the presence of the slaves, of having been at fault." No matter how innocent a slave might be—it availed him nothing, when accused by Mr. Gore of any misdemeanor. To be accused was to be convicted, and to be convicted was to be punished; the one always following the other with immutable certainty. To escape punishment was to escape accusation; and few slaves had the fortune to do either, under the overseership of Mr. Gore. He was just proud enough to demand the most debasing homage of the slave, and quite servile enough to crouch, himself, at the feet of the master. He was ambitious enough to be contented with nothing short of the highest rank of overseers, and persevering enough to reach the height of his ambition. He was cruel enough to inflict the severest punishment, artful enough to descend to the lowest trickery, and obdurate enough to be insensible to the voice of a reproving conscience. He was, of all the overseers, the most dreaded by the slaves. His presence was painful; his eye flashed confusion; and seldom was his sharp, shrill voice heard, without producing horror and trembling in their ranks.

Mr. Gore was a grave man, and, though a young man, he indulged in no jokes, said no funny words, seldom smiled. His words were in perfect keeping with his looks, and his looks were in perfect keeping with his words. Overseers will sometimes indulge in a witty word, even with the slaves; not so with Mr. Gore. He spoke but to command, and commanded but to be obeyed; he dealt sparingly with his words, and bountifully with his whip, never using the former where the latter would answer as well. When he whipped, he seemed to do so from a sense of duty, and feared no consequences. He did nothing reluctantly, no matter how disagreeable; always at his post, never inconsistent. He never promised but to fulfil. He was, in a word, a man of the most inflexible firmness and stone-like coolness.

His savage barbarity was equalled only by the consummate coolness with which he committed the grossest and most savage deeds upon the slaves under his charge. Mr. Gore once undertook to whip one of Colonel Lloyd's slaves, by the name of Demby. He had given Demby but few stripes, when, to get rid of the scourging, he ran and plunged himself into a creek, and stood there at the depth of his shoulders, refusing to come out. Mr. Gore told him that he would give him three calls, and that, if he did not come out at the third call, he would shoot him. The first call was given. Demby made no response, but stood his ground. The second and third calls were given with the same result. Mr. Gore then, without consultation or deliberation with any one, not even giving Demby an additional call, raised his musket to his face, taking deadly aim at his standing victim, and in an instant poor Demby was no more. His mangled body sank out of sight, and blood and brains marked the water where he had stood.

A thrill of horror flashed through every soul upon the plantation, excepting Mr. Gore. He alone seemed cool and collected. He was asked by Colonel Lloyd and my old master, why he resorted to this extraordinary expedient. His reply was, (as well as I can remember,) that Demby had become unmanageable. He was setting a dangerous example to the other slaves,—one which, if suffered to pass without some such demonstration on his part, would finally lead to the total subversion of all rule and order upon the plantation. He argued that if one slave refused to be corrected, and escaped with his life, the other slaves would soon copy the example; the result of which would be, the freedom of the slaves, and the enslavement of the whites. Mr. Gore's defence was satisfactory. He was continued in his station as overseer upon the home plantation. His fame as an overseer went abroad. His horrid crime was not even submitted to judicial investigation. It was committed in the presence of slaves, and they of course could neither institute a suit, nor testify against him; and thus the guilty perpetrator of one of the bloodiest and most foul murders goes unwhipped of justice, and uncensured by the community in which he lives. Mr. Gore lived in St. Michael's, Talbot county, Maryland, when I left there; and if he is still alive, he very probably lives there now; and if so, he is now, as he was then, as highly esteemed and as much respected as though his guilty soul had not been stained with his brother's blood.

I speak advisedly when I say this,—that killing a slave, or any colored person, in Talbot county, Maryland, is not treated as a crime, either by the courts or the community. Mr. Thomas Lanman, of St. Michael's, killed two slaves, one of whom he killed with a hatchet, by knocking his brains out. He used to boast of the commission of the awful and bloody deed. I have heard him do so laughingly, saying, among other things, that he was the only benefactor of his country in the company, and that when others would do as much as he had done, we should be relieved of "the d——d niggers."

The wife of Mr. Giles Hicks, living but a short distance from where I used to live, murdered my wife's cousin, a young girl between fifteen and sixteen years of age, mangling her person in the most horrible manner, breaking her nose and breastbone with a stick, so that the poor girl expired in a few hours afterward. She was immediately buried, but had not been in her untimely grave but a few hours before she was taken up and examined by the coroner, who decided that she had come to her death by severe beating. The offence for which this girl was thus murdered was this:—She had been set that night to mind Mrs. Hicks' baby, and during the night she fell asleep, and the baby cried. She, having lost her rest for several nights previous, did not hear the crying. They were both in the room with Mrs. Hicks. Mrs. Hicks, finding the girl slow to move, jumped from her bed, seized an oak stick of wood by the fireplace, and with it broke the girl's nose and breastbone, and thus ended her life. I will not say that this most horrid murder produced no sensation in the community. It did produce sensation, but not enough to bring the murderess to punishment. There was a warrant issued for her arrest, but it was never served. Thus she escaped not only punishment, but even the pain of being arraigned before a court for her horrid crime.

Whilst I am detailing bloody deeds which took place during my stay on Colonel Lloyd's plantation, I will briefly narrate another, which occurred about the same time as the murder of Demby by Mr. Gore.

Colonel Lloyd's slaves were in the habit of spending a part of their nights and Sundays in fishing for oysters, and in this way made up the deficiency of their scanty allowance. An old man belonging to Colonel Lloyd, while thus engaged, happened to get beyond the limits of Colonel Lloyd's, and on the premises of Mr. Beal Bondly. At this trespass, Mr. Bondly took offence, and with his musket came down to the shore, and blew its deadly contents into the poor old man.

Mr. Bondly came over to see Colonel Lloyd the next day, whether to pay him for his property, or to justify himself in what he had done, I know not. At any rate, this whole fiendish transaction was soon hushed up. There was very little said about it at all, and nothing done. It was a common saying, even among little white boys, that it was worth a half-cent to kill a "nigger," and a half-cent to bury one.

CHAPTER V.

As to my own treatment while I lived on Colonel Lloyd's plantation, it was very similar to that of the other slave children. I was not old enough to work in the field, and there being little else than field work to do, I had a great deal of leisure time. The most I had to do was to drive up the cows at evening, keep the fowls out of the garden, keep the front yard clean, and run of errands for my old master's daughter, Mrs. Lucretia Auld. The most of my leisure time I spent in helping Master Daniel Lloyd in finding his birds, after he had shot them. My connection with Master Daniel was of some advantage to me. He became quite attached to me, and was a sort of protector of me. He would not allow the older boys to impose upon me, and would divide his cakes with me.

I was seldom whipped by my old master, and suffered little from any thing else than hunger and cold. I suffered much from hunger, but much more from cold. In hottest summer and coldest winter, I was kept almost naked—no shoes, no stockings, no jacket, no trousers, nothing on but a coarse tow linen shirt, reaching only to my knees. I had no bed. I must have perished with cold, but that, the coldest nights, I used to steal a bag which was used for carrying corn to the mill. I would crawl into this bag, and there sleep on the cold, damp, clay floor, with my head in and feet out. My feet have been so cracked with the frost, that the pen with which I am writing might be laid in the gashes.

We were not regularly allowanced. Our food was coarse corn meal boiled. This was called *mush.* It was put into a large wooden tray or trough, and set down upon the ground. The children were then called, like so many pigs, and like so many pigs they would come and devour the mush; some with oyster-shells, others with pieces of shingle, some with naked hands, and none with spoons. He that ate fastest got most; he that was strongest secured the best place; and few left the trough satisfied.

I was probably either seven or eight years old when I left Colonel Lloyd's plantation. I left it with joy. I shall never forget the ecstasy with which I received the intelligence that my old master (Anthony) had determined to let me go to Baltimore, to live with Mr. Hugh Auld, brother to my old master's son-in-law, Captain Thomas Auld. I received this information about three days before my departure. They were three of the happiest days I ever enjoyed. I spent the most part of all these three days in the creek, washing off the plantation scurf, and preparing myself for my departure.

The pride of appearance which this would indicate was not my own. I spent the time in washing, not so much because I wished to, but because Mrs. Lucretia had told me I must get all the dead skin off my feet and knees before I could go to Baltimore; for the people in Baltimore were very cleanly, and would laugh at me if I looked dirty. Besides, she was going to give me a pair of trousers, which I should not put on unless I got all the dirt off me. The thought of owning a pair of trousers was great indeed! It was almost a sufficient motive, not only to make me take off what would be called by pig-drovers the mange, but the skin itself. I went at it in good earnest, working for the first time with the hope of reward.

The ties that ordinarily bind children to their homes were all suspended in my case. I found no severe trial in my departure. My home was charmless; it was not home to me; on parting from it, I could not feel that I was leaving any thing which I could have enjoyed by staying. My mother was dead, my grandmother lived far off, so that I seldom saw her. I had two sisters and one brother, that lived in the same house with me; but the early separation of us from our mother had well nigh blotted the fact of our relationship from our memories. I looked for home elsewhere, and was confident of finding none which I should relish less than the one which I was leaving. If, however, I found in my new home hardship, hunger, whipping, and nakedness, I had the consolation that I should not have escaped any one of them by staying. Having already had more than a taste of them in the house of my old master, and having endured them there, I very naturally inferred my ability to endure them elsewhere, and especially at Baltimore; for I had something of the feeling about Baltimore that is expressed in the proverb, that "being hanged in England is preferable to dying a natural death in Ireland." I had the strongest desire to see Baltimore. Cousin Tom, though not fluent in speech, had inspired me with that desire by his eloquent description of the place. I could never point out any thing at the Great House, no matter how beautiful or powerful, but that he had seen something at Baltimore far exceeding, both in beauty and strength, the object which I pointed out to him. Even the Great House itself, with all its pictures, was far inferior to many buildings in Baltimore. So strong was my desire, that I thought a gratification of it would fully compensate for whatever loss of comfort I should sustain by the exchange. I left without a regret, and with the highest hopes of future happiness.

We sailed out of Miles River for Baltimore on a Saturday morning. I remember only the day of the week, for at that time I had no knowledge of the days of the month, nor the months of the year. On setting sail, I walked aft, and gave to Colonel Lloyd's plantation what I hoped would be the last look. I then placed myself in the bows of the sloop, and there spent the remainder of the day in looking ahead, interesting myself in what was in the distance rather than in things near by or behind.

In the afternoon of that day, we reached Annapolis, the capital of the State. We stopped but a few moments, so that I had no time to go on shore. It was the first large town that I had ever seen, and though it would look small compared with some of our New England factory villages, I thought it a wonderful place for its size—more imposing even than the Great House Farm!

We arrived at Baltimore early on Sunday morning, landing at Smith's Wharf, not far from Bowley's Wharf. We had on board the sloop a large flock of sheep; and after aiding in driving them to the slaughter-house of Mr. Curtis on Loudon Slater's Hill, I was conducted by Rich, one of the hands belonging on board of the sloop, to my new home in Alliciana Street, near Mr. Gardner's ship-yard, on Fell's Point.

Mr. and Mrs. Auld were both at home, and met me at the door with their little son Thomas, to take care of whom I had been given. And here I saw what I had never seen before; it was a white face beaming with the most kindly emotions; it was the face of my new mistress, Sophia Auld. I wish I could describe the rapture that flashed through my soul as I beheld it. It was a new and strange sight to me, brightening up my pathway with the light of happiness. Little Thomas was told, there was his Freddy,—and I was told to take care of little Thomas; and thus I entered upon the duties of my new home with the most cheering prospect ahead.

I look upon my departure from Colonel Lloyd's plantation as one of the most interesting events of my life. It is possible, and even quite probable, that but for the mere circumstance of being removed from that plantation to Baltimore, I should have to-day, instead of being here seated by my own table, in the enjoyment of freedom and the happiness of home, writing this Narrative, been confined in the galling chains of slavery. Going to live at Baltimore laid the foundation, and opened the gateway, to all my subsequent prosperity. I have ever regarded it as the first plain manifestation of that kind Providence which has ever since attended me, and marked my life with so many favors. I regarded the selection of myself as being somewhat remarkable. There were a number of slave children that might have been sent from the plantation to Baltimore. There were those younger, those older, and those of the same age. I was chosen from among them all, and was the first, last, and only choice.

I may be deemed superstitious, and even egotistical, in regarding this event as a special interposition of divine Providence in my favor. But I should be false to the earliest sentiments of my soul, if I suppressed the opinion. I prefer to be true to myself, even at the hazard of incurring the ridicule of others, rather than to be false, and incur my own abhorrence. From my earliest recollection, I date the entertainment of a deep conviction that slavery would not always be able to hold me within its foul embrace; and in the darkest hours of my career in slavery, this living word of faith and spirit of hope departed not from me, but remained like ministering angels to cheer me through the gloom. This good spirit was from God, and to him I offer thanksgiving and praise.

CHAPTER VI.

My new mistress proved to be all she appeared when I first met her at the door,—a woman of the kindest heart and finest feelings. She had never had a slave under her control previously to myself, and prior to her marriage she had been dependent upon her own industry for a living. She was by trade a weaver; and by constant application to her business, she had been in a good degree preserved from the blighting and dehumanizing effects of slavery. I was utterly astonished at her goodness. I scarcely knew how to behave towards her. She was entirely unlike any other white woman I had ever seen. I could not approach her as I was accustomed to approach other white ladies. My early instruction was all out of place. The crouching servility, usually so acceptable a quality in a slave, did not answer when manifested towards her. Her favor was not gained by it; she seemed to be disturbed by it. She did not deem it impudent or unmannerly for a slave to look her in the face. The meanest slave was put fully at ease in her presence, and none left without feeling better for having seen her. Her face was made of heavenly smiles, and her voice of tranquil music.

But, alas! this kind heart had but a short time to remain such. The fatal poison of irresponsible power was already in her hands, and gradually commenced its infernal work. That cheerful eye, under the influence of slavery, eventually became red with rage; that voice, made all of sweet accord, changed to one of harsh and horrid discord; and that angelic face gave place to that of a demon. Thus is slavery the enemy of both the slave and the slaveholder.

Very soon after I went to live with Mr. and Mrs. Auld, she very kindly commenced to teach me the A, B, C. After I had learned this, she assisted me in learning to spell words of three or four letters. Just at this point of my progress, Mr. Auld found out what was going on, and at once forbade Mrs. Auld to instruct me further, telling her, among other things, that it was unlawful, as well as unsafe, to teach a slave to read. To use his own words, further, he said, "If you give a nigger an inch, he will take an ell. A nigger should know nothing but to obey his master—to do as he is told to do. Learning would *spoil* the best nigger in the world. Now," said he, "if you teach that nigger (speaking of myself) how to read, there would be no keeping him. It would forever unfit him to be a slave. He would at once become unmanageable, and of no value to his master. As to himself, it could do him no good, but a great deal of harm. It would make him discontented and unhappy." These words sank deep into my heart, stirred up sentiments within that lay slumbering, and called into existence an entirely new train of thought. It was a new and special revelation, explaining dark and mysterious things, with which my youthful understanding had struggled, but struggled in vain. I now understood what had been to me a most perplexing difficulty—to wit, the white man's power to enslave the black man. It was a grand achievement, and I prized it highly. From that moment, I understood the pathway from slavery to freedom. It was just what I wanted, and I got it at a time when I the least expected it. Whilst I was saddened by the thought of losing the aid of my kind mistress, I was gladdened by the invaluable instruction which, by the merest accident, I had gained from my master. Though conscious of the difficulty of learning without a teacher, I set out with high hope, and a fixed purpose, at whatever cost of trouble, to learn how to read. The very decided manner with which he spoke, and strove to impress his wife with the evil consequences of giving me instruction, served to convince me that he was deeply sensible of the truths he was uttering. It gave me the best assurance that I might rely with the utmost confidence on the results which, he said, would flow from teaching me to read. What he most dreaded, that I most desired. What he most loved, that I most hated. That which to him was a great evil, to be carefully shunned, was to me a great good, to be diligently sought; and the argument which he so warmly urged, against my learning to read, only served to inspire me with a desire and determination to learn. In learning to read, I owe almost as much to the bitter opposition of my master, as to the kindly aid of my mistress. I acknowledge the benefit of both.

I had resided but a short time in Baltimore before I observed a marked difference, in the treatment of slaves, from that which I had witnessed in the country. A city slave is almost a freeman, compared with a slave on the plantation. He is much better fed and clothed, and enjoys privileges altogether unknown to the slave on the plantation. There is a vestige of decency, a sense of shame, that does much to curb and check those outbreaks of atrocious cruelty so commonly enacted upon the plantation. He is a desperate slaveholder, who will shock the humanity of his non-slaveholding neighbors with the cries of his lacerated slave. Few are willing to incur the odium attaching to the reputation of being a cruel master; and above all things, they would not be known as not giving a slave enough to eat. Every city slaveholder is anxious to have it known of him, that he feeds his slaves well; and it is due to them to say, that most of them do give their slaves enough to eat. There are, however, some painful exceptions to this rule. Directly opposite to us, on Philpot Street, lived Mr. Thomas Hamilton. He owned two slaves. Their names were Henrietta and Mary. Henrietta was about twenty-two years of age, Mary was about fourteen; and of all the mangled and emaciated creatures I ever looked upon, these two were the most so. His heart must be harder than stone, that could look at these unmoved. The head, neck, and shoulders of Mary were literally cut to pieces. I have frequently felt her head, and found it nearly covered with festering sores, caused by the lash of her cruel mistress. I do not know that her master ever whipped her, but I have been an eye-witness to the cruelty of Mrs. Hamilton. I used to be in Mr. Hamilton's house nearly every day. Mrs. Hamilton used to sit in a large chair in the middle of the room, with a heavy cowskin always by her side, and scarce an hour passed during the day but was marked by the blood of one of these slaves. The girls seldom passed her without her saying, "Move faster, you *black gip!*" at the same time giving them a blow with the cowskin over the head or shoulders, often drawing the blood. She would then say, "Take that, you *black gip!*"—continuing, "If you don't move faster, I'll move you!" Added to the cruel lashings to which these slaves were subjected, they were kept nearly half-starved. They seldom knew what it was to eat a full meal. I have seen Mary contending with the pigs for the offal thrown into the street. So much was Mary kicked and cut to pieces, that she was oftener called "*pecked*" than by her name.

CHAPTER VII.

I LIVED in Master Hugh's family about seven years. During this time, I succeeded in learning to read and write. In accomplishing this, I was compelled to resort to various stratagems. I had no regular teacher. My mistress, who had kindly commenced to instruct me, had, in compliance with the advice and direction of her husband, not only ceased to instruct, but had set her face against my being instructed by any one else. It is due, however, to my mistress to say of her, that she did not adopt this course of treatment immediately. She at first lacked the depravity indispensable to shutting me up in mental darkness. It was at least necessary for her to have some training in the exercise of irresponsible power, to make her equal to the task of treating me as though I were a brute.

My mistress was, as I have said, a kind and tender-hearted woman; and in the simplicity of her soul she commenced, when I first went to live with her, to treat me as she supposed one human being ought to treat another. In entering upon the duties of a slaveholder, she did not seem to perceive that I sustained to her the relation of a mere chattel, and that for her to treat me as a human being was not only wrong, but dangerously so. Slavery proved as injurious to her as it did to me. When I went there, she was a pious, warm, and tender-hearted woman. There was no sorrow or suffering for which she had not a tear. She had bread for the hungry, clothes for the naked, and comfort for every mourner that came within her reach. Slavery soon proved its ability to divest her of these heavenly qualities. Under its influence, the tender heart became stone, and the lamb-like disposition gave way to one of tiger-like fierceness. The first step in her downward course was in her ceasing to instruct me. She now commenced to practise her husband's precepts. She finally became even more violent in her opposition than her husband himself. She was not satisfied with simply doing as well as he had commanded; she seemed anxious to do better. Nothing seemed to make her more angry than to see me with a newspaper. She seemed to think that here lay the danger. I have had her rush at me with a face made all up of fury, and snatch from me a newspaper, in a manner that fully revealed her apprehension. She was an apt woman; and a little experience soon demonstrated, to her satisfaction, that education and slavery were incompatible with each other.

From this time I was most narrowly watched. If I was in a separate room any considerable length of time, I was sure to be suspected of having a book, and was at once called to give an account of myself. All this, however, was too late. The first step had been taken. Mistress, in teaching me the alphabet, had given me the *inch,* and no precaution could prevent me from taking the *ell.*

The plan which I adopted, and the one by which I was most successful, was that of making friends of all the little white boys whom I met in the street. As many of these as I could, I converted into teachers. With their kindly aid, obtained at different times and in different places, I finally succeeded in learning to read. When I was sent of errands, I always took my book with me, and by going one part of my errand quickly, I found time to get a lesson before my return. I used also to carry bread with me, enough of which was always in the house, and to which I was always welcome; for I was much better off in this regard than many of the poor white children in the neighborhood. This bread I used to bestow on the hungry little urchins, who, in return, would give me the more valuable bread of knowledge. I am strongly tempted to give the names of two or three of those little boys, as a testimonial of the gratitude and affection I bear them; but prudence forbids;—not that it would injure me, but it might embarrass them; for it is almost an unpardonable offence to teach slaves to read in this Christian country. It is enough to say of the dear little fellows, that they lived on Philpot Street, very near Durgin and Bailey's ship-yard. I used to talk this matter of slavery over with them. I would sometimes say to them, I wished I could be as free as they would be when they got to be men. "You will be free as soon as you are twenty-one, *but I am a slave for life!* Have not I as good a right to be free as you have?" These words used to trouble them; they would express for me the liveliest sympathy, and console me with the hope that something would occur by which I might be free.

I was now about twelve years old, and the thought of being *a slave for life* began to bear heavily upon my heart. Just about this time, I got hold of a book entitled "The Columbian Orator." Every opportunity I got, I used to read this book. Among much of other interesting matter, I found in it a dialogue between a master and his slave. The slave was represented as having run away from his master three times. The dialogue represented the conversation which took place between them, when the slave was retaken the third time. In this dialogue, the whole argument in behalf of slavery was brought forward by the master, all of which was disposed of by the slave. The slave was made to say some very smart as well as impressive things in reply to his master—things which had the desired though unexpected effect; for the conversation resulted in the voluntary emancipation of the slave on the part of the master.

In the same book, I met with one of Sheridan's mighty speeches on and in behalf of Catholic emancipation. These were choice documents to me. I read them over and over again with unabated interest. They gave tongue to interesting thoughts of my own soul, which had frequently flashed through my mind, and died away for want of utterance. The moral which I gained from the dialogue was the power of truth over the conscience of even a slaveholder. What I got from Sheridan was a bold denunciation of slavery, and a powerful vindication of human rights. The reading of these documents enabled me to utter my thoughts, and to meet the arguments brought forward to sustain slavery; but while they relieved me of one difficulty, they brought on another even more painful than the one of which I was relieved. The more I read, the more I was led to abhor and detest my enslavers. I could regard them in no other light than a band of successful robbers, who had left their homes, and gone to Africa, and stolen us from our homes, and in a strange land reduced us to slavery. I loathed them as being the meanest as well as the most wicked of men. As I read and contemplated the subject, behold! that very discontentment which Master Hugh had predicted would follow my learning to read had already come, to torment and sting my soul to unutterable anguish. As I writhed under it, I would at times feel that learning to read had been a curse rather than a blessing. It had given me a view of my wretched condition, without the remedy. It opened my eyes to the horrible pit, but to no ladder upon which to get out. In moments of agony, I envied my fellow-slaves for their stupidity. I have often wished myself a beast. I preferred the condition of the meanest reptile to my own. Any thing, no matter what, to get rid of thinking! It was this everlasting thinking of my condition that tormented me. There was no getting rid of it. It was pressed upon me by every object within sight or hearing, animate or inanimate. The silver trump of freedom had roused my soul to eternal wakefulness. Freedom now appeared, to disappear no more forever. It was heard in every sound, and seen in every thing. It was ever present to torment me with a sense of my wretched condition. I saw nothing without seeing it, I heard nothing without hearing it, and felt nothing without feeling it. It looked from every star, it smiled in every calm, breathed in every wind, and moved in every storm.

I often found myself regretting my own existence, and wished myself dead; and but for the hope of being free, I have no doubt but that I should have killed myself, or done something for which I should have been killed. While in this state of mind, I was eager to hear any one speak of slavery. I was a ready listener. Every little while, I could hear something about the abolitionists. It was some time before I found what the word meant. It was always used in such connections as to make it an interesting word to me. If a slave ran away and succeeded in getting clear, or if a slave killed his master, set fire to a barn, or did any thing very wrong in the mind of a slaveholder, it was spoken of as the fruit of *abolition*. Hearing the word in this connection very often, I set about learning what it meant. The dictionary afforded me little or no help. I found it was "the act of abolishing;" but then I did not know what was to be abolished. Here I was perplexed. I did not dare to ask any one about its meaning, for I was satisfied that it was something they wanted me to know very little about. After a patient waiting, I got one of our city papers, containing an account of the number of petitions from the north, praying for the abolition of slavery in the District of Columbia, and of the slave trade between the States. From this time I understood the words *abolition* and *abolitionist,* and always drew near when that word was spoken, expecting to hear something of importance to myself and fellow-slaves. The light broke in upon me by degrees. I went one day down on the wharf of Mr. Waters; and seeing two Irishmen unloading a scow of stone, I went, unasked, and helped them. When we had finished, one of them came to me and asked me if I were a slave. I told him I was. He asked, "Are ye a slave for life?" I told him that I was. The good Irishman seemed to be deeply affected by the statement. He said to the other that it was a pity so fine a little fellow as myself should be a slave for life. He said it was a shame to hold me. They both advised me to run away to the north; that I should find friends there, and that I should be free. I pretended not to be interested in what they said, and treated them as if I did not understand them; for I feared they might be treacherous. White men have been known to encourage slaves to escape, and then, to get the reward, catch them and return them to their masters. I was afraid that these seemingly good men might use me so; but I nevertheless remembered their advice, and from that time I resolved to run away. I looked forward to a time at which it would be safe for me to escape. I was too young to think of doing so immediately; besides, I wished to learn how to write, as I might have occasion to write my own pass. I consoled myself with the hope that I should one day find a good chance. Meanwhile, I would learn to write.

The idea as to how I might learn to write was suggested to me by being in Durgin and Bailey's ship-yard, and frequently seeing the ship carpenters, after hewing, and getting a piece of timber ready for use, write on the timber the name of that part of the ship for which it was intended. When a piece of timber was intended for the larboard side, it would be marked thus—"L." When a piece was for the starboard side, it would be marked thus—"S." A piece for the larboard side forward, would be marked thus—"L.F." When a piece was for starboard side forward, it would be marked thus—"S.F." For larboard aft, it would be marked thus—"L.A." For starboard aft, it would be marked thus—"S.A." I soon learned the names of these letters, and for what they were intended when placed upon a piece of timber in the ship-yard. I immediately commenced copying them, and in a short time was able to make the four letters named. After that, when I met with any boy who I knew could write, I would tell him I could write as well as he. The next word would be, "I don't believe you. Let me see you try it." I would then make the letters which I had been so fortunate as to learn, and ask him to beat that. In this way I got a good many lessons in writing, which it is quite possible I should never have gotten in any other way. During this time, my copy-book was the board fence, brick wall, and pavement; my pen and ink was a lump of chalk. With these, I learned mainly how to write. I then commenced and continued copying the italics in Webster's Spelling Book, until I could make them all without looking on the book. By this time, my little Master Thomas had gone to school, and learned how to write, and had written over a number of copy-books. These had been brought home, and shown to some of our near neighbors, and then laid aside. My mistress used to go to class meeting at the Wilk Street meeting-house every Monday afternoon, and leave me to take care of the house. When left thus, I used to spend the time in writing in the spaces left in Master Thomas's copy-book, copying what he had written. I continued to do this until I could write a hand very similar to that of Master Thomas. Thus, after a long, tedious effort for years, I finally succeeded in learning how to write.

CHAPTER VIII.

In a very short time after I went to live at Baltimore, my old master's youngest son, Richard, died; and in about three years and six months after his death, my old master, Captain Anthony, died, leaving only his son, Andrew, and daughter, Lucretia, to share his estate. He died while on a visit to see his daughter at Hillsborough. Cut off thus unexpectedly, he left no will as to the disposal of his property. It was therefore necessary to have a valuation of the property, that it might be equally divided between Mrs. Lucretia and Master Andrew. I was immediately sent for, to be valued with the other property. Here again my feelings rose up in detestation of slavery. I had now a new conception of my degraded condition. Prior to this, I had become, if not insensible to my lot, at least partly so. I left Baltimore with a young heart overborne with sadness, and a soul full of apprehension. I took passage with Captain Rowe, in the schooner Wild Cat, and, after a sail of about twenty-four hours, I found myself near the place of my birth. I had now been absent from it almost, if not quite, five years. I, however, remembered the place very well. I was only about five years old when I left it, to go and live with my old master on Colonel Lloyd's plantation; so that I was now between ten and eleven years old.

We were all ranked together at the valuation. Men and women, old and young, married and single, were ranked with horses, sheep, and swine. There were horses and men, cattle and women, pigs and children, all holding the same rank in the scale of being, and all were subjected to the same narrow examination. Silvery-headed age and sprightly youth, maids and matrons, had to undergo the same indelicate inspection. At this moment, I saw more clearly than ever the brutalizing effects of slavery upon both slave and slaveholder.

After the valuation, then came the division. I have no language to express the high excitement and deep anxiety which were felt among us poor slaves during this time. Our fate for life was now to be decided. We had no more voice in that decision than the brutes among whom we were ranked. A single word from the white men was enough—against all our wishes, prayers, and entreaties—to sunder forever the dearest friends, dearest kindred, and strongest ties known to human beings. In addition to the pain of separation, there was the horrid dread of falling into the hands of Master Andrew. He was known to us all as being a most cruel wretch,—a common drunkard, who had, by his reckless mismanagement and profligate dissipation, already wasted a large portion of his father's property. We all felt that we might as well be sold at once to the Georgia traders, as to pass into his hands; for we knew that that would be our inevitable condition,—a condition held by us all in the utmost horror and dread.

I suffered more anxiety than most of my fellow-slaves. I had known what it was to be kindly treated; they had known nothing of the kind. They had seen little or nothing of the world. They were in very deed men and women of sorrow, and acquainted with grief. Their backs had been made familiar with the bloody lash, so that they had become callous; mine was yet tender; for while at Baltimore I got few whippings, and few slaves could boast of a kinder master and mistress than myself; and the thought of passing out of their hands into those of Master Andrew—a man who, but a few days before, to give me a sample of his bloody disposition, took my little brother by the throat, threw him on the ground, and with the heel of his boot stamped upon his head till the blood gushed from his nose and ears—was well calculated to make me anxious as to my fate. After he had committed this savage outrage upon my brother, he turned to me, and said that was the way he meant to serve me one of these days,—meaning, I suppose, when I came into his possession.

Thanks to a kind Providence, I fell to the portion of Mrs. Lucretia, and was sent immediately back to Baltimore, to live again in the family of Master Hugh. Their joy at my return equalled their sorrow at my departure. It was a glad day to me. I had escaped a fate worse than lion's jaws. I was absent from Baltimore, for the purpose of valuation and division, just about one month, and it seemed to have been six.

Very soon after my return to Baltimore, my mistress, Lucretia, died, leaving her husband and one child, Amanda; and in a very short time after her death, Master Andrew died. Now all the property of my old master, slaves included, was in the hands of strangers,—strangers who had nothing to do with accumulating it. Not a slave was left free. All remained slaves, from the youngest to the oldest. If any one thing in my experience, more than another, served to deepen my conviction of the infernal character of slavery, and to fill me with unutterable loathing of slaveholders, it was their base ingratitude to my poor old grandmother. She had served my old master faithfully from youth to old age. She had been the source of all his wealth; she had peopled his plantation with slaves; she had become a great grandmother in his service. She had rocked him in infancy, attended him in childhood, served him through life, and at his death wiped from his icy brow the cold death-sweat, and closed his eyes forever. She was nevertheless left a slave—a slave for life—a slave in the hands of strangers; and in their hands she saw her children, her grandchildren, and her great-grandchildren, divided, like so many sheep, without being gratified with the small privilege of a single word, as to their or her own destiny. And, to cap the climax of their base ingratitude and fiendish barbarity, my grandmother, who was now very old, having outlived my old master and all his children, having seen the beginning and end of all of them, and her present owners finding she was of but little value, her frame already racked with the pains of old age, and complete helplessness fast stealing over her once active limbs, they took her to the woods, built her a little hut, put up a little mud-chimney, and then made her welcome to the privilege of supporting herself there in perfect loneliness; thus virtually turning her out to die! If my poor old grandmother now lives, she lives to suffer in utter loneliness; she lives to remember and mourn over the loss of children, the loss of grandchildren, and the loss of great-grandchildren. They are, in the language of the slave's poet, Whittier,—

"Gone, gone, sold and gone
To the rice swamp dank and lone,
Where the slave-whip ceaseless swings,
Where the noisome insect stings,
Where the fever-demon strews
Poison with the falling dews,
Where the sickly sunbeams glare
Through the hot and misty air:—
Gone, gone, sold and gone
To the rice swamp dank and lone,
From Virginia's hills and waters—
Woe is me, my stolen daughters!"

The hearth is desolate. The children, the unconscious children, who once sang and danced in her presence, are gone. She gropes her way, in the darkness of age, for a drink of water. Instead of the voices of her children, she hears by day the moans of the dove, and by night the screams of the hideous owl. All is gloom. The grave is at the door. And now, when weighed down by the pains and aches of old age, when the head inclines to the feet, when the beginning and ending of human existence meet, and helpless infancy and painful old age combine together—at this time, this most needful time, the time for the exercise of that tenderness and affection which children only can exercise towards a declining parent—my poor old grandmother, the devoted mother of twelve children, is left all alone, in yonder little hut, before a few dim embers. She stands—she sits—she staggers—she falls—she groans—she dies—and there are none of her children or grandchildren present, to wipe from her wrinkled brow the cold sweat of death, or to place beneath the sod her fallen remains. Will not a righteous God visit for these things?

In about two years after the death of Mrs. Lucretia, Master Thomas married his second wife. Her name was Rowena Hamilton. She was the eldest daughter of Mr. William Hamilton. Master now lived in St. Michael's. Not long after his marriage, a misunderstanding took place between himself and Master Hugh; and as a means of punishing his brother, he took me from him to live with himself at St. Michael's. Here I underwent another most painful separation. It, however, was not so severe as the one I dreaded at the division of property; for, during this interval, a great change had taken place in Master Hugh and his once kind and affectionate wife. The influence of brandy upon him, and of slavery upon her, had effected a disastrous change in the characters of both; so that, as far as they were concerned, I thought I had little to lose by the change. But it was not to them that I was attached. It was to those little Baltimore boys that I felt the strongest attachment. I had received many good lessons from them, and was still receiving them, and the thought of leaving them was painful indeed. I was leaving, too, without the hope of ever being allowed to return. Master Thomas had said he would never let me return again. The barrier betwixt himself and his brother he considered impassable.

I then had to regret that I did not at least make the attempt to carry out my resolution to run away; for the chances of success are tenfold greater from the city than from the country.

I sailed from Baltimore for St. Michael's in the sloop Amanda, Captain Edward Dodson. On my passage, I paid particular attention to the direction which the steamboats took to go to Philadelphia. I found, instead of going down, on reaching North Point they went up the bay, in a north-easterly direction. I deemed this knowledge of the utmost importance. My determination to run away was again revived. I resolved to wait only so long as the offering of a favorable opportunity. When that came, I was determined to be off.

CHAPTER IX.

I HAVE now reached a period of my life when I can give dates. I left Baltimore, and went to live with Master Thomas Auld, at St. Michael's, in March, 1832. It was now more than seven years since I lived with him in the family of my old master, on Colonel Lloyd's plantation. We of course were now almost entire strangers to each other. He was to me a new master, and I to him a new slave. I was ignorant of his temper and disposition; he was equally so of mine. A very short time, however, brought us into full acquaintance with each other. I was made acquainted with his wife not less than with himself.

They were well matched, being equally mean and cruel. I was now, for the first time during a space of more than seven years, made to feel the painful gnawings of hunger—a something which I had not experienced before since I left Colonel Lloyd's plantation. It went hard enough with me then, when I could look back to no period at which I had enjoyed a sufficiency. It was tenfold harder after living in Master Hugh's family, where I had always had enough to eat, and of that which was good. I have said Master Thomas was a mean man. He was so. Not to give a slave enough to eat, is regarded as the most aggravated development of meanness even among slaveholders. The rule is, no matter how coarse the food, only let there be enough of it. This is the theory; and in the part of Maryland from which I came, it is the general practice,—though there are many exceptions. Master Thomas gave us enough of neither coarse nor fine food. There were four slaves of us in the kitchen—my sister Eliza, my aunt Priscilla, Henny, and myself; and we were allowed less than half of a bushel of corn-meal per week, and very little else, either in the shape of meat or vegetables. It was not enough for us to subsist upon. We were therefore reduced to the wretched necessity of living at the expense of our neighbors. This we did by begging and stealing, whichever came handy in the time of need, the one being considered as legitimate as the other. A great many times have we poor creatures been nearly perishing with hunger, when food in abundance lay mouldering in the safe and smoke-house, and our pious mistress was aware of the fact; and yet that mistress and her husband would kneel every morning, and pray that God would bless them in basket and store!

Bad as all slaveholders are, we seldom meet one destitute of every element of character commanding respect. My master was one of this rare sort. I do not know of one single noble act ever performed by him. The leading trait in his character was meanness; and if there were any other element in his nature, it was made subject to this. He was mean; and, like most other mean men, he lacked the ability to conceal his meanness. Captain Auld was not born a slaveholder. He had been a poor man, master only of a Bay craft. He came into possession of all his slaves by marriage; and of all men, adopted slaveholders are the worst. He was cruel, but cowardly. He commanded without firmness. In the enforcement of his rules, he was at times rigid, and at times lax. At times, he spoke to his slaves with the firmness of Napoleon and the fury of a demon; at other times, he might well be mistaken for an inquirer who had lost his way. He did nothing of himself. He might have passed for a lion, but for his ears. In all things noble which he attempted, his own meanness shone most conspicuous. His airs, words, and actions, were the airs, words, and actions of born slaveholders, and, being assumed, were awkward enough. He was not even a good imitator. He possessed all the disposition to deceive, but wanted the power. Having no resources within himself, he was compelled to be the copyist of many, and being such, he was forever the victim of inconsistency; and of consequence he was an object of contempt, and was held as such even by his slaves. The luxury of having slaves of his own to wait upon him was something new and unprepared for. He was a slaveholder without the ability to hold slaves. He found himself incapable of managing his slaves either by force, fear, or fraud. We seldom called him "master;" we generally called him "Captain Auld," and were hardly disposed to title him at all. I doubt not that our conduct had much to do with making him appear awkward, and of consequence fretful. Our want of reverence for him must have perplexed him greatly. He wished to have us call him master, but lacked the firmness necessary to command us to do so. His wife used to insist upon our calling him so, but to no purpose. In August, 1832, my master attended a Methodist camp-meeting held in the Bay-side, Talbot county, and there experienced religion. I indulged a faint hope that his conversion would lead him to emancipate his slaves, and that, if he did not do this, it would, at any rate, make him more kind and humane. I was disappointed in both these respects. It neither made him to be humane to his slaves, nor to emancipate them. If it had any effect on his character, it made him more cruel and hateful in all his ways; for I believe him to have been a much worse man after his conversion than before. Prior to his conversion, he relied upon his own depravity to shield and sustain him in his savage barbarity; but after his conversion, he found religious sanction and support for his slaveholding cruelty. He made the greatest pretensions to piety. His house was the house of prayer. He prayed morning, noon, and night. He very soon distinguished himself among his brethren, and was soon made a class-leader and exhorter. His activity in revivals was great, and he proved himself an instrument in the hands of the church in converting many souls. His house was the preachers' home. They used to take great pleasure in coming there to put up; for while he starved us, he stuffed them. We have had three or four preachers there at a time. The names of those who used to come most frequently while I lived there, were Mr. Storks, Mr. Ewery, Mr. Humphry, and Mr. Hickey. I have also seen Mr. George Cookman at our house. We slaves loved Mr. Cookman. We believed him to be a good man. We thought him instrumental in getting Mr. Samuel Harrison, a very rich slaveholder, to emancipate his slaves; and by some means got the impression that he was laboring to effect the emancipation of all the slaves. When he was at our house, we were sure to be called in to prayers. When the others were there, we were sometimes called in and sometimes not. Mr. Cookman took more notice of us than either of the other ministers. He could not come among us without betraying his sympathy for us, and, stupid as we were, we had the sagacity to see it.

While I lived with my master in St. Michael's, there was a white young man, a Mr. Wilson, who proposed to keep a Sabbath school for the instruction of such slaves as might be disposed to learn to read the New Testament. We met but three times, when Mr. West and Mr. Fairbanks, both class-leaders, with many others, came upon us with sticks and other missiles, drove us off, and forbade us to meet again. Thus ended our little Sabbath school in the pious town of St. Michael's.

I have said my master found religious sanction for his cruelty. As an example, I will state one of many facts going to prove the charge. I have seen him tie up a lame young woman, and whip her with a heavy cowskin upon her naked shoulders, causing the warm red blood to drip; and, in justification of the bloody deed, he would quote this passage of Scripture—"He that knoweth his master's will, and doeth it not, shall be beaten with many stripes."

Master would keep this lacerated young woman tied up in this horrid situation four or five hours at a time. I have known him to tie her up early in the morning, and whip her before breakfast; leave her, go to his store, return at dinner, and whip her again, cutting her in the places already made raw with his cruel lash. The secret of master's cruelty toward "Henny" is found in the fact of her being almost helpless. When quite a child, she fell into the fire, and burned herself horribly. Her hands were so burnt that she never got the use of them. She could do very little but bear heavy burdens. She was to master a bill of expense; and as he was a mean man, she was a constant offence to him. He seemed desirous of getting the poor girl out of existence. He gave her away once to his sister; but, being a poor gift, she was not disposed to keep her. Finally, my benevolent master, to use his own words, "set her adrift to take care of herself." Here was a recently-converted man, holding on upon the mother, and at the same time turning out her helpless child, to starve and die! Master Thomas was one of the many pious slaveholders who hold slaves for the very charitable purpose of taking care of them.

My master and myself had quite a number of differences. He found me unsuitable to his purpose. My city life, he said, had had a very pernicious effect upon me. It had almost ruined me for every good purpose, and fitted me for every thing which was bad. One of my greatest faults was that of letting his horse run away, and go down to his father-in-law's farm, which was about five miles from St. Michael's. I would then have to go after it. My reason for this kind of carelessness, or carefulness, was, that I could always get something to eat when I went there. Master William Hamilton, my master's father-in-law, always gave his slaves enough to eat. I never left there hungry, no matter how great the need of my speedy return. Master Thomas at length said he would stand it no longer. I had lived with him nine months, during which time he had given me a number of severe whippings, all to no good purpose. He resolved to put me out, as he said, to be broken; and, for this purpose, he let me for one year to a man named Edward Covey. Mr. Covey was a poor man, a farm-renter. He rented the place upon which he lived, as also the hands with which he tilled it. Mr. Covey had acquired a very high reputation for breaking young slaves, and this reputation was of immense value to him. It enabled him to get his farm tilled with much less expense to himself than he could have had it done without such a reputation. Some slaveholders thought it not much loss to allow Mr. Covey to have their slaves one year, for the sake of the training to which they were subjected, without any other compensation. He could hire young help with great ease, in consequence of this reputation. Added to the natural good qualities of Mr. Covey, he was a professor of religion—a pious soul—a member and a class-leader in the Methodist church. All of this added weight to his reputation as a "nigger-breaker." I was aware of all the facts, having been made acquainted with them by a young man who had lived there. I nevertheless made the change gladly; for I was sure of getting enough to eat, which is not the smallest consideration to a hungry man.

CHAPTER X.

I LEFT Master Thomas's house, and went to live with Mr. Covey, on the 1st of January, 1833. I was now, for the first time in my life, a field hand. In my new employment, I found myself even more awkward than a country boy appeared to be in a large city. I had been at my new home but one week before Mr. Covey gave me a very severe whipping, cutting my back, causing the blood to run, and raising ridges on my flesh as large as my little finger. The details of this affair are as follows: Mr. Covey sent me, very early in the morning of one of our coldest days in the month of January, to the woods, to get a load of wood. He gave me a team of unbroken oxen. He told me which was the in-hand ox, and which the off-hand one. He then tied the end of a large rope around the horns of the in-hand ox, and gave me the other end of it, and told me, if the oxen started to run, that I must hold on upon the rope. I had never driven oxen before, and of course I was very awkward. I, however, succeeded in getting to the edge of the woods with little difficulty; but I had got a very few rods into the woods, when the oxen took fright, and started full tilt, carrying the cart against trees, and over stumps, in the most frightful manner. I expected every moment that my brains would be dashed out against the trees. After running thus for a considerable distance, they finally upset the cart, dashing it with great force against a tree, and threw themselves into a dense thicket. How I escaped death, I do not know. There I was, entirely alone, in a thick wood, in a place new to me. My cart was upset and shattered, my oxen were entangled among the young trees, and there was none to help me. After a long spell of effort, I succeeded in getting my cart righted, my oxen disentangled, and again yoked to the cart. I now proceeded with my team to the place where I had, the day before, been chopping wood, and loaded my cart pretty heavily, thinking in this way to tame my oxen. I then proceeded on my way home. I had now consumed one half of the day. I got out of the woods safely, and now felt out of danger. I stopped my oxen to open the gate; and just as I did so, before I could get hold of my ox-rope, the oxen again started, rushed through the gate, catching it between the wheel and the body of the cart, tearing it to pieces, and coming within a few inches of crushing me against the gate-post. Thus twice, in one short day, I escaped death by the merest chance. On my return, I told Mr. Covey what had happened, and how it happened. He ordered me to return to the woods again immediately. I did so, and he followed on after me. Just as I got into the woods, he came up and told me to stop my cart, and that he would teach me how to trifle away my time, and break gates. He then went to a large gum-tree, and with his axe cut three large switches, and, after trimming them up neatly with his pocket-knife, he ordered me to take off my clothes. I made him no answer, but stood with my clothes on. He repeated his order. I still made him no answer, nor did I move to strip myself. Upon this he rushed at me with the fierceness of a tiger, tore off my clothes, and lashed me till he had worn out his switches, cutting me so savagely as to leave the marks visible for a long time after. This whipping was the first of a number just like it, and for similar offences.

I lived with Mr. Covey one year. During the first six months, of that year, scarce a week passed without his whipping me. I was seldom free from a sore back. My awkwardness was almost always his excuse for whipping me. We were worked fully up to the point of endurance. Long before day we were up, our horses fed, and by the first approach of day we were off to the field with our hoes and ploughing teams. Mr. Covey gave us enough to eat, but scarce time to eat it. We were often less than five minutes taking our meals. We were often in the field from the first approach of day till its last lingering ray had left us; and at saving-fodder time, midnight often caught us in the field binding blades.

Covey would be out with us. The way he used to stand it, was this. He would spend the most of his afternoons in bed. He would then come out fresh in the evening, ready to urge us on with his word, example, and frequently with the whip. Mr. Covey was one of the few slaveholders who could and did work with his hands. He was a hard-working man. He knew by himself just what a man or a boy could do. There was no deceiving him. His work went on in his absence almost as well as in his presence; and he had the faculty of making us feel that he was ever present with us. This he did by surprising us. He seldom approached the spot where we were at work openly, if he could do it secretly. He always aimed at taking us by surprise. Such was his cunning, that we used to call him, among ourselves, "the snake." When we were at work in the cornfield, he would sometimes crawl on his hands and knees to avoid detection, and all at once he would rise nearly in our midst, and scream out, "Ha, ha! Come, come! Dash on, dash on!" This being his mode of attack, it was never safe to stop a single minute. His comings were like a thief in the night. He appeared to us as being ever at hand. He was under every tree, behind every stump, in every bush, and at every window, on the plantation. He would sometimes mount his horse, as if bound to St. Michael's, a distance of seven miles, and in half an hour afterwards you would see him coiled up in the corner of the wood-fence, watching every motion of the slaves. He would, for this purpose, leave his horse tied up in the woods. Again, he would sometimes walk up to us, and give us orders as though he was upon the point of starting on a long journey, turn his back upon us, and make as though he was going to the house to get ready; and, before he would get half way thither, he would turn short and crawl into a fence-corner, or behind some tree, and there watch us till the going down of the sun.

Mr. Covey's *forte* consisted in his power to deceive. His life was devoted to planning and perpetrating the grossest deceptions. Every thing he possessed in the shape of learning or religion, he made conform to his disposition to deceive. He seemed to think himself equal to deceiving the Almighty. He would make a short prayer in the morning, and a long prayer at night; and, strange as it may seem, few men would at times appear more devotional than he. The exercises of his family devotions were always commenced with singing; and, as he was a very poor singer himself, the duty of raising the hymn generally came upon me. He would read his hymn, and nod at me to commence. I would at times do so; at others, I would not. My non-compliance would almost always produce much confusion. To show himself independent of me, he would start and stagger through with his hymn in the most discordant manner. In this state of mind, he prayed with more than ordinary spirit. Poor man! such was his disposition, and success at deceiving, I do verily believe that he sometimes deceived himself into the solemn belief, that he was a sincere worshipper of the most high God; and this, too, at a time when he may be said to have been guilty of compelling his woman slave to commit the sin of adultery. The facts in the case are these: Mr. Covey was a poor man; he was just commencing in life; he was only able to buy one slave; and, shocking as is the fact, he bought her, as he said, for *a breeder.* This woman was named Caroline. Mr. Covey bought her from Mr. Thomas Lowe, about six miles from St. Michael's. She was a large, able-bodied woman, about twenty years old. She had already given birth to one child, which proved her to be just what he wanted. After buying her, he hired a married man of Mr. Samuel Harrison, to live with him one year; and him he used to fasten up with her every night! The result was, that, at the end of the year, the miserable woman gave birth to twins. At this result Mr. Covey seemed to be highly pleased, both with the man and the wretched woman. Such was his joy, and that of his wife, that nothing they could do for Caroline during her confinement was too good, or too hard, to be done. The children were regarded as being quite an addition to his wealth.

If at any one time of my life more than another, I was made to drink the bitterest dregs of slavery, that time was during the first six months of my stay with Mr. Covey. We were worked in all weathers. It was never too hot or too cold; it could never rain, blow, hail, or snow, too hard for us to work in the field. Work, work, work, was scarcely more the order of the day than of the night. The longest days were too short for him, and the shortest nights too long for him. I was somewhat unmanageable when I first went there, but a few months of this discipline tamed me. Mr. Covey succeeded in breaking me. I was broken in body, soul, and spirit. My natural elasticity was crushed, my intellect languished, the disposition to read departed, the cheerful spark that lingered about my eye died; the dark night of slavery closed in upon me; and behold a man transformed into a brute!

Sunday was my only leisure time. I spent this in a sort of beast-like stupor, between sleep and wake, under some large tree. At times I would rise up, a flash of energetic freedom would dart through my soul, accompanied with a faint beam of hope, that flickered for a moment, and then vanished. I sank down again, mourning over my wretched condition. I was sometimes prompted to take my life, and that of Covey, but was prevented by a combination of hope and fear. My sufferings on this plantation seem now like a dream rather than a stern reality.

Our house stood within a few rods of the Chesapeake Bay, whose broad bosom was ever white with sails from every quarter of the habitable globe. Those beautiful vessels, robed in purest white, so delightful to the eye of freemen, were to me so many shrouded ghosts, to terrify and torment me with thoughts of my wretched condition. I have often, in the deep stillness of a summer's Sabbath, stood all alone upon the lofty banks of that noble bay, and traced, with saddened heart and tearful eye, the countless number of sails moving off to the mighty ocean. The sight of these always affected me powerfully. My thoughts would compel utterance; and there, with no audience but the Almighty, I would pour out my soul's complaint, in my rude way, with an apostrophe to the moving multitude of ships:—

"You are loosed from your moorings, and are free; I am fast in my chains, and am a slave! You move merrily before the gentle gale, and I sadly before the bloody whip! You are freedom's swift-winged angels, that fly round the world; I am confined in bands of iron! O that I were free! O, that I were on one of your gallant decks, and under your protecting wing! Alas! betwixt me and you, the turbid waters roll. Go on, go on. O that I could also go! Could I but swim! If I could fly! O, why was I born a man, of whom to make a brute! The glad ship is gone; she hides in the dim distance. I am left in the hottest hell of unending slavery. O God, save me! God, deliver me! Let me be free! Is there any God? Why am I a slave? I will run away. I will not stand it. Get caught, or get clear, I'll try it. I had as well die with ague as the fever. I have only one life to lose. I had as well be killed running as die standing. Only think of it; one hundred miles straight north, and I am free! Try it? Yes! God helping me, I will. It cannot be that I shall live and die a slave. I will take to the water. This very bay shall yet bear me into freedom. The steamboats steered in a north-east course from North Point. I will do the same; and when I get to the head of the bay, I will turn my canoe adrift, and walk straight through Delaware into Pennsylvania. When I get there, I shall not be required to have a pass; I can travel without being disturbed. Let but the first opportunity offer, and, come what will, I am off. Meanwhile, I will try to bear up under the yoke. I am not the only slave in the world. Why should I fret? I can bear as much as any of them. Besides, I am but a boy, and all boys are bound to some one. It may be that my misery in slavery will only increase my happiness when I get free. There is a better day coming."

Thus I used to think, and thus I used to speak to myself; goaded almost to madness at one moment, and at the next reconciling myself to my wretched lot.

I have already intimated that my condition was much worse, during the first six months of my stay at Mr. Covey's, than in the last six. The circumstances leading to the change in Mr. Covey's course toward me form an epoch in my humble history. You have seen how a man was made a slave; you shall see how a slave was made a man. On one of the hottest days of the month of August, 1833, Bill Smith, William Hughes, a slave named Eli, and myself, were engaged in fanning wheat. Hughes was clearing the fanned wheat from before the fan, Eli was turning, Smith was feeding, and I was carrying wheat to the fan. The work was simple, requiring strength rather than intellect; yet, to one entirely unused to such work, it came very hard. About three o'clock of that day, I broke down; my strength failed me; I was seized with a violent aching of the head, attended with extreme dizziness; I trembled in every limb. Finding what was coming, I nerved myself up, feeling it would never do to stop work. I stood as long as I could stagger to the hopper with grain. When I could stand no longer, I fell, and felt as if held down by some immense weight. The fan of course stopped; every one had his own work to do; and no one could do the work of the other, and have his own go on at the same time.

Mr. Covey was at the house, about one hundred yards from the treading-yard where we were fanning. On hearing the fan stop, he left immediately, and came to the spot where we were. He hastily inquired what the matter was. Bill answered that I was sick, and there was no one to bring wheat to the fan. I had by this time crawled away under the side of the post and rail-fence by which the yard was enclosed, hoping to find relief by getting out of the sun. He then asked where I was. He was told by one of the hands. He came to the spot, and, after looking at me awhile, asked me what was the matter. I told him as well as I could, for I scarce had strength to speak. He then gave me a savage kick in the side, and told me to get up. I tried to do so, but fell back in the attempt. He gave me another kick, and again told me to rise. I again tried, and succeeded in gaining my feet; but, stooping to get to the tub with which I was feeding the fan, I again staggered and fell. While down in this situation, Mr. Covey took up the hickory slat with which Hughes had been striking off the half-bushel measure, and with it gave me a heavy blow upon the head, making a large wound, and the blood ran freely; and with this again told me to get up. I made no effort to comply, having now made up my mind to let him do his worst. In a short time after receiving this blow, my head grew better. Mr. Covey had now left me to my fate. At this moment I resolved, for the first time, to go to my master, enter a complaint, and ask his protection. In order to do this, I must that afternoon walk seven miles; and this, under the circumstances, was truly a severe undertaking. I was exceedingly feeble; made so as much by the kicks and blows which I received, as by the severe fit of sickness to which I had been subjected. I, however, watched my chance, while Covey was looking in an opposite direction, and started for St. Michael's. I succeeded in getting a considerable distance on my way to the woods, when Covey discovered me, and called after me to come back, threatening what he would do if I did not come. I disregarded both his calls and his threats, and made my way to the woods as fast as my feeble state would allow; and thinking I might be overhauled by him if I kept the road, I walked through the woods, keeping far enough from the road to avoid detection, and near enough to prevent losing my way. I had not gone far before my little strength again failed me. I could go no farther. I fell down, and lay for a considerable time. The blood was yet oozing from the wound on my head. For a time I thought I should bleed to death; and think now that I should have done so, but that the blood so matted my hair as to stop the wound. After lying there about three quarters of an hour, I nerved myself up again, and started on my way, through bogs and briers, barefooted and bare-headed, tearing my feet sometimes at nearly every step; and after a journey of about seven miles, occupying some five hours to perform it, I arrived at master's store. I then presented an appearance enough to affect any but a heart of iron. From the crown of my head to my feet, I was covered with blood. My hair was all clotted with dust and blood; my shirt was stiff with blood. My legs and feet were torn in sundry places with briers and thorns, and were also covered with blood. I suppose I looked like a man who had escaped a den of wild beasts, and barely escaped them. In this state I appeared before my master, humbly entreating him to interpose his authority for my protection. I told him all the circumstances as well as I could, and it seemed, as I spoke, at times to affect him. He would then walk the floor, and seek to justify Covey by saying he expected I deserved it. He asked me what I wanted. I told him, to let me get a new home; that as sure as I lived with Mr. Covey again, I should live with but to die with him; that Covey would surely kill me; he was in a fair way for it. Master Thomas ridiculed the idea that there was any danger of Mr. Covey's killing me, and said that he knew Mr. Covey; that he was a good man, and that he could not think of taking me from him; that, should he do so, he would lose the whole year's wages; that I belonged to Mr. Covey for one year, and that I must go back to him, come what might; and that I must not trouble him with any more stories, or that he would himself *get hold of me.* After threatening me thus, he gave me a very large dose of salts, telling me that I might remain in St. Michael's that night, (it being quite late,) but that I must be off back to Mr. Covey's early in the morning; and that if I did not, he would *get hold of me,* which meant that he would whip me. I remained all night, and, according to his orders, I started off to Covey's in the morning, (Saturday morning,) wearied in body and broken in spirit. I got no supper that night, or breakfast that morning. I reached Covey's about nine o'clock; and just as I was getting over the fence that divided Mrs. Kemp's fields from ours, out ran Covey with his cowskin, to give me another whipping. Before he could reach me, I succeeded in getting to the cornfield; and as the corn was very high, it afforded me the means of hiding. He seemed very angry, and searched for me a long time. My behavior was altogether unaccountable. He finally gave up the chase, thinking, I suppose, that I must come home for something to eat; he would give himself no further trouble in looking for me. I spent that day mostly in the woods, having the alternative before me,—to go home and be whipped to death, or stay in the woods and be starved to death. That night, I fell in with Sandy Jenkins, a slave with whom I was somewhat acquainted. Sandy had a free wife who lived about four miles from Mr. Covey's; and it being Saturday, he was on his way to see her. I told him my circumstances, and he very kindly invited me to go home with him. I went home with him, and talked this whole matter over, and got his advice as to what course it was best for me to pursue. I found Sandy an old adviser. He told me, with great solemnity, I must go back to Covey; but that before I went, I must go with him into another part of the woods, where there was a certain *root,* which, if I would take some of it with me, carrying it *always on my right side,* would render it impossible for Mr. Covey, or any other white man, to whip me. He said he had carried it for years; and since he had done so, he had never received a blow, and never expected to while he carried it. I at first rejected the idea, that the simple carrying of a root in my pocket would have any such effect as he had said, and was not disposed to take it; but Sandy impressed the necessity with much earnestness, telling me it could do no harm, if it did no good. To please him, I at length took the root, and, according to his direction, carried it upon my right side. This was Sunday morning. I immediately started for home; and upon entering the yard gate, out came Mr. Covey on his way to meeting. He spoke to me very kindly, bade me drive the pigs from a lot near by, and passed on towards the church. Now, this singular conduct of Mr. Covey really made me begin to think that there was something in the *root* which Sandy had given me; and had it been on any other day than Sunday, I could have attributed the conduct to no other cause than the influence of that root; and as it was, I was half inclined to think the *root* to be something more than I at first had taken it to be. All went well till Monday morning. On this morning, the virtue of the *root* was fully tested. Long before daylight, I was called to go and rub, curry, and feed, the horses. I obeyed, and was glad to obey. But whilst thus engaged, whilst in the act of throwing down some blades from the loft, Mr. Covey entered the stable with a long rope; and just as I was half out of the loft, he caught hold of my legs, and was about tying me. As soon as I found what he was up to, I gave a sudden spring, and as I did so, he holding to my legs, I was brought sprawling on the stable floor. Mr. Covey seemed now to think he had me, and could do what he pleased; but at this moment—from whence came the spirit I don't know—I resolved to fight; and, suiting my action to the resolution, I seized Covey hard by the throat; and as I did so, I rose. He held on to me, and I to him. My resistance was so entirely unexpected, that Covey seemed taken all aback. He trembled like a leaf. This gave me assurance, and I held him uneasy, causing the blood to run where I touched him with the ends of my fingers. Mr. Covey soon called out to Hughes for help. Hughes came, and, while Covey held me, attempted to tie my right hand. While he was in the act of doing so, I watched my chance, and gave him a heavy kick close under the ribs. This kick fairly sickened Hughes, so that he left me in the hands of Mr. Covey. This kick had the effect of not only weakening Hughes, but Covey also. When he saw Hughes bending over with pain, his courage quailed. He asked me if I meant to persist in my resistance. I told him I did, come what might; that he had used me like a brute for six months, and that I was determined to be used so no longer. With that, he strove to drag me to a stick that was lying just out of the stable door. He meant to knock me down. But just as he was leaning over to get the stick, I seized him with both hands by his collar, and brought him by a sudden snatch to the ground. By this time, Bill came. Covey called upon him for assistance. Bill wanted to know what he could do. Covey said, "Take hold of him, take hold of him!" Bill said his master hired him out to work, and not to help to whip me; so he left Covey and myself to fight our own battle out. We were at it for nearly two hours. Covey at length let me go, puffing and blowing at a great rate, saying that if I had not resisted, he would not have whipped me half so much. The truth was, that he had not whipped me at all. I considered him as getting entirely the worst end of the bargain; for he had drawn no blood from me, but I had from him. The whole six months afterwards, that I spent with Mr. Covey, he never laid the weight of his finger upon me in anger. He would occasionally say, he didn't want to get hold of me again. "No," thought I, "you need not; for you will come off worse than you did before."

This battle with Mr. Covey was the turning-point in my career as a slave. It rekindled the few expiring embers of freedom, and revived within me a sense of my own manhood. It recalled the departed self-confidence, and inspired me again with a determination to be free. The gratification afforded by the triumph was a full compensation for whatever else might follow, even death itself. He only can understand the deep satisfaction which I experienced, who has himself repelled by force the bloody arm of slavery. I felt as I never felt before. It was a glorious resurrection, from the tomb of slavery, to the heaven of freedom. My long crushed spirit rose, cowardice departed, bold defiance took its place; and I now resolved that, however long I might remain a slave in form, the day had passed forever when I could be a slave in fact. I did not hesitate to let it be known of me, that the white man who expected to succeed in whipping, must also succeed in killing me.

From this time I was never again what might be called fairly whipped, though I remained a slave four years afterwards. I had several fights, but was never whipped.

It was for a long time a matter of surprise to me why Mr. Covey did not immediately have me taken by the constable to the whipping-post, and there regularly whipped for the crime of raising my hand against a white man in defence of myself. And the only explanation I can now think of does not entirely satisfy me; but such as it is, I will give it. Mr. Covey enjoyed the most unbounded reputation for being a first-rate overseer and negro-breaker. It was of considerable importance to him. That reputation was at stake; and had he sent me—a boy about sixteen years old—to the public whipping-post, his reputation would have been lost; so, to save his reputation, he suffered me to go unpunished.

My term of actual service to Mr. Edward Covey ended on Christmas day, 1833. The days between Christmas and New Year's day are allowed as holidays; and, accordingly, we were not required to perform any labor, more than to feed and take care of the stock. This time we regarded as our own, by the grace of our masters; and we therefore used or abused it nearly as we pleased. Those of us who had families at a distance, were generally allowed to spend the whole six days in their society. This time, however, was spent in various ways. The sober, staid, thinking and industrious ones of our number would employ themselves in making corn-brooms, mats, horse-collars, and baskets; and another class of us would spend the time in hunting opossums, hares, and coons. But by far the larger part engaged in such sports and merriments as ball playing, wrestling, running foot-races, fiddling, dancing, and drinking whisky; and this latter mode of spending the time was by far the most agreeable to the feelings of our masters. A slave who would work during the holidays was considered by our masters as scarcely deserving them. He was regarded as one who rejected the favor of his master. It was deemed a disgrace not to get drunk at Christmas; and he was regarded as lazy indeed, who had not provided himself with the necessary means, during the year, to get whisky enough to last him through Christmas.

From what I know of the effect of these holidays upon the slave, I believe them to be among the most effective means in the hands of the slaveholder in keeping down the spirit of insurrection. Were the slaveholders at once to abandon this practice, I have not the slightest doubt it would lead to an immediate insurrection among the slaves. These holidays serve as conductors, or safety-valves, to carry off the rebellious spirit of enslaved humanity. But for these, the slave would be forced up to the wildest desperation; and woe betide the slaveholder, the day he ventures to remove or hinder the operation of those conductors! I warn him that, in such an event, a spirit will go forth in their midst, more to be dreaded than the most appalling earthquake.

The holidays are part and parcel of the gross fraud, wrong, and inhumanity of slavery. They are professedly a custom established by the benevolence of the slaveholders; but I undertake to say, it is the result of selfishness, and one of the grossest frauds committed upon the down-trodden slave. They do not give the slaves this time because they would not like to have their work during its continuance, but because they know it would be unsafe to deprive them of it. This will be seen by the fact, that the slaveholders like to have their slaves spend those days just in such a manner as to make them as glad of their ending as of their beginning. Their object seems to be, to disgust their slaves with freedom, by plunging them into the lowest depths of dissipation. For instance, the slaveholders not only like to see the slave drink of his own accord, but will adopt various plans to make him drunk. One plan is, to make bets on their slaves, as to who can drink the most whisky without getting drunk; and in this way they succeed in getting whole multitudes to drink to excess. Thus, when the slave asks for virtuous freedom, the cunning slaveholder, knowing his ignorance, cheats him with a dose of vicious dissipation, artfully labelled with the name of liberty. The most of us used to drink it down, and the result was just what might be supposed: many of us were led to think that there was little to choose between liberty and slavery. We felt, and very properly too, that we had almost as well be slaves to man as to rum. So, when the holidays ended, we staggered up from the filth of our wallowing, took a long breath, and marched to the field,—feeling, upon the whole, rather glad to go, from what our master had deceived us into a belief was freedom, back to the arms of slavery.

I have said that this mode of treatment is a part of the whole system of fraud and inhumanity of slavery. It is so. The mode here adopted to disgust the slave with freedom, by allowing him to see only the abuse of it, is carried out in other things. For instance, a slave loves molasses; he steals some. His master, in many cases, goes off to town, and buys a large quantity; he returns, takes his whip, and commands the slave to eat the molasses, until the poor fellow is made sick at the very mention of it. The same mode is sometimes adopted to make the slaves refrain from asking for more food than their regular allowance. A slave runs through his allowance, and applies for more. His master is enraged at him; but, not willing to send him off without food, gives him more than is necessary, and compels him to eat it within a given time. Then, if he complains that he cannot eat it, he is said to be satisfied neither full nor fasting, and is whipped for being hard to please! I have an abundance of such illustrations of the same principle, drawn from my own observation, but think the cases I have cited sufficient. The practice is a very common one.

On the first of January, 1834, I left Mr. Covey, and went to live with Mr. William Freeland, who lived about three miles from St. Michael's. I soon found Mr. Freeland a very different man from Mr. Covey. Though not rich, he was what would be called an educated southern gentleman. Mr. Covey, as I have shown, was a well-trained negro-breaker and slave-driver. The former (slaveholder though he was) seemed to possess some regard for honor, some reverence for justice, and some respect for humanity. The latter seemed totally insensible to all such sentiments. Mr. Freeland had many of the faults peculiar to slaveholders, such as being very passionate and fretful; but I must do him the justice to say, that he was exceedingly free from those degrading vices to which Mr. Covey was constantly addicted. The one was open and frank, and we always knew where to find him. The other was a most artful deceiver, and could be understood only by such as were skilful enough to detect his cunningly-devised frauds. Another advantage I gained in my new master was, he made no pretensions to, or profession of, religion; and this, in my opinion, was truly a great advantage. I assert most unhesitatingly, that the religion of the south is a mere covering for the most horrid crimes,—a justifier of the most appalling barbarity,—a sanctifier of the most hateful frauds,—and a dark shelter, under which the darkest, foulest, grossest, and most infernal deeds of slaveholders find the strongest protection. Were I to be again reduced to the chains of slavery, next to that enslavement, I should regard being the slave of a religious master the greatest calamity that could befall me. For of all slaveholders with whom I have ever met, religious slaveholders are the worst. I have ever found them the meanest and basest, the most cruel and cowardly, of all others. It was my unhappy lot not only to belong to a religious slaveholder, but to live in a community of such religionists. Very near Mr. Freeland lived the Rev. Daniel Weeden, and in the same neighborhood lived the Rev. Rigby Hopkins. These were members and ministers in the Reformed Methodist Church. Mr. Weeden owned, among others, a woman slave, whose name I have forgotten. This woman's back, for weeks, was kept literally raw, made so by the lash of this merciless, *religious* wretch. He used to hire hands. His maxim was, Behave well or behave ill, it is the duty of a master occasionally to whip a slave, to remind him of his master's authority. Such was his theory, and such his practice.

Mr. Hopkins was even worse than Mr. Weeden. His chief boast was his ability to manage slaves. The peculiar feature of his government was that of whipping slaves in advance of deserving it. He always managed to have one or more of his slaves to whip every Monday morning. He did this to alarm their fears, and strike terror into those who escaped. His plan was to whip for the smallest offences, to prevent the commission of large ones. Mr. Hopkins could always find some excuse for whipping a slave. It would astonish one, unaccustomed to a slaveholding life, to see with what wonderful ease a slaveholder can find things, of which to make occasion to whip a slave. A mere look, word, or motion,—a mistake, accident, or want of power,—are all matters for which a slave may be whipped at any time. Does a slave look dissatisfied? It is said, he has the devil in him, and it must be whipped out.

Does he speak loudly when spoken to by his master? Then he is getting high-minded, and should be taken down a button-hole lower. Does he forget to pull off his hat at the approach of a white person? Then he is wanting in reverence, and should be whipped for it. Does he ever venture to vindicate his conduct, when censured for it? Then he is guilty of impudence,—one of the greatest crimes of which a slave can be guilty. Does he ever venture to suggest a different mode of doing things from that pointed out by his master? He is indeed presumptuous, and getting above himself; and nothing less than a flogging will do for him. Does he, while ploughing, break a plough,—or, while hoeing, break a hoe? It is owing to his carelessness, and for it a slave must always be whipped. Mr. Hopkins could always find something of this sort to justify the use of the lash, and he seldom failed to embrace such opportunities. There was not a man in the whole county, with whom the slaves who had the privilege of getting their own home, would not prefer to live, rather than with this Rev. Mr. Hopkins. And yet there was not a man any where round, who made higher professions of religion, or was more active in revivals,—more attentive to the class, love-feast, prayer and preaching meetings, or more devotional in his family,—who prayed earlier, later, louder, and longer,—than this same reverend slave-driver, Rigby Hopkins.

But to return to Mr. Freeland, and to my experience while in his employment. He, like Mr. Covey, gave us enough to eat; but, unlike Mr. Covey, he also gave us sufficient time to take our meals. He worked us hard, but always between sunrise and sunset. He required a good deal of work to be done, but gave us good tools with which to work. His farm was large, but he employed hands enough to work it, and with ease, compared with many of his neighbors. My treatment, while in his employment, was heavenly, compared with what I experienced at the hands of Mr. Edward Covey.

Mr. Freeland was himself the owner of but two slaves. Their names were Henry Harris and John Harris. The rest of his hands he hired. These consisted of myself, Sandy Jenkins,* and Handy Caldwell. Henry and John were

*This is the same man who gave me the roots to prevent my being whipped by Mr. Covey. He was "a clever soul." We used frequently to talk about the fight with Covey, and as often as we did so, he would claim my success as the result of the roots which he gave me. This superstition is very common among the more ignorant slaves. A slave seldom dies but that his death is attributed to trickery.

quite intelligent, and in a very little while after I went there, I succeeded in creating in them a strong desire to learn how to read. This desire soon sprang up in the others also. They very soon mustered up some old spelling-books, and nothing would do but that I must keep a Sabbath school. I agreed to do so, and accordingly devoted my Sundays to teaching these my loved fellow-slaves how to read. Neither of them knew his letters when I went there. Some of the slaves of the neighboring farms found what was going on, and also availed themselves of this little opportunity to learn to read. It was understood, among all who came, that there must be as little display about it as possible. It was necessary to keep our religious masters at St. Michael's unacquainted with the fact, that, instead of spending the Sabbath in wrestling, boxing, and drinking whisky, we were trying to learn how to read the will of God; for they had much rather see us engaged in those degrading sports, than to see us behaving like intellectual, moral, and accountable beings. My blood boils as I think of the bloody manner in which Messrs. Wright Fairbanks and Garrison West, both class-leaders in connection with many others, rushed in upon us with sticks and stones, and broke up our virtuous little Sabbath school, at St. Michael's—all calling themselves Christians! humble followers of the Lord Jesus Christ! But I am again digressing.

I held my Sabbath school at the house of a free colored man, whose name I deem it imprudent to mention; for should it be known, it might embarrass him greatly, though the crime of holding the school was committed ten years ago. I had at one time over forty scholars, and those of the right sort, ardently desiring to learn. They were of all ages, though mostly men and women. I look back to those Sundays with an amount of pleasure not to be expressed. They were great days to my soul. The work of instructing my dear fellow-slaves was the sweetest engagement with which I was ever blessed. We loved each other, and to leave them at the close of the Sabbath was a severe cross indeed. When I think that these precious souls are to-day shut up in the prison-house of slavery, my feelings overcome me, and I am almost ready to ask, "Does a righteous God govern the universe? and for what does he hold the thunders in his right hand, if not to smite the oppressor, and deliver the spoiled out of the hand of the spoiler?" These dear souls came not to Sabbath school because it was popular to do so, nor did I teach them because it was reputable to be thus engaged. Every moment they spent in that school, they were liable to be taken up, and given thirty-nine lashes. They came because they wished to learn. Their minds had been starved by their cruel masters. They had been shut up in mental darkness. I taught them, because it was the delight of my soul to be doing something that looked like bettering the condition of my race. I kept up my school nearly the whole year I lived with Mr. Freeland; and, beside my Sabbath school, I devoted three evenings in the week, during the winter, to teaching the slaves at home. And I have the happiness to know, that several of those who came to the Sabbath school learned how to read; and that one, at least, is now free through my agency.

The year passed off smoothly. It seemed only about half as long as the year which preceded it. I went through it without receiving a single blow. I will give Mr. Freeland the credit of being the best master I ever had, *till I became my own master.* For the ease with which I passed the year, I was, however, somewhat indebted to the society of my fellow-slaves. They were noble souls; they not only possessed loving hearts, but brave ones. We were linked and interlinked with each other. I loved them with a love stronger than any thing I have experienced since. It is sometimes said that we slaves do not love and confide in each other. In answer to this assertion, I can say, I never loved any or confided in any people more than my fellow-slaves, and especially those with whom I lived at Mr. Freeland's. I believe we would have died for each other. We never undertook to do any thing, of any importance, without a mutual consultation. We never moved separately. We were one; and as much so by our tempers and dispositions, as by the mutual hardships to which we were necessarily subjected by our condition as slaves.

At the close of the year 1834, Mr. Freeland again hired me of my master, for the year 1835. But, by this time, I began to want to live *upon free land* as well as *with Freeland;* and I was no longer content, therefore, to live with him or any other slaveholder. I began, with the commencement of the year, to prepare myself for a final struggle, which should decide my fate one way or the other. My tendency was upward. I was fast approaching manhood, and year after year had passed, and I was still a slave. These thoughts roused me—I must do something. I therefore resolved that 1835 should not pass without witnessing an attempt, on my part, to secure my liberty. But I was not willing to cherish this determination alone. My fellow-slaves were dear to me. I was anxious to have them participate with me in this, my life-giving determination. I therefore, though with great prudence, commenced early to ascertain their views and feelings in regard to their condition, and to imbue their minds with thoughts of freedom. I bent myself to devising ways and means for our escape, and meanwhile strove, on all fitting occasions, to impress them with the gross fraud and inhumanity of slavery. I went first to Henry, next to John, then to the others. I found, in them all, warm hearts and noble spirits. They were ready to hear, and ready to act when a feasible plan should be proposed. This was what I wanted. I talked to them of our want of manhood, if we submitted to our enslavement without at least one noble effort to be free. We met often, and consulted frequently, and told our hopes and fears, recounted the difficulties, real and imagined, which we should be called on to meet. At times we were almost disposed to give up, and try to content ourselves with our wretched lot; at others, we were firm and unbending in our determination to go. Whenever we suggested any plan, there was shrinking—the odds were fearful. Our path was beset with the greatest obstacles; and if we succeeded in gaining the end of it, our right to be free was yet questionable—we were yet liable to be returned to bondage. We could see no spot, this side of the ocean, where we could be free. We knew nothing about Canada. Our knowledge of the north did not extend farther than New York; and to go there, and be forever harassed with the frightful liability of being returned to slavery—with the certainty of being treated tenfold worse than before—the thought was truly a horrible one, and one which it was not easy to overcome. The case sometimes stood thus: At every gate through which we were to pass, we saw a watchman—at every ferry a guard—on every bridge a sentinel—and in every wood a patrol. We were hemmed in upon every side. Here were the difficulties, real or imagined—the good to be sought, and the evil to be shunned. On the one hand, there stood slavery, a stern reality, glaring frightfully upon us,—its robes already crimsoned with the blood of millions, and even now feasting itself greedily upon our own flesh. On the other hand, away back in the dim distance, under the flickering light of the north star, behind some craggy hill or snow-covered mountain, stood a doubtful freedom—half frozen—beckoning us to come and share its hospitality. This in itself was sometimes enough to stagger us; but when we permitted ourselves to survey the road, we were frequently appalled. Upon either side we saw grim death, assuming the most horrid shapes. Now it was starvation, causing us to eat our own flesh;—now we were contending with the waves, and were drowned;—now we were overtaken, and torn to pieces by the fangs of the terrible bloodhound. We were stung by scorpions, chased by wild beasts, bitten by snakes, and finally, after having nearly reached the desired spot,—after swimming rivers, encountering wild beasts, sleeping in the woods, suffering hunger and nakedness,—we were overtaken by our pursuers, and, in our resistance, we were shot dead upon the spot! I say, this picture sometimes appalled us, and made us

> "rather bear those ills we had,
> Than fly to others, that we knew not of."

In coming to a fixed determination to run away, we did more than Patrick Henry, when he resolved upon liberty or death. With us it was a doubtful liberty at most, and almost certain death if we failed. For my part, I should prefer death to hopeless bondage.

Sandy, one of our number, gave up the notion, but still encouraged us. Our company then consisted of Henry Harris, John Harris, Henry Bailey, Charles Roberts, and myself. Henry Bailey was my uncle, and belonged to my master. Charles married my aunt: he belonged to my master's father-in-law, Mr. William Hamilton.

The plan we finally concluded upon was, to get a large canoe belonging to Mr. Hamilton, and upon the Saturday night previous to Easter holidays, paddle directly up the Chesapeake Bay. On our arrival at the head of the bay, a distance of seventy or eighty miles from where we lived, it was our purpose to turn our canoe adrift, and follow the guidance of the north star till we got beyond the limits of Maryland. Our reason for taking the water route was, that we were less liable to be suspected as runaways; we hoped to be regarded as fishermen; whereas, if we should take the land route, we should be subjected to interruptions of almost every kind. Any one having a white face, and being so disposed, could stop us, and subject us to examination.

The week before our intended start, I wrote several protections, one for each of us. As well as I can remember, they were in the following words:—

> "This is to certify that I, the undersigned, have given the bearer, my servant, full liberty to go to Baltimore, and spend the Easter holidays. Written with mine own hand, &c., 1835.
>
> "William Hamilton,
>
> "Near St. Michael's, in Talbot County, Maryland."

We were not going to Baltimore; but, in going up the bay, we went toward Baltimore, and these protections were only intended to protect us while on the bay.

As the time drew near for our departure, our anxiety became more and more intense. It was truly a matter of life and death with us. The strength of our determination was about to be fully tested. At this time, I was very active in explaining every difficulty, removing every doubt, dispelling every fear, and inspiring all with the firmness indispensable to success in our undertaking; assuring them that half was gained the instant we made the move; we had talked long enough; we were now ready to move; if not now, we never should be; and if we did not intend to move now, we had as well fold our arms, sit down, and acknowledge ourselves fit only to be slaves. This, none of us were prepared to acknowledge. Every man stood firm; and in our last meeting, we pledged ourselves afresh, and in the most solemn manner, that, at the time appointed, we would certainly start in pursuit of freedom. This was in the middle of the week, at the end of which we were to be off. We went, as usual, to our several fields of labor, but with bosoms highly agitated with thoughts of our truly hazardous undertaking. We tried to conceal our feelings as much as possible; and I think we succeeded very well.

After a painful waiting, the Saturday morning, whose night was to witness our departure, came. I hailed it with joy, bring what of sadness it might. Friday night was a sleepless one for me. I probably felt more anxious than the rest, because I was, by common consent, at the head of the whole affair. The responsibility of success or failure lay heavily upon me. The glory of the one, and the confusion of the other, were alike mine. The first two hours of that morning were such as I never experienced before, and hope never to again. Early in the morning, we went, as usual, to the field. We were spreading the manure; and all at once, while thus engaged, I was overwhelmed with an indescribable feeling, in the fulness of which I turned to Sandy, who was near by, and said, "We are betrayed!" "Well," said he, "that thought has this moment struck me." We said no more. I was never more certain of any thing.

The horn was blown as usual, and we went up from the field to the house for breakfast. I went for the form, more than for want of any thing to eat that morning. Just as I got to the house, in looking out at the lane gate, I saw four white men, with two colored men. The white men were on horseback, and the colored ones were walking behind, as if tied. I watched them a few moments till they got up to our lane gate. Here they halted, and tied the colored men to the gate-post. I was not yet certain as to what the matter was. In a few moments, in rode Mr. Hamilton, with a speed betokening great excitement. He came to the door, and inquired if Master William was in. He was told he was at the barn. Mr. Hamilton, without dismounting, rode up to the barn with extraordinary speed. In a few moments, he and Mr. Freeland returned to the house. By this time, the three constables rode up, and in great haste dismounted, tied their horses, and met Master William and Mr. Hamilton returning from the barn; and after talking awhile, they all walked up to the kitchen door. There was no one in the kitchen but myself and John. Henry and Sandy were up at the barn. Mr. Freeland put his head in at the door, and called me by my name, saying, there were some gentlemen at the door who wished to see me. I stepped to the door, and inquired what they wanted. They at once seized me, and, without giving me any satisfaction, tied me—lashing my hands closely together. I insisted upon knowing what the matter was. They at length said, that they had learned I had been in a "scrape," and that I was to be examined before my master; and if their information proved false, I should not be hurt.

In a few moments, they succeeded in tying John. They then turned to Henry, who had by this time returned, and commanded him to cross his hands. "I won't!" said Henry, in a firm tone, indicating his readiness to meet the consequences of his refusal. "Won't you?" said Tom Graham, the constable. "No, I won't!" said Henry, in a still stronger tone. With this, two of the constables pulled out their shining pistols, and swore, by their Creator, that they would make him cross his hands or kill him. Each cocked his pistol, and, with fingers on the trigger, walked up to Henry, saying, at the same time, if he did not cross his hands, they would blow his damned heart out. "Shoot me, shoot me!" said Henry; "you can't kill me but once. Shoot, shoot,—and be damned! *I won't be tied!*" This he said in a tone of loud defiance; and at the same time, with a motion as quick as lightning, he with one single stroke dashed the pistols from the hand of each constable. As he did this, all hands fell upon him, and, after beating him some time, they finally overpowered him, and got him tied.

During the scuffle, I managed, I know not how, to get my pass out, and, without being discovered, put it into the fire. We were all now tied; and just as we were to leave for Easton jail, Betsy Freeland, mother of William Freeland, came to the door with her hands full of biscuits, and divided them between Henry and John. She then delivered herself of a speech, to the following effect:—addressing herself to me, she said, "*You devil! You yellow devil!* it was you that put it into the heads of Henry and John to run away. But for you, you long-legged mulatto devil! Henry nor John would never have thought of such a thing." I made no reply, and was immediately hurried off towards St. Michael's. Just a moment previous to the scuffle with Henry, Mr. Hamilton suggested the propriety of making a search for the protections which he had understood Frederick had written for himself and the rest. But, just at the moment he was about carrying his proposal into effect, his aid was needed in helping to tie Henry; and the excitement attending the scuffle caused them either to forget, or to deem it unsafe, under the circumstances, to search. So we were not yet convicted of the intention to run away.

When we got about half way to St. Michael's, while the constables having us in charge were looking ahead, Henry inquired of me what he should do with his pass. I told him to eat it with his biscuit, and own nothing; and we passed the word around, "*Own nothing;*" and "*Own nothing!*" said we all. Our confidence in each other was unshaken. We were resolved to succeed or fail together, after the calamity had befallen us as much as before. We were now prepared for any thing. We were to be dragged that morning fifteen miles behind horses, and then to be placed in the Easton jail. When we reached St. Michael's, we underwent a sort of examination. We all denied that we ever intended to run away. We did this more to bring out the evidence against us, than from any hope of getting clear of being sold; for, as I have said, we were ready for that. The fact was, we cared but little where we went, so we went together. Our greatest concern was about separation. We dreaded that more than any thing this side of death. We found the evidence against us to be the testimony of one person; our master would not tell who it was; but we came to a unanimous decision among ourselves as to who their informant was. We were sent off to the jail at Easton. When we got there, we were delivered up to the sheriff, Mr. Joseph Graham, and by him placed in jail. Henry, John, and myself, were placed in one room together—Charles, and Henry Bailey, in another. Their object in separating us was to hinder concert.

We had been in jail scarcely twenty minutes, when a swarm of slave traders, and agents for slave traders, flocked into jail to look at us, and to ascertain if we were for sale. Such a set of beings I never saw before! I felt myself surrounded by so many fiends from perdition. A band of pirates never looked more like their father, the devil. They laughed and grinned over us, saying, "Ah, my boys! we have got you, haven't we?" And after taunting us in various ways, they one by one went into an examination of us, with intent to ascertain our value. They would impudently ask us if we would not like to have them for our masters. We would make them no answer, and leave them to find out as best they could. Then they would curse and swear at us, telling us that they could take the devil out of us in a very little while, if we were only in their hands.

While in jail, we found ourselves in much more comfortable quarters than we expected when we went there. We did not get much to eat, nor that which was very good; but we had a good clean room, from the windows of which we could see what was going on in the street, which was very much better than if we had been placed in one of the dark, damp cells. Upon the whole, we got along very well, so far as the jail and its keeper were concerned. Immediately after the holidays were over, contrary to all our expectations, Mr. Hamilton and Mr. Freeland came up to Easton, and took Charles, the two Henrys, and John, out of jail, and carried them home, leaving me alone. I regarded this separation as a final one. It caused me more pain than any thing else in the whole transaction. I was ready for any thing rather than separation. I supposed that they had consulted together, and had decided that, as I was the whole cause of the intention of the others to run away, it was hard to make the innocent suffer with the guilty; and that they had, therefore, concluded to take the others home, and sell me, as a warning to the others that remained. It is due to the noble Henry to say, he seemed almost as reluctant at leaving the prison as at leaving home to come to the prison. But we knew we should, in all probability, be separated, if we were sold; and since he was in their hands, he concluded to go peaceably home.

I was now left to my fate. I was all alone, and within the walls of a stone prison. But a few days before, and I was full of hope. I expected to have been safe in a land of freedom; but now I was covered with gloom, sunk down to the utmost despair. I thought the possibility of freedom was gone. I was kept in this way about one week, at the end of which, Captain Auld, my master, to my surprise and utter astonishment, came up, and took me out, with the intention of sending me, with a gentleman of his acquaintance, into Alabama. But, from some cause or other, he did not send me to Alabama, but concluded to send me back to Baltimore, to live again with his brother Hugh, and to learn a trade.

Thus, after an absence of three years and one month, I was once more permitted to return to my old home at Baltimore. My master sent me away, because there existed against me a very great prejudice in the community, and he feared I might be killed.

In a few weeks after I went to Baltimore, Master Hugh hired me to Mr. William Gardner, an extensive ship-builder, on Fell's Point. I was put there to learn how to calk. It, however, proved a very unfavorable place for the accomplishment of this object. Mr. Gardner was engaged that spring in building two large man-of-war brigs, professedly for the Mexican government. The vessels were to be launched in the July of that year, and in failure thereof, Mr. Gardner was to lose a considerable sum; so that when I entered, all was hurry. There was no time to learn any thing. Every man had to do that which he knew how to do. In entering the ship-yard, my orders from Mr. Gardner were, to do whatever the carpenters commanded me to do. This was placing me at the beck and call of about seventy-five men. I was to regard all these as masters. Their word was to be my law. My situation was a most trying one. At times I needed a dozen pair of hands. I was called a dozen ways in the space of a single minute. Three or four voices would strike my ear at the same moment. It was—"Fred., come help me to cant this timber here."—"Fred., come carry this timber yonder."—"Fred., bring that roller here."—"Fred., go get a fresh can of water."—"Fred., come help saw off the end of this timber."—"Fred., go quick, and get the crowbar."—"Fred., hold on the end of this fall."—"Fred., go to the blacksmith's shop, and get a new punch."—"Hurra, Fred.! run and bring me a cold chisel."—"I say, Fred., bear a hand, and get up a fire as quick as lightning under that steam-box."—"Halloo, nigger! come, turn this grindstone."—"Come, come! move, move! and *bowse* this timber forward."—"I say, darky, blast your eyes, why don't you heat up some pitch?"—"Halloo! halloo! halloo!" (Three voices at the same time.) "Come here!—Go there!—Hold on where you are! Damn you, if you move, I'll knock your brains out!"

This was my school for eight months; and I might have remained there longer, but for a most horrid fight I had with four of the white apprentices, in which my left eye was nearly knocked out, and I was horribly mangled in other respects. The facts in the case were these: Until a very little while after

I went there, white and black ship-carpenters worked side by side, and no one seemed to see any impropriety in it. All hands seemed to be very well satisfied. Many of the black carpenters were freemen. Things seemed to be going on very well. All at once, the white carpenters knocked off, and said they would not work with free colored workmen. Their reason for this, as alleged, was, that if free colored carpenters were encouraged, they would soon take the trade into their own hands, and poor white men would be thrown out of employment. They therefore felt called upon at once to put a stop to it. And, taking advantage of Mr. Gardner's necessities, they broke off, swearing they would work no longer, unless he would discharge his black carpenters. Now, though this did not extend to me in form, it did reach me in fact. My fellow-apprentices very soon began to feel it degrading to them to work with me. They began to put on airs, and talk about the "niggers" taking the country, saying we all ought to be killed; and, being encouraged by the journeymen, they commenced making my condition as hard as they could, by hectoring me around, and sometimes striking me. I, of course, kept the vow I made after the fight with Mr. Covey, and struck back again, regardless of consequences; and while I kept them from combining, I succeeded very well; for I could whip the whole of them, taking them separately. They, however, at length combined, and came upon me, armed with sticks, stones, and heavy handspikes. One came in front with a half brick. There was one at each side of me, and one behind me. While I was attending to those in front, and on either side, the one behind ran up with the handspike, and struck me a heavy blow upon the head. It stunned me. I fell, and with this they all ran upon me, and fell to beating me with their fists. I let them lay on for a while, gathering strength. In an instant, I gave a sudden surge, and rose to my hands and knees. Just as I did that, one of their number gave me, with his heavy boot, a powerful kick in the left eye. My eyeball seemed to have burst. When they saw my eye closed, and badly swollen, they left me. With this I seized the handspike, and for a time pursued them. But here the carpenters interfered, and I thought I might as well give it up. It was impossible to stand my hand against so many. All this took place in sight of not less than fifty white ship-carpenters, and not one interposed a friendly word; but some cried, "Kill the damned nigger! Kill him! kill him! He struck a white person." I found my only chance for life was in flight. I succeeded in getting away without an additional blow, and barely so; for to strike a white man is death by Lynch law,—and that was the law in Mr. Gardner's ship-yard; nor is there much of any other out of Mr. Gardner's ship-yard, within the bounds of the Slave States.

I went directly home, and told the story of my wrongs to Master Hugh; and I am happy to say of him, irreligious as he was, his conduct was heavenly, compared with that of his brother Thomas under similar circumstances. He listened attentively to my narration of the circumstances leading to the savage outrage, and gave many proofs of his strong indignation at it. The heart of my once overkind mistress was again melted into pity. My puffed-out eye and blood-covered face moved her to tears. She took a chair by me, washed the blood from my face, and, with a mother's tenderness, bound up my head, covering the wounded eye with a lean piece of fresh beef. It was almost compensation for my sufferings to witness, once more, a manifestation of kindness from this, my once affectionate old mistress. Master Hugh was very much enraged. He gave expression to his feelings by pouring out curses upon the heads of those who did the deed. As soon as I got a little the better of my bruises, he took me with him to Esquire Watson's, on Bond Street, to see what could be done about the matter. Mr. Watson inquired who saw the assault committed. Master Hugh told him it was done in Mr. Gardner's ship-yard, at mid-day, where there was a large company of men at work. "As to that," he said, "the deed was done, and there was no question as to who did it." His answer was, he could do nothing in the case, unless some white man would come forward and testify. He could issue no warrant on my word. If I had been killed in the presence of a thousand colored people, their testimony combined would have been insufficient to have arrested one of the murderers. Master Hugh, for once, was compelled to say this state of things was too bad. Of course, it was impossible to get any white man to volunteer his testimony in my behalf, and against the white young men. Even those who may have sympathized with me were not prepared to do this. It required a degree of courage unknown to them to do so; for just at that time, the slightest manifestation of humanity toward a colored person was denounced as abolitionism, and that name subjected its bearer to frightful liabilities. The watchwords of the bloody-minded in that region, and in those days, were, "Damn the abolitionists!" and "Damn the niggers!" There was nothing done, and probably nothing would have been done if I had been killed. Such was, and such remains, the state of things in the Christian city of Baltimore.

Master Hugh, finding he could get no redress, refused to let me go back again to Mr. Gardner. He kept me himself, and his wife dressed my wound till I was again restored to health. He then took me into the ship-yard of which he was foreman, in the employment of Mr. Walter Price. There I was immediately set to calking, and very soon learned the art of using my mallet and irons. In the course of one year from the time I left Mr. Gardner's, I was able to command the highest wages given to the most experienced calkers. I was now of some importance to my master. I was bringing him from six to seven dollars per week. I sometimes brought him nine dollars per week: my wages were a dollar and a half a day. After learning how to calk, I sought my own employment, made my own contracts, and collected the money which I earned. My pathway became much more smooth than before; my condition was now much more comfortable. When I could get no calking to do, I did nothing. During these leisure times, those old notions about freedom would steal over me again. When in Mr. Gardner's employment, I was kept in such a perpetual whirl of excitement, I could think of nothing, scarcely, but my life; and in thinking of my life, I almost forgot my liberty. I have observed this in my experience of slavery,—that whenever my condition was improved, instead of its increasing my contentment, it only increased my desire to be free, and set me to thinking of plans to gain my freedom. I have found that, to make a contented slave, it is necessary to make a thoughtless one. It is necessary to darken his moral and mental vision, and, as far as possible, to annihilate the power of reason. He must be able to detect no inconsistencies in slavery; he must be made to feel that slavery is right; and he can be brought to that only when he ceases to be a man.

I was now getting, as I have said, one dollar and fifty cents per day. I contracted for it; I earned it; it was paid to me; it was rightfully my own; yet, upon each returning Saturday night, I was compelled to deliver every cent of that money to Master Hugh. And why? Not because he earned it,—not because he had any hand in earning it,—not because I owed it to him,—nor because he possessed the slightest shadow of a right to it; but solely because he had the power to compel me to give it up. The right of the grim-visaged pirate upon the high seas is exactly the same.

CHAPTER XI.

I NOW come to that part of my life during which I planned, and finally succeeded in making, my escape from slavery. But before narrating any of the peculiar circumstances, I deem it proper to make known my intention not to state all the facts connected with the transaction. My reasons for pursuing this course may be understood from the following: First, were I to give a minute statement of all the facts, it is not only possible, but quite probable, that others would thereby be involved in the most embarrassing difficulties. Secondly, such a statement would most undoubtedly induce greater vigilance on the part of slaveholders than has existed heretofore among them; which would, of course, be the means of guarding a door whereby some dear brother bondman might escape his galling chains. I deeply regret the necessity that impels me to suppress any thing of importance connected with my experience in slavery. It would afford me great pleasure indeed, as well as materially add to the interest of my narrative, were I at liberty to gratify a curiosity, which I know exists in the minds of many, by an accurate statement of all the facts pertaining to my most fortunate escape. But I must deprive myself of this pleasure, and the curious of the gratification which such a statement would afford. I would allow myself to suffer under the greatest imputations which evil-minded men might suggest, rather than exculpate myself, and thereby run the hazard of closing the slightest avenue by which a brother slave might clear himself of the chains and fetters of slavery.

I have never approved of the very public manner in which some of our western friends have conducted what they call the *underground railroad*, but which, I think, by their open declarations, has been made most emphatically the *upperground railroad.* I honor those good men and women for their noble daring, and applaud them for willingly subjecting themselves to bloody persecution, by openly avowing their participation in the escape of slaves. I, however, can see very little good resulting from such a course, either to themselves or the slaves escaping; while, upon the other hand, I see and feel assured that those open declarations are a positive evil to the slaves remaining, who are seeking to escape. They do nothing towards enlightening the slave, whilst they do much towards enlightening the master. They stimulate him to greater watchfulness, and enhance his power to capture his slave. We owe something to the slaves south of the line as well as to those north of it; and in aiding the latter on their way to freedom, we should be careful to do nothing which would be likely to hinder the former from escaping from slavery. I would keep the merciless slaveholder profoundly ignorant of the means of flight adopted by the slave. I would leave him to imagine himself surrounded by myriads of invisible tormentors, ever ready to snatch from his infernal grasp his trembling prey. Let him be left to feel his way in the dark; let darkness commensurate with his crime hover over him; and let him feel that at every step he takes, in pursuit of the flying bondman, he is running the frightful risk of having his hot brains dashed out by an invisible agency. Let us render the tyrant no aid; let us not hold the light by which he can trace the footprints of our flying brother. But enough of this. I will now proceed to the statement of those facts, connected with my escape, for which I am alone responsible, and for which no one can be made to suffer but myself.

In the early part of the year 1838, I became quite restless. I could see no reason why I should, at the end of each week, pour the reward of my toil into the purse of my master. When I carried to him my weekly wages, he would, after counting the money, look me in the face with a robber-like fierceness, and ask, "Is this all?" He was satisfied with nothing less than the last cent. He would, however, when I made him six dollars, sometimes give me six cents, to encourage me. It had the opposite effect. I regarded it as a sort of admission of my right to the whole. The fact that he gave me any part of my wages was proof, to my mind, that he believed me entitled to the whole of them. I always felt worse for having received any thing; for I feared that the giving me a few cents would ease his conscience, and make him feel himself to be a pretty honorable sort of robber. My discontent grew upon me. I was ever on the look-out for means of escape; and, finding no direct means, I determined to try to hire my time, with a view of getting money with which to make my escape. In the spring of 1838, when Master Thomas came to Baltimore to purchase his spring goods, I got an opportunity, and applied to him to allow me to hire my time. He unhesitatingly refused my request, and told me this was another stratagem by which to escape. He told me I could go nowhere but that he could get me; and that, in the event of my running away, he should spare no pains in his efforts to catch me. He exhorted me to content myself, and be obedient. He told me, if I would be happy, I must lay out no plans for the future. He said, if I behaved myself properly, he would take care of me. Indeed, he advised me to complete thoughtlessness of the future, and taught me to depend solely upon him for happiness. He seemed to see fully the pressing necessity of setting aside my intellectual nature, in order to contentment in slavery. But in spite of him, and even in spite of myself, I continued to think, and to think about the injustice of my enslavement, and the means of escape.

About two months after this, I applied to Master Hugh for the privilege of hiring my time. He was not acquainted with the fact that I had applied to Master Thomas, and had been refused. He too, at first, seemed disposed to refuse; but, after some reflection, he granted me the privilege, and proposed the following terms: I was to be allowed all my time, make all contracts with those for whom I worked, and find my own employment; and, in return for this liberty, I was to pay him three dollars at the end of each week, find myself in calking tools, and in board and clothing. My board was two dollars and a half per week. This, with the wear and tear of clothing and calking tools, made my regular expenses about six dollars per week. This amount I was compelled to make up, or relinquish the privilege of hiring my time. Rain or shine, work or no work, at the end of each week the money must be forthcoming, or I must give up my privilege. This arrangement, it will be perceived, was decidedly in my master's favor. It relieved him of all need of looking after me. His money was sure. He received all the benefits of slaveholding without its evils; while I endured all the evils of a slave, and suffered all the care and anxiety of a freeman. I found it a hard bargain. But, hard as it was, I thought it better than the old mode of getting along. It was a step towards freedom to be allowed to bear the responsibilities of a freeman, and I was determined to hold on upon it. I bent myself to the work of making money. I was ready to work at night as well as day, and by the most untiring perseverance and industry, I made enough to meet my expenses, and lay up a little money every week. I went on thus from May till August. Master Hugh then refused to allow me to hire my time longer. The ground for his refusal was a failure on my part, one Saturday night, to pay him for my week's time. This failure was occasioned by my attending a camp meeting about ten miles from Baltimore. During the week, I had entered into an engagement with a number of young friends to start from Baltimore to the camp ground early Saturday evening; and being detained by my employer, I was unable to go down to Master Hugh's without disappointing the company. I knew that Master Hugh was in no special need of the money that night. I therefore decided to go to camp meeting, and upon my return to pay him the three dollars. I staid at the camp meeting one day longer than I intended when I left. But as soon as I returned, I called upon him to pay him what he considered his due. I found him very angry; he could scarce restrain his wrath. He said he had a great mind to give me a severe whipping. He wished to know how I dared go out of the city without asking his permission. I told him I hired my time, and while I paid him the price which he asked for it, I did not know that I was bound to ask him when and where I should go. This reply troubled him; and, after reflecting a few moments, he turned to me, and said I should hire my time no longer; the next thing he should know of, I would be running away. Upon the same plea, he told me to bring my tools and clothing home forthwith. I did so; but instead of seeking work, as I had been accustomed to do previously to hiring my time, I spent the whole week without the performance of a single stroke of work. I did this in retaliation. Saturday night, he called upon me as usual for my week's wages. I told him I had no wages; I had done no work that week. Here we were upon the point of coming to blows. He raved, and swore his determination to get hold of me. I did not allow myself a single word; but was resolved, if he laid the weight of his hand upon me, it should be blow for blow. He did not strike me, but told me that he would find me in constant employment in future. I thought the matter over during the next day, Sunday, and finally resolved upon the third day of September, as the day upon which I would make a second attempt to secure my freedom. I now had three weeks during which to prepare for my journey. Early on Monday morning, before Master Hugh had time to make any engagement for me, I went out and got employment of Mr. Butler, at his ship-yard near the drawbridge, upon what is called the City Block, thus making it unnecessary for him to seek employment for me. At the end of the week, I brought him between eight and nine dollars. He seemed very well pleased, and asked me why I did not do the same the week before. He little knew what my plans were. My object in working steadily was to remove any suspicion he might entertain of my intent to run away; and in this I succeeded admirably. I suppose he thought I was never better satisfied with my condition than at the very time during which I was planning my escape. The second week passed, and again I carried him my full wages; and so well pleased was he, that he gave me twenty-five cents, (quite a large sum for a slaveholder to give a slave,) and bade me to make good use of it. I told him I would.

Things went on without very smoothly indeed, but within there was trouble. It is impossible for me to describe my feelings as the time of my contemplated start drew near. I had a number of warm-hearted friends in Baltimore,—friends that I loved almost as I did my life,—and the thought of being separated from them forever was painful beyond expression. It is my opinion that thousands would escape from slavery, who now remain, but for the strong cords of affection that bind them to their friends. The thought of leaving my friends was decidedly the most painful thought with which I had to contend. The love of them was my tender point, and shook my decision more than all things else. Besides the pain of separation, the dread and apprehension of a failure exceeded what I had experienced at my first attempt. The appalling defeat I then sustained returned to torment me. I felt assured that, if I failed in this attempt, my case would be a hopeless one—it would seal my fate as a slave forever. I could not hope to get off with any thing less than the severest punishment, and being placed beyond the means of escape. It required no very vivid imagination to depict the most frightful scenes through which I should have to pass, in case I failed. The wretchedness of slavery, and the blessedness of freedom, were perpetually before me. It was life and death to me. But I remained firm, and, according to my resolution, on the third day of September, 1838, I left my chains, and succeeded in reaching New York without the slightest interruption of any kind. How I did so,—what means I adopted,—in what direction I travelled, and by what mode of conveyance,—I must leave unexplained, for the reasons before mentioned.

I have been frequently asked how I felt when I found myself in a free State. I have never been able to answer the question with any satisfaction to myself. It was a moment of the highest excitement I ever experienced. I suppose I felt as one may imagine the unarmed mariner to feel when he is rescued by a friendly man-of-war from the pursuit of a pirate. In writing to a dear friend, immediately after my arrival at New York, I said I felt like one who had escaped a den of hungry lions. This state of mind, however, very soon subsided; and I was again seized with a feeling of great insecurity and loneliness. I was yet liable to be taken back, and subjected to all the tortures of slavery. This in itself was enough to damp the ardor of my enthusiasm. But the loneliness overcame me. There I was in the midst of thousands, and yet a perfect stranger; without home and without friends, in the midst of thousands of my own brethren—children of a common Father, and yet I dared not unfold to any one of them my sad condition. I was afraid to speak to any one for fear of speaking to the wrong one, and thereby falling into the hands of money-loving kidnappers, whose business it was to lie in wait for the panting fugitive, as the ferocious beasts of the forest lie in wait for their prey. The motto which I adopted when I started from slavery was this—"Trust no man!" I saw in every white man an enemy, and in almost every colored man cause for distrust. It was a most painful situation; and, to understand it, one must needs experience it, or imagine himself in similar circumstances. Let him be a fugitive slave in a strange land—a land given up to be the hunting-ground for slaveholders—whose inhabitants are legalized kidnappers—where he is every moment subjected to the terrible liability of being seized upon by his fellow-men, as the hideous crocodile seizes upon his prey!—I say, let him place himself in my situation—without home or friends—without money or credit—wanting shelter, and no one to give it—wanting bread, and no money to buy it,—and at the same time let him feel that he is pursued by merciless men-hunters, and in total darkness as to what to do, where to go, or where to stay,—perfectly helpless both as to the means of defence and means of escape,—in the midst of plenty, yet suffering the terrible gnawings of hunger,—in the midst of houses, yet having no home,—among fellow-men, yet feeling as if in the midst of wild beasts, whose greediness to swallow up the trembling and half-famished fugitive is only equalled by that with which the monsters of the deep swallow up the helpless fish upon which they subsist,—I say, let him be placed in this most trying situation,—the situation in which I was placed,—then, and not till then, will he fully appreciate the hardships of, and know how to sympathize with, the toil-worn and whip-scarred fugitive slave.

Thank Heaven, I remained but a short time in this distressed situation. I was relieved from it by the humane hand of Mr. DAVID RUGGLES, whose vigilance, kindness, and perseverance, I shall never forget. I am glad of an opportunity to express, as far as words can, the love and gratitude I bear him. Mr. Ruggles is now afflicted with blindness, and is himself in need of the same kind offices which he was once so forward in the performance of toward others. I had been in New York but a few days, when Mr. Ruggles sought me out, and very kindly took me to his boarding-house at the corner of Church and Lespenard Streets. Mr. Ruggles was then very deeply engaged in the memorable *Darg* case, as well as attending to a number of other fugitive slaves, devising ways and means for their successful escape; and, though watched and hemmed in on almost every side, he seemed to be more than a match for his enemies.

Very soon after I went to Mr. Ruggles, he wished to know of me where I wanted to go; as he deemed it unsafe for me to remain in New York. I told him I was a calker, and should like to go where I could get work. I thought of going to Canada; but he decided against it, and in favor of my going to New Bedford, thinking I should be able to get work there at my trade. At this time, Anna,* my intended wife, came on; for I wrote to her immediately after my arrival at New York, (notwithstanding my homeless, houseless, and helpless condition,) informing her of my successful flight, and wishing her to come on forthwith. In a few days after her arrival, Mr. Ruggles called in the Rev. J. W. C. Pennington, who, in the presence of Mr. Ruggles, Mrs. Michaels, and two or three others, performed the marriage ceremony, and gave us a certificate, of which the following is an exact copy:—

> "THIS may certify, that I joined together in holy matrimony Frederick Johnson† and Anna Murray, as man and wife, in the presence of Mr. David Ruggles and Mrs. Michaels.
>
> "JAMES W. C. PENNINGTON.
>
> "*New York, Sept.* 15, 1838."

Upon receiving this certificate, and a five-dollar bill from Mr. Ruggles, I shouldered one part of our baggage, and Anna took up the other, and we set out forthwith to take passage on board of the steamboat John W. Richmond for Newport, on our way to New Bedford. Mr. Ruggles gave me a letter to a Mr. Shaw in Newport, and told me, in case my money did not serve me to New Bedford, to stop in Newport and obtain further assistance; but upon our arrival at Newport, we were so anxious to get to a place of safety, that, notwithstanding we lacked the necessary money to pay our fare, we decided

*She was free.

†I had changed my name from Frederick *Bailey* to that of *Johnson.*

to take seats in the stage, and promise to pay when we got to New Bedford. We were encouraged to do this by two excellent gentlemen, residents of New Bedford, whose names I afterward ascertained to be Joseph Ricketson and William C. Taber. They seemed at once to understand our circumstances, and gave us such assurance of their friendliness as put us fully at ease in their presence. It was good indeed to meet with such friends, at such a time. Upon reaching New Bedford, we were directed to the house of Mr. Nathan Johnson, by whom we were kindly received, and hospitably provided for. Both Mr. and Mrs. Johnson took a deep and lively interest in our welfare. They proved themselves quite worthy of the name of abolitionists. When the stage-driver found us unable to pay our fare, he held on upon our baggage as security for the debt. I had but to mention the fact to Mr. Johnson, and he forthwith advanced the money.

We now began to feel a degree of safety, and to prepare ourselves for the duties and responsibilities of a life of freedom. On the morning after our arrival at New Bedford, while at the breakfast-table, the question arose as to what name I should be called by. The name given me by my mother was, "Frederick Augustus Washington Bailey." I, however, had dispensed with the two middle names long before I left Maryland so that I was generally known by the name of "Frederick Bailey." I started from Baltimore bearing the name of "Stanley." When I got to New York, I again changed my name to "Frederick Johnson," and thought that would be the last change. But when I got to New Bedford, I found it necessary again to change my name. The reason of this necessity was, that there were so many Johnsons in New Bedford, it was already quite difficult to distinguish between them. I gave Mr. Johnson the privilege of choosing me a name, but told him he must not take from me the name of "Frederick." I must hold on to that, to preserve a sense of my identity. Mr. Johnson had just been reading the "Lady of the Lake," and at once suggested that my name be "Douglass." From that time until now I have been called "Frederick Douglass;" and as I am more widely known by that name than by any of the others, I shall continue to use it as my own.

I was quite disappointed at the general appearance of things in New Bedford. The impression which I had received respecting the character and condition of the people of the north, I found to be singularly erroneous. I had very strangely supposed, while in slavery, that few of the comforts, and scarcely any of the luxuries, of life were enjoyed at the north, compared with what were enjoyed by the slaveholders of the south. I probably came to this conclusion from the fact that northern people owned no slaves. I supposed that they were about upon a level with the non-slaveholding population of the south. I knew *they* were exceedingly poor, and I had been accustomed to regard their poverty as the necessary consequence of their being non-slaveholders. I had somehow imbibed the opinion that, in the absence of slaves, there could be no wealth, and very little refinement. And upon coming to the north, I expected to meet with a rough, hard-handed, and uncultivated population, living in the most Spartan-like simplicity, knowing nothing of the ease, luxury, pomp, and grandeur of southern slaveholders. Such being my conjectures, any one acquainted with the appearance of New Bedford may very readily infer how palpably I must have seen my mistake.

In the afternoon of the day when I reached New Bedford, I visited the wharves, to take a view of the shipping. Here I found myself surrounded with the strongest proofs of wealth. Lying at the wharves, and riding in the stream, I saw many ships of the finest model, in the best order, and of the largest size. Upon the right and left, I was walled in by granite warehouses of the widest dimensions, stowed to their utmost capacity with the necessaries and comforts of life. Added to this, almost every body seemed to be at work, but noiselessly so, compared with what I had been accustomed to in Baltimore. There were no loud songs heard from those engaged in loading and unloading ships. I heard no deep oaths or horrid curses on the laborer. I saw no whipping of men; but all seemed to go smoothly on. Every man appeared to understand his work, and went at it with a sober, yet cheerful earnestness, which betokened the deep interest which he felt in what he was doing, as well as a sense of his own dignity as a man. To me this looked exceedingly strange. From the wharves I strolled around and over the town, gazing with wonder and admiration at the splendid churches, beautiful dwellings, and finely-cultivated gardens; evincing an amount of wealth, comfort, taste, and refinement, such as I had never seen in any part of slaveholding Maryland.

Every thing looked clean, new, and beautiful. I saw few or no dilapidated houses, with poverty-stricken inmates; no half-naked children and barefooted women, such as I had been accustomed to see in Hillsborough, Easton, St. Michael's, and Baltimore. The people looked more able, stronger, healthier, and happier, than those of Maryland. I was for once made glad by a view of extreme wealth, without being saddened by seeing extreme poverty. But the most astonishing as well as the most interesting thing to me was the condition of the colored people, a great many of whom, like myself, had escaped thither as a refuge from the hunters of men. I found many, who had not been seven years out of their chains, living in finer houses, and evidently enjoying more of the comforts of life, than the average of slaveholders in Maryland. I will venture to assert that my friend Mr. Nathan Johnson (of whom I can say with a grateful heart, "I was hungry, and he gave me meat; I was thirsty, and he gave me drink; I was a stranger, and he took me in") lived in a neater house; dined at a better table; took, paid for, and read, more newspapers; better understood the moral, religious, and political character of the nation,—than nine tenths of the slaveholders in Talbot county, Maryland. Yet Mr. Johnson was a working man. His hands were hardened by toil, and not his alone, but those also of Mrs. Johnson. I found the colored people much more spirited than I had supposed they would be. I found among them a determination to protect each other from the blood-thirsty kidnapper, at all hazards. Soon after my arrival, I was told of a circumstance which illustrated their spirit. A colored man and a fugitive slave were on unfriendly terms. The former was heard to threaten the latter with informing his master of his whereabouts. Straightway a meeting was called among the colored people, under the stereotyped notice, "Business of importance!" The betrayer was invited to attend. The people came at the appointed hour, and organized the meeting by appointing a very religious old gentleman as president, who, I believe, made a prayer, after which he addressed the meeting as follows: "*Friends, we have got him here, and I would recommend that you young men just take him outside the door, and kill him!*" With this, a number of them bolted at him; but they were intercepted by some more timid than themselves, and the betrayer escaped their vengeance, and has not been seen in New Bedford since. I believe there have been no more such threats, and should there be hereafter, I doubt not that death would be the consequence.

I found employment, the third day after my arrival, in stowing a sloop with a load of oil. It was new, dirty, and hard work for me; but I went at it with a glad heart and a willing hand. I was now my own master. It was a happy moment, the rapture of which can be understood only by those who have been slaves. It was the first work, the reward of which was to be entirely my own. There was no Master Hugh standing ready, the moment I earned the money, to rob me of it. I worked that day with a pleasure I had never before experienced. I was at work for myself and my newly-married wife. It was to me the starting-point of a new existence. When I got through with that job, I went in pursuit of a job of calking; but such was the strength of prejudice against color, among the white calkers, that they refused to work with me, and of course I could get no employment.* Finding my trade of no immediate benefit, I threw off my calking habiliments, and prepared myself to do any kind of work I could get to do. Mr. Johnson kindly let me have his wood-horse and saw, and I very soon found myself a plenty of work. There was no work too hard—none too dirty. I was ready to saw wood, shovel coal, carry the hod, sweep the chimney, or roll oil casks,—all of which I did for nearly three years in New Bedford, before I became known to the anti-slavery world.

In about four months after I went to New Bedford, there came a young man to me, and inquired if I did not wish to take the "Liberator." I told him I did; but, just having made my escape from slavery, I remarked that I was unable to pay for it then. I, however, finally became a subscriber to it. The paper came, and I read it from week to week with such feelings as it would be quite idle for me to attempt to describe. The paper became my meat and my drink. My soul was set all on fire. Its sympathy for my brethren in bonds—its scathing denunciations of slaveholders—its faithful exposures of slavery—and its powerful attacks upon the upholders of the institution—sent a thrill of joy through my soul, such as I had never felt before!

I had not long been a reader of the "Liberator," before I got a pretty correct idea of the principles, measures, and spirit of the anti-slavery reform. I took right hold of the cause. I could do but little; but what I could, I did with a joyful heart, and never felt happier than when in an anti-slavery meeting. I seldom had much to say at the meetings, because what I wanted to say was said so much better by others. But, while attending an anti-slavery convention at Nantucket, on the 11th of August, 1841, I felt strongly moved to speak, and was at the same time much urged to do so by Mr. William C. Coffin, a gentleman who had heard me speak in the colored people's meeting at New Bedford. It was a severe cross, and I took it up reluctantly. The truth was,

*I am told that colored persons can now get employment at calking in New Bedford—a result of anti-slavery effort.

I felt myself a slave, and the idea of speaking to white people weighed me down. I spoke but a few moments, when I felt a degree of freedom, and said what I desired with considerable ease. From that time until now, I have been engaged in pleading the cause of my brethren—with what success, and with what devotion, I leave those acquainted with my labors to decide.

APPENDIX.

I FIND, on reading over the foregoing Narrative that I have, in several instances, spoken in such a tone and manner, respecting religion, as may possibly lead those unacquainted with my religious views to suppose me an opponent of all religion. To remove the liability to such misapprehension, I deem it proper to append the following brief explanation. What I have said respecting and against religion, I mean strictly to apply to the *slaveholding religion* of this land, and with no reference whatever to Christianity proper; for, between the Christianity of this land, and the Christianity of Christ, I recognize the widest possible difference—so wide, that to receive the one as good, pure, and holy, is of necessity to reject the other as bad, corrupt, and wicked. To be the friend of the one, is of necessity to be the enemy of the other. I love the pure, peaceable, and impartial Christianity of Christ: I therefore hate the corrupt, slaveholding, women-whipping, cradle-plundering, partial and hypocritical Christianity of this land. Indeed, I can see no reason, but the most deceitful one, for calling the religion of this land Christianity. I look upon it as the climax of all misnomers, the boldest of all frauds, and the grossest of all libels. Never was there a clearer case of "stealing the livery of the court of heaven to serve the devil in." I am filled with unutterable loathing when I contemplate the religious pomp and show, together with the horrible inconsistencies, which every where surround me. We have men-stealers for ministers, women-whippers for missionaries, and cradle-plunderers for church members. The man who wields the blood-clotted cowskin during the week fills the pulpit on Sunday, and claims to be a minister of the meek and lowly Jesus. The man who robs me of my earnings at the end of each week meets me as a class-leader on Sunday morning, to show me the way of life, and the path of salvation. He who sells my sister, for purposes of prostitution, stands forth as the pious advocate of purity. He who proclaims it a religious duty to read the Bible denies me the right of learning to read the name of the God who made me. He who is the religious advocate of marriage robs whole millions of its sacred influence, and leaves them to the ravages of wholesale pollution. The warm defender of the sacredness of the family relation is the same that scatters whole families,—sundering husbands and wives, parents and children, sisters and brothers,—leaving the hut vacant, and the hearth desolate. We see the thief preaching against theft, and the adulterer against adultery. We have men sold to build churches, women sold to support the gospel, and babes sold to purchase Bibles for the *poor heathen! all for the glory of God and the good of souls!* The slave auctioneer's bell and the church-going bell chime in with each other, and the bitter cries of the heart-broken slave are drowned in the religious shouts of his pious master. Revivals of religion and revivals in the slave-trade go hand in hand together. The slave prison and the church stand near each other. The clanking of fetters and the rattling of chains in the prison, and the pious psalm and solemn prayer in the church, may be heard at the same time. The dealers in the bodies and souls of men erect their stand in the presence of the pulpit, and they mutually help each other. The dealer gives his blood-stained gold to support the pulpit, and the pulpit, in return, covers his infernal business with the garb of Christianity. Here we have religion and robbery the allies of each other; slavery and piety linked and interlinked; preachers of the gospel united with slaveholders! A horrible sight, to see devils dressed in angels' robes, and hell presenting the semblance of paradise.

"Just God! and these are they,
Who minister at thine altar, God of right!
Men who their hands, with prayer and blessing, lay
On Israel's ark of light.

"What! preach, and kidnap men?
Give thanks, and rob thy own afflicted poor?
Talk of thy glorious liberty, and then
Bolt hard the captive's door?

"What! servants of thy own
Merciful Son, who came to seek and save
The homeless and the outcast, fettering down
The tasked and plundered slave!

"Pilate and Herod friends!
Chief priests and rulers, as of old, combine!
Just God and holy! is that church which lends
Strength to the spoiler thine?"—*Whittier.*

The Christianity of America is a Christianity, of whose votaries it may be as truly said, as it was of the ancient scribes and Pharisees, "They bind heavy burdens, and grievous to be borne, and lay them on men's shoulders, but they themselves will not move them with one of their fingers. All their works they do for to be seen of men.—They love the uppermost rooms at feasts, and the chief seats in the synagogues, ... and to be called of men, Rabbi, Rabbi.—But woe unto you, scribes and Pharisees, hypocrites! for ye shut up the kingdom of heaven against men; for ye neither go in yourselves, neither suffer ye them that are entering to go in. Ye devour widows' houses, and for a pretence make long prayers; therefore ye shall receive the greater damnation. Ye compass sea and land to make one proselyte, and when he is made, ye make him twofold more the child of hell than yourselves.—Woe unto you, scribes and Pharisees, hypocrites! for ye pay tithe of mint, and anise, and cumin, and have omitted the weightier matters of the law, judgment, mercy, and faith; these ought ye to have done, and not to leave the other undone. Ye blind guides! which strain at a gnat, and swallow a camel. Woe unto you, scribes and Pharisees, hypocrites! for ye make clean the outside of the cup and of the platter; but within, they are full of extortion and excess.—Woe unto you, scribes and Pharisees, hypocrites! for ye are like unto whited sepulchres, which indeed appear beautiful outward, but are within full of dead men's bones and of all uncleanness. Even so ye also outwardly appear righteous unto men, but within ye are full of hypocrisy and iniquity."

Dark and terrible as is this picture, I hold it to be strictly true of the overwhelming mass of professed Christians in America. They strain at a gnat, and swallow a camel. Could any thing be more true of our churches? They would be shocked at the proposition of fellowshipping a *sheep*-stealer; and at the same time they hug to their communion a *man*-stealer, and brand me with being an infidel, if I find fault with them for it. They attend with Pharisaical strictness to the outward forms of religion, and at the same time neglect the weightier matters of the law, judgment, mercy, and faith. They are always ready to sacrifice, but seldom to show mercy. These are they who are represented as professing to love God whom they have not seen, whilst they hate their brother whom they have seen. They love the heathen on the other side of the globe. They can pray for him, pay money to have the Bible put into his hand, and missionaries to instruct him; while they despise and totally neglect the heathen at their own doors.

Such is, very briefly, my view of the religion of this land; and to avoid any misunderstanding, growing out of the use of general terms, I mean, by the religion of this land, that which is revealed in the words, deeds, and actions, of those bodies, north and south, calling themselves Christian churches, and yet in union with slaveholders. It is against religion, as represented by these bodies, that I feel it my duty to testify.

I conclude these remarks by copying the following portrait of the religion of the south, (which is, by communion and fellowship, the religion of the north,) which I soberly affirm is "true to the life," and without caricature or the slightest exaggeration. It is said to have been drawn, several years before the present anti-slavery agitation began, by a northern Methodist preacher, who, while residing at the south, had an opportunity to see slaveholding morals, manners, and piety, with his own eyes. "Shall I not visit for these things? saith the Lord. Shall not my soul be avenged on such a nation as this?"

"A PARODY.

"Come, saints and sinners, hear me tell
How pious priests whip Jack and Nell,
And women buy and children sell,
And preach all sinners down to hell,
And sing of heavenly union.

"They'll bleat and baa, dona like goats,
Gorge down black sheep, and strain at motes,
Array their backs in fine black coats,
Then seize their negroes by their throats,
And choke, for heavenly union.

"They'll church you if you sip a dram,
And damn you if you steal a lamb;
Yet rob old Tony, Doll, and Sam,

Of human rights, and bread and ham;
Kidnapper's heavenly union.

"They'll loudly talk of Christ's reward,
And bind his image with a cord,
And scold, and swing the lash abhorred,
And sell their brother in the Lord
To handcuffed heavenly union.

"They'll read and sing a sacred song,
And make a prayer both loud and long,
And teach the right and do the wrong,
Hailing the brother, sister throng,
With words of heavenly union.

"We wonder how such saints can sing,
Or praise the Lord upon the wing,
Who roar, and scold, and whip, and sting,
And to their slaves and mammon cling,
In guilty conscience union.

"They'll raise tobacco, corn, and rye,
And drive, and thieve, and cheat, and lie,
And lay up treasures in the sky,
By making switch and cowskin fly,
In hope of heavenly union.

"They'll crack old Tony on the skull,
And preach and roar like Bashan bull,
Or braying ass, of mischief full,
Then seize old Jacob by the wool,
And pull for heavenly union.

"A roaring, ranting, sleek man-thief,
Who lived on mutton, veal, and beef,
Yet never would afford relief
To needy, sable sons of grief,
Was big with heavenly union.

" 'Love not the world,' the preacher said,
And winked his eye, and shook his head;
He seized on Tom, and Dick, and Ned,
Cut short their meat, and clothes, and bread,
Yet still loved heavenly union.

"Another preacher whining spoke
Of One whose heart for sinners broke:
He tied old Nanny to an oak,
And drew the blood at every stroke,
And prayed for heavenly union.

"Two others oped their iron jaws,
And waved their children-stealing paws;
There sat their children in gewgaws;
By stinting negroes' backs and maws,
They kept up heavenly union.

"All good from Jack another takes,
And entertains their flirts and rakes,
Who dress as sleek as glossy snakes,
And cram their mouths with sweetened cakes;
And this goes down for union."

Sincerely and earnestly hoping that this little book may do something toward throwing light on the American slave system, and hastening the glad day of deliverance to the millions of my brethren in bonds—faithfully relying upon the power of truth, love, and justice, for success in my humble efforts—and solemnly pledging my self anew to the sacred cause,—I subscribe myself,

FREDERICK DOUGLASS.

LYNN, *Mass., April* 28, 1845.

THE END.

Historical Context

The pre–Civil War documents collected here verify Douglass's description of Maryland slavery, as well as the details of his own slave life. As primary sources, they attest to the slave laws of Maryland, the religious justifications for and against slavery, the rising antislavery sentiments, and the culture of slavery during Douglass's lifetime. They also show the evolution of the antebellum debate on human bondage and, along with similar writings, may well have influenced the young Douglass's thinking.

The Doctrines and Discipline of the Methodist Episcopal Church, in America: "Of Slavery" (1798)

In the *Narrative*'s appendix, Douglass declares that he hates the "corrupt, slaveholding, women-whipping, cradle-plundering, partial and hypocritical Christianity of this land." He denounces the religious protestations of Thomas and Hugh Auld, who owned him, and most of the Maryland whites whom he comes to know well. Douglass's accusations of hypocrisy on the part of the largely Methodist slaveholding class of the Eastern Shore had a solid basis in fact. As slave owners, these individuals, including the Methodist clergy, generally ignored their own denomination's strong condemnation of the immorality of slavery as set down in section IX of *The Doctrines and Discipline of the Methodist Episcopal Church, in America,* promulgated in 1798. In 1844 the Methodist denomination finally split over the issue of permitting its bishops to own slaves. SOURCE: *The Doctrines and Discipline of the Methodist Episcopal Church, in America. With Explanatory Notes by Thomas Coke and Francis Asbury.* 10th ed. (Philadelphia: Printed by Henry Tuckniss, 1798).

Section IX
Of Slavery.

QUEST. *WHAT regulations shall be made for the extirpation of the crying evil of African slavery?*

ANSW. 1. We declare, that we are more than ever convinced of the great evil of the African slavery which still exists in these United States; and do most earnestly recommend to the yearly conferences, quarterly meeting, and to those who have the oversight of districts and circuits, to be exceedingly cautious what persons they admit to official stations in our church; and in the case of future admission to official stations, to require such security of those who hold slaves, for the emancipation of them, immediately or gradually, as the laws of the states respectively, and the circumstances of the case will admit: and we do fully authorise all the yearly conferences to make whatever regulations they judge proper, in the present case, respecting the admission of persons to official stations in our church.

Slavery Defended from Scripture, against the Attacks of the Abolitionists: Excerpt (1842)

Alexander McCaine

In the *Narrative,* Douglass charges Maryland Methodist ministers with perverting Christian principles to defend the morality of slavery. Many such ministers felt, to the contrary, that it was the abolitionists who twisted the words of the Bible to claim that God disapproved of human bondage. One of them, the Reverend Alexander McCaine (1768–1857), a Dublin-born educator and minister in Baltimore, as well as a champion of the rights of that city's white artisans, produced a deeply researched tract, excerpted below, demonstrating the Bible's support for slavery. SOURCE: Alexander McCaine, *Slavery Defended from Scripture, against the Attacks of the Abolitionists, in a Speech Delivered before the General Conference of the Methodist Protestant Church in Baltimore* (Baltimore: Wm. Woodby, 1842).

[T]he doctrine of the abolitionists is at war with the doctrine of the Bible. The abolitionists say, slavery is a "great moral evil," and, of consequence, that the slaveholder is a *great sinner.* If this be true, Abraham was a great sinner, and so were all the slaveholders in the Patriarchal and Jewish Churches. And yet, with these very great sinners did a Holy God hold communion, and to them did He impart his grace. A clear proof, that slavery is *not* a moral evil; or, that God held fellowship with those who were sinners; which is repugnant to every idea that we have of God, and contrary to every declaration which is recorded in his word. If, however, they should say, that slavery *was not* a moral evil under the law, but *is* a moral evil under the gospel, I demand proof for the assertion. I require of them to state the basis of the distinction. Do they make the distinction to grow out of the nature and quality of the thing itself? or do they make it by the authority of God's word? It is unphilosophical and absurd to make the distinction from the thing itself, for under both dispensations its nature and essence are the same. And it is unscriptural to say it was right under the law, but it is wrong under the gospel. So that if they strive to avoid one horn of the dilemma, they will fall upon the other—and if they labor to shun Scylla, they will inevitably be shipwrecked upon Charibdis.

Walker's Appeal to the Coloured Citizens of the World: Excerpt (1829)

David Walker

In the *Narrative,* Douglass condemns men of God who use Scripture to defend slavery. In 1829, David Walker, a free black, published his *Appeal,* defending slaves' right to revolt against their masters; and like Douglass, he challenges the religious justification of slavery. In this excerpt, Walker recalls hearing a minister preach of slaves' inferiority and warns his readers of God's vengeful wrath if slavery is allowed to persist. SOURCE: David Walker, *Walker's Appeal in Four Articles, together with a Preamble to the Coloured Citizens of the World, but in Particular, and Very Expressly to those of the United States of America* (Boston: David Walker, 1829).

I remember a Camp Meeting in South Carolina, for which I embarked in a Steam Boat at Charleston, and having been five or six hours on the water, we at last arrived at the place of hearing, where was a very great concourse of people, who were no doubt, collected together to hear the word of God. . . . Myself and boat companions, having been there a little while, we were all called up to hear; I among the rest went up and took my seat—being seated, I fixed myself in a complete position to hear the word of my Savior and to receive such as I thought was authenticated by the Holy Scriptures; but to my no ordinary astonishment, our Reverend gentleman got up and told us (coloured people) that slaves must be obedient to their masters—must do their duty to their masters or be whipped—the whip was made for the backs of fools, &c. Here I pause for a moment, to give the world time to consider what was my surprise, to hear such preaching from a minister of my Master, whose very gospel is that of peace and not of blood and whips, as this pretended preacher tried to make us believe. What the American preachers can think of us, I aver this day before my God, I have never been able to define. . . . I tell you Americans! that unless you speedily alter your course, *you* and your *Country are gone!!!!!!* For God Almighty will tear up the very face of the earth!!! Will not that very remarkable passage of Scripture be fulfilled on Christian Americans? Hear it Americans!! "He that is unjust, let him be unjust still:—and he which is filthy, let him be filthy still: and he that is righteous, let him be righteous still: and he that is holy, let him be holy still." I hope that the Americans may hear, but I am afraid that they have done us so much injury, and are so firm in the belief that our Creator made us to be an inheritance to them for ever, that their hearts will be hardened, so that their destruction may be sure. This language, perhaps is too harsh for the American's delicate ears. But Oh Americans! Americans!! I warn you in the name of the Lord, (whether you will hear, or forbear,) to repent and reform, or you are ruined!!!

"Insurrection of the Blacks" (1831)

Niles Weekly Register

In the early morning of 22 August 1831 in Southampton County, Virginia, Nat Turner led a rebellion that lasted less than three days. In that time, sixty to eighty slaves joined the insurrection, raising arms against their masters and white townspeople, including women and children. This early account from the Baltimore *Niles Weekly Register,* dated 27 August, describes the uprising and names the known victims. Though quickly suppressed by authorities, this widely publicized rebellion produced both a tightening of white controls over African Americans in the Chesapeake region and a new round of public debate over slavery's future. SOURCE: "Insurrection of the Blacks," Baltimore *Niles Weekly Register,* 27 August 1831.

A gentleman arrived here yesterday express from Suffolk, with intelligence from the upper part of Southampton county, stating that a band of insurgent slaves (some of them believed to be runaways from the neighboring swamps), had turned out on Sunday night last, and murdered several whole families, amounting to 40 or 50 individuals. Some of the families were named, and among them was that of Mrs. Catharine Whitehead, sister of our worthy townsman, Dr. N. C. Whitehead, who, with her son and five daughters, fell a sacrifice to the savage ferocity of these demons in human shape.

The insurrection was represented as one of a most alarming character, though it is believed to have originated only in a design to plunder, and not with a view to a more important object—as Mrs. Whitehead, being a wealthy lady, was supposed to have had a large sum of money in her house. Unfortunately a large number of the effective male population was absent at camp meeting in Gates county, some miles off, a circumstance which gave a temporary security to the brigands in the perpetration of their butcheries; and the panic which they struck at the moment prevented the assembling of a force sufficient to check their career.

As soon as this intelligence was received, our authorities met, and decided on making an immediate application to col. *House,* commanding at Fortress Monroe, who at 6 o'clock this morning embarked on board the steam boat Hampton, with three companies and a piece of artillery for Suffolk. These troops were re-inforced in the roads by detachments from the U.S. ships Warren and Natchez, the whole amounting to nearly 300 men.

To-day another express arrived from Suffolk; confirming the disastrous news of the preceding one, and adding still more to the number of the slain. The insurgents are believed to have from 100 to 150 mounted men, and about the same number on foot. They are armed with fowling pieces, clubs, &c. and have had a rencontre with a small number of the militia, who killed six and took eight of them prisoners. They are said to be on their way to South Quay, probably making their way for the Dismal Swamp, in which they will be able to remain for a short time in security. For my part, I have no fears of their doing much further mischief. There is very little disaffection in the slaves generally, and they cannot muster a force sufficient to effect any object of importance. The few who have thus rushed headlong into the arena, will be shot down like crows or captured and made examples of. The militia are collecting in all the neighboring counties, and the utmost vigilance prevails.

"Extract from a Discourse Delivered before the New-York Society for Promoting the Manumission of Slaves" (1797)

Samuel Miller

In his youth, Douglass read from Caleb Bingham's very popular primer, *The Columbian Orator,* which, despite its name, contained excerpts from essays and poems as well as speeches by both Americans and Europeans. The selections demonstrated not only Bingham's fervent patriotism but also his advocacy for many reforms, especially abolitionism. The book became Douglass's key text during his slave years as he gained literacy; it helped him formulate his antislavery arguments and stirred his desire for freedom. Douglass wrote, "The more I read, the more I was led to abhor and detest my slavers." The following is an essay from the *Orator* that Douglass would have read. Written by a white New York minister, Samuel Miller, it condemns American slave traders and describes Africa as a shameful monument to the slaving activities of Europe and America. SOURCE: Samuel Miller, "Extract from a Discourse Delivered before the New-York Society for Promoting the Manumission of Slaves, April 12, 1797," in Caleb Bingham, ed., *The Columbian Orator: Containing a Variety of Original and Selected Pieces, together with Rules; Calculated to Improve Youth and Others in the Ornamental and Useful Art of Eloquence* (1797; Boston: J. H. A. Frost, 1827).

I HAVE hitherto confined myself to the consideration of slavery as it exists among ourselves, and of that unjust domination which is exercised over the Africans and their descendants, who are already in our country. It is with a regret and indignation which I am unable to express, that I call your attention to the conduct of some among us, who, instead of diminishing, strive to increase the evil in question.

While the friends of humanity, in Europe and America, are weeping over their injured fellow-creatures, and directing their ingenuity and their labors to the removal of so disgraceful a monument of cruelty and avarice, there are not wanting men, who claim the tide, and enjoy the privileges of American citizens who still employ themselves in the odious traffic of human flesh.

Yes, in direct opposition to public sentiment, and a law of the land, there are ships fitted out, every year, in the ports of the United States, to transport the inhabitants of Africa, from their native shores, and consign them to all the torments of West-India oppression.

Fellow citizens! is Justice asleep? Is Humanity discouraged and silent, on account of the many injuries she has sustained? Were not this the case, methinks the pursuit of the beasts of the forest would be forgotten, and such monsters of wickedness would, in their stead, be hunted from the abodes of men.

Oh AFRICA! unhappy, ill-fated region! how long shall thy savage inhabitants have reason to utter complaints, and to imprecate the vengeance of Heaven against civilization and Christianity? Is it not enough that nature's God has consigned thee to arid plains, to noxious vapours, to devouring beasts of prey, and to all the scorching influences of the torrid zone? Must rapine and violence, captivity and slavery, be superadded to thy torments; and be inflicted too by men, who wear the garb of justice and humanity, who boast the principles of a sublime morality; and who hypocritically adopt the accents of the benevolent religion of Jesus?

Oh AFRICA! thou loud proclaimer of the rapacity, the treachery, and cruelty of civilized man! Thou everlasting monument of European and American disgrace! "Remember not against us our offences, nor the offences of our forefathers; be tender in the great day of inquiry; and show a Christian world, that thou canst suffer, and forgive!"

Declaration of Sentiments of the American Anti-Slavery Society: "Preamble" (1833)

The American Anti-Slavery Society, founded in Philadelphia in December 1833, promoted the immediate emancipation of all slaves and defended this position through moral arguments. The most active member in the early society, William Lloyd Garrison, an abolitionist editor in Boston, wrote this preamble for the society's *Declaration of Sentiments.* After escaping to freedom, Douglass became a strong admirer of Garrison and a hired traveling lecturer for the society. SOURCE: American Anti-Slavery Society, *Declaration of Sentiments of the American Anti-Slavery Society: Adopted at the Formation of Said*

Society, in Philadelphia, on the 4th Day of December, 1833 (New York: American Anti-Slavery Society, 1833), 3.

PREAMBLE
TO THE CONSTITUTION OF THE AMERICAN ANTI-SLAVERY SOCIETY.

Whereas, the Most High God "hath made of one blood all nations of men to dwell on all the face of the earth," and hath commanded them to love their neighbors as themselves; and whereas, our national existence is based upon this principle, as recognized in the Declaration of Independence, "that all men are created equal, and that they are endowed by their Creator with certain inalienable rights, among which are life, liberty, and the pursuit of happiness;" and whereas, after the lapse of nearly sixty years, since the faith and honor of the American people were pledged to this avowal, before Almighty God, and the world, nearly one-sixth part of the nation are held in bondage by their fellow-citizens; and whereas, Slavery is contrary to the principles of natural justice, of our republican form of Government, and of the Christian Religion, and is destructive to the prosperity of the country, while it is endangering the peace, union, and liberty of the States: and whereas, we believe it the duty and interest of the masters, immediately to emancipate their slaves, and that no scheme of expatriation, either voluntary or by compulsion, can remove this great and increasing evil: and whereas, we believe that it is practicable, by appeals to the consciences, hearts, and interests of the people, to awaken a public sentiment throughout the nation, that will be opposed to the continuance of Slavery in any part of the Republic, and by effecting the speedy abolition of Slavery, prevent a general convulsion; and whereas, we believe we owe it to the oppressed, to our fellow-citizens who hold slaves, to our whole country, to posterity, and to God, to do all that is lawfully in our power to bring about the extinction of Slavery, we do hereby agree, with a prayerful reliance on the Divine aid, to form ourselves into a society, to be governed by the following Constitution.

"I Have Come to Tell You Something about Slavery" (1841)

Frederick Douglass

Massachusetts abolitionists recruited Frederick Douglass to lecture on slavery shortly after he first spoke at one of their conventions in Nantucket in August 1841. The following document is the oldest surviving text of a speech by the young Douglass, given just a few months later in Lynn, Massachusetts. A Philadelphia abolitionist, Edward M. Davis, visiting Lynn, reported on the speech for the *Pennsylvania Freeman*, noting that "it thrilled through every one present, and compelled them to feel for the Wrongs he had endured." In early speeches such as this one, Douglass rehearsed the themes of southern brutality toward slaves and northern prejudice toward emancipated blacks that he would incorporate into the *Narrative*. In the speech Douglass also recollects the impact of reading a speech by John Quincy Adams published in *The Columbian Orator*. SOURCE: Frederick Douglass, "I Have Come to Tell You Something about Slavery: An Address Delivered in Lynn, Massachusetts, in October 1841," *Pennsylvania Freeman*, 20 October 1841.

My friends, I have come to tell you something about slavery—what *I know* of it, as I have *felt* it. When I came North, I was astonished to find that abolitionists knew so much about it, that they were acquainted with its deadly effects as well as if they had lived in its midst. But though they can give you its history—though they can depict its horrors, they cannot speak as I can from *experience;* they cannot refer you to a back covered with scars, as I can; for I have felt these wounds; I have suffered under the lash without the power of resisting. Yes, my blood has sprung out as the lash embedded itself in my flesh. And yet my master has the reputation of being a pious man and a good Christian. [. . .]

A large portion of the slaves *know* that they have a right to their liberty. —It is often talked about and read of, for some of us know how to read, although all our knowledge is gained in secret.

I well remember getting possession of a speech by John Quincy Adams, made in Congress about slavery and freedom, and reading it to my fellow slaves. Oh! what joy and gladness it produced to know that so great, so good a man was pleading for us, and further, to know that there was a large and growing class of people in the north called abolitionists, who were moving for our freedom. This is known all through the south, and cherished with gratitude. It has increased the slaves' hope for liberty. Without it his heart would faint within him; his patience would be exhausted. On the agitation of this subject he has built his highest hopes. [. . .]

Emancipation, my friends, is that cure for slavery and its evils. It alone will give to the South peace and quietness. It will blot out the insults we have borne, will heal the wounds we have endured, and are even now groaning under, will pacify the resentment which would kindle to a blaze were it not for your exertions, and, though it may never unite the many kindred and dear friends which slavery has torn asunder, it will be received with gratitude and a forgiving spirit. Ah! how the slave yearns for it, that he may be secure from the lash, that he may enjoy his family, and no more be tortured with the worst feature of slavery, the separation of friends and families. The whip we can bear without a murmur, compared to the idea of *separation.* Oh, my friends, you cannot feel the slave's misery, when he is separated from his kindred. The agony of the mother when parting from her children cannot be told. There is nothing we so much dread as to be sold farther south. My friends, we are not taught from books; there is a law against teaching us, although I have heard some folks say we could not learn if we had a chance. The northern people say so, but the south do not believe it, or they would not have laws with heavy penalties to prevent it. The northern people think that if slavery were abolished, we would all come north. They may be more afraid of the free colored people and the runaway slaves going South. We would all seek our home and our friends, but, more than all, to escape from northern prejudice, would we go to the south. Prejudice against color is stronger north than south; it hangs around my neck like a heavy weight. It presses me out from among my fellow men, and, although I have met it at every step the three years I have been out of southern slavery, I have been able, in spite of its influence, "to take good care of myself."

Bill of Sale Manumitting Douglass (1846)

Hugh Auld

Douglass's concern for his personal safety after the publication of the *Narrative* led friends and admirers, made during his first antislavery tour of the

British Isles, to undertake his manumission. In August 1846, Anna Richardson, an English Quaker abolitionist, wrote Hugh Auld asking him whether Douglass's freedom had a price. Auld replied in October that he would manumit Douglass for £150. The money arrived in late November, and Hugh hurriedly arranged the legal transfer of Douglass from his brother Thomas to himself. On 5 December 1846, Hugh Auld filed Douglass's manumission papers in Baltimore County.

To all whom it may concern: Be it known, that I, Hugh Auld, of the city of Baltimore, in Baltimore county, in the state of Maryland, for divers good causes and considerations, me thereunto moving, have released from slavery, liberated, manumitted, and set free, and by these presents do hereby release from slavery, liberate, manumit, and set free, MY NEGRO MAN, named FREDERICK BAILY, otherwise called DOUGLASS, being of the age of twenty-eight years, or thereabouts, and able to work and gain a sufficient livelihood and maintenance; and him the said negro man, named FREDERICK BAILY, otherwise called FREDERICK DOUGLASS, I do declare to be henceforth free, manumitted, and discharged from all manner of servitude to me, my executors, and administrators forever.

In witness whereof, I, the said Hugh Auld, have hereunto set my hand and seal, the fifth of December, in the year one thousand eight hundred and forty-six. HUGH AULD.

Sealed and delivered in presence of T. Hanson Belt.

James N. S. T. Wright.

Douglass and His Contemporary Critics

Contemporary commentary about Douglass's autobiography gives clues about the impact of the *Narrative* on the antebellum debate over slavery. Douglass himself could not avoid joining in the discussion. When a white Marylander questioned the *Narrative*'s accuracy, Douglass published a blistering rebuttal, reproduced below. The other selections are representative book reviews, both positive and negative, published in the first year after the *Narrative* appeared in print. The controversy stirred by Douglass's life story generated greater sales for his book than those garnered by any other slave narrative and catapulted him before the age of thirty into the status of the nation's most influential African American.

Review of the *Narrative* (1845)

Anonymous

Anonymously written, the following review of the *Narrative,* published in the Lynn (Massachusetts) *Pioneer* and reprinted in the Boston *Liberator,* pronounced that Douglass's book would forever alter the political landscape of slavery. According to its author, the *Narrative* was the most important book that the American press had ever published; it would spark the "flames of liberty" that would sweep across the nation, burning the country's proslavery laws and sentiments to the ground. The reviewer correctly prophesied that the book would sell at least twenty thousand copies in the United States and as many abroad. SOURCE: "Frederick Douglass," Lynn *Pioneer,* n.d., reprinted in the Boston *Liberator,* 30 May 1845.

My readers will be delighted to learn that Frederick Douglass—the fugitive slave—has at last concluded his narrative. All who know the wonderful gifts of friend Douglass know that his narrative must, in the nature of things, be written with great power. It is so indeed. It is the most thrilling work which the American press ever issued—*and the most important.* If it does not open the eyes of this people, they must be petrified into eternal sleep.

The picture it presents of slavery is too horrible to look upon, and yet it is but a faint *picture* of what to millions is a vivid *life*. It is evidently drawn with a nice eye, and the coloring is chaste and subdued, rather than extravagant or overwrought. Thrilling as it is, and full of the most burning eloquence, it is yet simple and unimpassioned. Its eloquence is the eloquence of truth, and so is as simple and touching as the impulses of childhood. There are passages in it which would brighten the reputation of any living author,—while the book, as a whole, judged as a mere work of art[,] would widen the fame of Bunyan or De Foe [Defoe]. A spirit of the loftiest integrity, and a vein of the purest religious sentiment, runs through its pages, and it must leave on every mind a deep conviction of the author's strength of mind and purity of heart. I predict for it a sale of at least twenty thousand in this country, and equally great in Europe. It will leave a mark upon this age which the busy finger of time will deepen at every touch. It will generate a public sentiment in this nation, in the presence of which our pro-slavery laws and constitutions shall be like chaff in the presence of fire. It contains the spark which will kindle up the smoldering embers of freedom in a million souls, and light up our whole continent with the flames of liberty. Great efforts will be made in the name of the Constitution and the Bible, of James Polk and the Apostle Paul, to suppress it: but it will run through this nation from house to house, and from heart to heart, as the wild fire, *finding wings in every wind which blows,* flies across the tall and boundless prairies. Its stirring incidents will fasten themselves on the eager minds of the youth of this country with hooks of steel. The politics of the land will stand abashed before it, while her more corrupt religion will wish to sink back into the hot womb which gave it birth. It will fall in among the churches and state-houses of the land like a bomb-shell, and those who madly undertake to pick it to pieces will share the fate of that poor New-Yorker who attempted something of the kind on a bomb-shell picked up on the shores of Jersey, i.e., they will be blowed to atoms at the first blow. —*Lynn Pioneer*

Review of the *Narrative* (1845)

Margaret Fuller

Perhaps no review of Douglass's *Narrative* reached a wider reading audience than the one written by Margaret Fuller for the New York *Tribune*, which then had the nation's largest circulation. Fuller was a leading Transcendentalist, journalist, and women's rights advocate who joined the *Tribune*'s staff in 1844. A year after writing this review, she became a foreign correspondent for the *Tribune*, covering the political revolutions sweeping Europe. SOURCE: Margaret Fuller, review of *Narrative of the Life of Frederick Douglass, an American Slave, Written by Himself*, New York *Tribune*, 12 June 1845.

Frederick Douglass has been for some time a prominent member of the Abolition party. He is said to be an excellent speaker—can speak from a thorough personal experience—and has upon the audience, beside[s], the influence of a strong character and uncommon talents. In the book before us he has put into the story of his life the thoughts, the feelings and the adventures that have been so affecting through the living voice; nor are they less so from the printed page. He has had the courage to name the persons, times and places, thus exposing himself to obvious danger, and setting the seal on his deep convictions as to the religious need of speaking the whole truth. Considered merely as a narrative, we have never read one more simple, true, coherent, and warm with genuine feeling. It is an excellent piece of writing, and on that score to be prized as a specimen of the powers of the Black Race, which Prejudice persists in disputing. We prize highly all evidence of this kind, and it is becoming more abundant. The Cross of the Legion of Honor has just been conferred in France on Dumas and Souliè, both celebrated in the path of light literature. Dumas, whose father was a General in the French Army, is a Mulatto; Souliè, a Quadroon. He went from New-Orleans, where, though to the eye a white man, yet, as known to have African blood in his veins, he could never have enjoyed the privileges due to a human being. Leaving the Land of Freedom, he found himself free to develop the powers that God had given.

Two wise and candid thinkers,—the Scotchman, Kinment, prematurely lost to this country, of which he was so faithful and generous a student, and the late Dr. Channing,—both thought that the African Race had in them a peculiar element, which if it could be assimilated with those imported among us from Europe, would give to genius a development, and to the energies of character a balance and harmony beyond what has been seen heretofore in the history of the world. Such an element is indicated in the lowest estate by a talent for melody, a ready skill at imitation and adaptation, an almost indestructible elasticity of nature. It is to be remarked, in the writings both of Soulìè and Dumas, full of faults but glowing with plastic life and fertile in invention. The same torrid energy and saccharine fulness may be felt in the writings of this Douglass, though his life being one of action or resistance, was less favorable to *such* powers than one of a more joyous flow might have been.

The book is prefaced by two communications,—one from Garrison, and one from Wendell Phillips[.] That from the former is in his usual over emphatic style. His motives and his course have been noble and generous. We look upon him with high respect, but he has indulged in violent invective and denunciation till he has spoiled the temper of his mind. Like a man who has been in the habit of screaming himself hoarse to make the deaf hear, he can no longer pitch his voice on a key agreeable to common ears. Mr. Phillips's remarks are equally decided, without this exaggeration in the tone Douglass himself seems very just and temperate. We feel that his view, even of those who have injured him most, may be relied upon. He knows how to allow for motives and influences. Upon the subject of Religion, he speaks with great force, and not more than our own sympathies can respond to. The inconsistencies of Slaveholding professors of religion cry to Heaven. We are not disposed to detest, or refuse communion with them. Their blindness is but one form of that prevalent fallacy which substitutes a creed for a faith, a ritual for a life. We have seen too much of this system of atonement not to know that those who adopt it often began with good intentions, and are, at any rate, in their mistakes worthy of the deepest pity. But that is no reason why the truth should not be uttered, trumpet-tongued, about the thing. "Bring no more vain oblations"; sermons must daily be preached anew on that text. Kings, five hundred years ago, built Churches with the spoils of War; Clergymen to-day command Slaves to obey a Gospel which they will not allow them to read, and call themselves Christians amid the curses of their fellow men.—The world ought to get on a little faster than that, if there be really any principle of improvement in it. The Kingdom of Heaven may not at the beginning have dropped seed larger than a mustard-seed, but even from that we had a right to expect a fuller growth than can be believed to exist, when we read such a book as this of Douglass. Unspeakably affecting is the fact that he never saw his mother at all by day-light.

> "I do not recollect of ever seeing my mother by the light of day. She was with me in the night. She would lie down with me, and get me to sleep, but long before I waked she was gone."

The following extract presents a suitable answer to the hacknied argument drawn by the defender of Slavery from the songs of the Slave, and is also a good specimen of the powers of observation and manly heart of the writer. We wish that every one may read his book and see what a mind might have been stifled in bondage,—what a man may be subjected to the insults of spendthrift dandies, or the blows of mercenary brutes, in whom there is no whiteness except of the skin, no humanity except in the outward form, and of whom the Avenger will not fail yet to demand—"Where is thy brother?"

[The review here reprinted selections from the Narrative, describing conditions Douglass observed on Edward Lloyd's Great House Farm.]

Copies of the work may be had of W. H. Graham, Tribune Buildings. Price, 50 cents.

Review of the *Narrative* (1845)

Maria Weston Chapman

In 1840 the American abolition movement split over tactical disputes regarding women's rights, politics, and religion. The following year the abolitionist wing led by William Lloyd Garrison, editor of the Boston *Liberator,* hired Douglass as a lecturer. One of Garrison's ablest lieutenants in the 1840s was Maria Weston Chapman. The widow of a wealthy Boston merchant, Chapman was a tireless organizer and fundraiser for abolition. She wrote a review of Douglass's *Narrative* for the Garrisonians' official periodical, the New York *National Anti-Slavery Standard.* SOURCE: Maria Weston Chapman, "*Narrative of the Life of Frederick Douglass,*" New York *National Anti-Slavery Standard,* 12 June 1845.

This book ought to be read by all before whose mental blindness visions of happy slaves continually dance. It is the story of the life of a man of great intellectual power, in the very circumstances so often alluded to by the advocates for the longer continuance of Slavery;—in the Northernmost of the slave States, and under kind masters. No wonder that those States patronize the Colonization Society for the removal of characters so dangerous to the perpetuity of Slavery. Once, the kind master made a merit of giving *such* a slave his freedom on condition of consenting to go to Liberia. *Nous avons changé tout cela;* the anti-slavery enterprise has drawn to itself the most effectual advocates from the victims of the system it opposes. It has, while shaking that system to its foundation, been unavoidably and incidentally the means of freeing and educating in their own native country, more of these single victims, than the Colonization Society, while doing its best to uphold Slavery, has been able to doom to African exile.

All pro-slavery men, all Abolitionists, and all those who are merely indifferent should buy this book. It will convince the first class, confirm the second, and by the mere interest of its delineation, amply satisfy the third. It is illustrated by a remarkably good engraving of the author. The condition of the infant and of the aged slave, the sorrowful songs of bondage so often quoted by Northern men as an excuse for standing aloof from the Anti-Slavery enterprise, and the swell of heart with which the thought of freedom fills the bosom of the fugitive, are all dwelt upon with that deep impressment which artistical skill strives in vain with melancholy experience, to equal. "I never saw my mother in the day-time. She used to travel in the evening twelve miles to see me, and return before morning." Shall not the simple pathos of this fact, one of a class of facts necessary in Slavery, raise the soul of every mother that reads it?

We have no space for extracts this week, nor do we wish to lessen the value of the narrative to purchasers by forestalling its deeply interesting contents. It is accompanied by a letter from Wendell Phillips, which so truly expresses our own feelings, that we subjoin it.—c. [That letter from Wendell Phillips is reproduced in the *Narrative* as prefatory material.]

"Gleams of Light" (1845)

A Citizen of Maryland

Written anonymously by "A Citizen of Maryland" and published in the Boston *Liberator* on 26 September 1845, this review asserts the validity of Douglass's *Narrative* on the authority of its author's own familial relation to Colonel Edward Lloyd. The reviewer bemoans the negative impact of slavery on both the white and the black population of the South and predicts that the *Narrative* will "do much good" and bring hope to those who despise slavery. SOURCE: A Citizen of Maryland, "Gleams of Light," Boston *Liberator,* 26 September 1845.

A Baltimore correspondent of the Albany Patriot writes to the editor of that paper a letter, which contains the following interesting and encouraging statements:

We can buy anti-slavery documents now in this city at Shurtz & Wilde's Periodical Bookstore. The following are for sale: Review of West India Emancipation, by a Virginian; Biscom's and Peck's Pamphlets; Wayland and Fuller's Letters; and 'Slavery in Maryland,' by John L. Carey of this city, Editor of the Baltimore American. Frederick Douglass's Narrative is now circulating and being read in this city, and five hundred copies are still wanted here. They would be read with avidity, and do much good. And thus Garrison, who is proscribed here in person, would be heard in Baltimore, in the burning language of his Preface to the Narrative.

One word in regard to the truth of the narrative. I have made some inquiry, and have reason to believe his statements are true. Col. Edward Lloyd's relatives are my relatives! Let this suffice for the present. There is one particular slave mentioned in the book that I have often heard spoken of; that is, poor 'Jake,' who was bought by my brother-in-law, a nephew of Col. L. The northern people fight slavery at a distance: I have to fight it every day, and every where, in all the highways and byways of life. I board with a slaveholder, and am waited on by a slave, and see all the laziness and inefficiency on the part of the whites, and the *puttering,* do-nothing, sulky habits of the poor blacks. Every thing about slavery is mean, dirty, lazy, hateful, and *undignified.* There is nothing about it to promote self-respect, or any other noble or virtuous feeling.

Dr. Stewart, a noble-minded philanthropist, the owner of 150 slaves and a plantation, is now writing a pamphlet on slavery and emancipation, and in favor of the freedom of the slaves. Dr. S. is a brother of Gen. Stewart of this city, of whom your correspondent some months since stated, that he sold a colored woman by whom he had children with her offspring, his own flesh and blood, to Hope H. Slatter. No wonder Dr. Stewart is disgusted with slavery, when his own brother is such a monster of iniquity.

We are full of hope in this State. The 'Saturday Visitor' is our leader. Pray for us, till hope is lost in victory.

A CITIZEN OF MARYLAND

"To Tell the Public.—Falsehood Refuted" (1845)

A. C. C. Thompson

A. C. C. Thompson, an acquaintance of both the Lloyd and the Auld families, conducted a public debate in the press with Douglass regarding the truthfulness of the *Narrative.* In a letter published in the *Delaware Republican* on 12 December 1845, Thompson stated that he knew Douglass as a slave by the name of Frederick Bailey, who was too unlearned to write such a book. Thompson railed against the negative portrayals of Colonel Edward Lloyd, Thomas Auld, Captain Aaron Anthony, Austin Gore, Giles Hicks, Thomas Lambdin, and Edward Covey, drawing on his personal relationships with these men to repudiate Douglass's descriptions of them. Douglass welcomed Thompson's letters, recognizing that they served as a "triumphant vindication of truth" against his proslavery critics who claimed that the *Narrative* was completely fabricated. SOURCE: A. C. C. Thompson, "To Tell the Public.—Falsehood Refuted," New York *National Anti-Slavery Standard,* 25 November 1845; reprinted in the Boston *Liberator,* 12 December 1845.

Refuge of Oppression.

From the Delaware Republican.
TO THE PUBLIC.
FALSEHOOD REFUTED.

It is with considerable regret that I find myself measurably compelled to appear before the public; but my attention has lately been arrested by a pamphlet which has been freely circulated in Wilmington and elsewhere, with the following superscription:—*Extract from a Narrative of Frederick Douglass, an American Slave, written by himself.*

And although I am aware that no sensible, unprejudiced person will credit such a ridiculous publication, which bears the glaring impress of falsehood on every page, yet I deem it expedient that I should give the public some information respecting the validity of this narrative, because I was for many years a citizen of the section of country where the scenes of the above mentioned narrative are laid; and am intimately acquainted with most of the gentlemen whose characters are so shamefully traduced, and I am also aware, that the Narrative was not written by the professed author; but from statements of this runaway slave, some evil designed person or persons have composed this catalogue of lies to excite the indignation of the public opinion against the slaveholders of the South; and have even attempted to plunge their venomous fangs in the vitals of the church.

I shall, therefore, briefly notice some of the most glaring falsehoods contained in the aforesaid Narrative, and give a true representation of the character of those gentlemen, who have been censured in such an uncharitable manner, as murderers, hypocrites, and everything else that is vile.

I indulge no animosity against the fabricators and circulators of the Narrative, neither do I know them; but I positively declare the whole to be a budget of falsehoods, from beginning to end.

1st. The identity of the author. About eight years ago, I knew this recreant slave by the name of Frederick Bailey, (instead of Douglass.) He then lived with Mr. Edward Covy, and was an unlearned, and rather an ordinary negro, and am confident he was not capable of writing the Narrative alluded to; for none but an educated man, and one who had some knowledge of the rules of grammar, could write so correctly. Although, to make the imposition at all credible, the composer has labored to write it in as plain a style as possible: consequently, the detection of this first falsehood proves the whole production to be notoriously untrue.

Again[:] 'It is a common custom in the part of Maryland from which I ran away, to separate children from their mothers at a very early age.'

This also I know to be false. There is no such custom prevalent in that section of the country; but, on the contrary, the children are raised with their mothers, and generally live with them in the same house, except in some few instances where the mother is hired out as a cook or laborer in some other family.

The gentlemen whose names are so prominently set forth in the said Narrative are Col. Edward Lloyd, Capt. Anthony, Austin Gore, Thomas Lamdin, (not Lanman,) Giles Hicks, Thomas Auld, and Edward Covy. Most of these persons I am intimately acquainted with, and shall give a brief sketch of their characters as follows:

Col. Edward Lloyd was one of the most wealthy and respectable planters in the State of Maryland. He was at one time the Governor of the State, and for several years, a member of the Legislature. He owned several thousand acres of land, and between 4 and 500 slaves. He died before I had much knowledge of him; but I know that he was a kind and charitable man, and in every respect an honorable and worthy citizen.

Most of the same slaves are now owned by his three sons, and they manage their servants in the same manner as did their father; and I know there are no such barbarities committed on their plantations.

Could it be possible that charitable feeling men could murder human beings, with as little remorse of conscience, as the narrative of this infamous libel wishes to make us believe; and that the laws of Maryland, which operate *alike upon black and white,* bond or free, could permit such foul murders to pass unnoticed? No! it is impossible; and every sensible man knows that these false accusations are the ebullition of an unchristian prejudice.

Captain Anthony and Giles Hicks, I know but little of. The accused murderer, Mr. Gore, is a respectable citizen, living near St. Michaels, and I believe a worthy member of the Methodist Episcopal Church: he was formerly an overseer for Col. Lloyd, and at this time, all who know him, think him anything but a murderer.

Thomas Lamdin, who, it is said, (in the Narrative,) boasted so frequently of his murders, is at this time an honest school teacher in the District where I formerly lived; and all the harm that can be said of him is, that he is too good-natured and harmless to injure any person but himself.

Capt. Thomas Auld, whose hypocritical meanness is so strongly depicted in the aforesaid Narrative, was for many years a respectable merchant in the town of St. Michaels, and an honorable and worthy member of the Methodist E. Church, and only notable for his integrity and irreproachable Christian character. He is now retired from the turmoil of a mercantile life, and engaged in the worthy occupation of tilling the soil, little dreaming of the foul accusations that are circulated against him.

Edward Covy, the renowned 'negro breaker,' is also a plain, honest farmer, and a tried and faithful member of the Methodist E. Church. Mr. Covy lived for several years on a farm adjoining my father's at which time this runaway negro lived with him, and I am well aware that no such bloody tragedy as is recorded in that lying Narrative ever occurred on Mr. Covy's farm. All that can be said of Mr. Covy is that he is a good Christian, and a hard working man, and makes every one around him work and treats them well. By his honest industry, he has purchased a fine farm, and is now reaping the reward of his labor.

Such are the characters of the men whom the imposers of this dirty Narrative have so uncharitably traduced, and by blending these false accusations with the Methodist religion of the South, they wish to lacerate her already bleeding wounds.

I was raised among slaves, and have also owned them, and am well aware that the slaves live better and fare better in many respects than the free blacks.

Yet, I am positively opposed to slavery, for I know it is a great evil; but *the evil falls not upon the slave,* but on the owner.

Intrigue and false accusations will never liberate the slave of the South; but, on the contrary, every such attempt will only forge for them new and stronger fetters.

Let the tender-hearted philanthropist of the North speak truth and love towards their southern brethren, and make a liberal application of their gold for the removing the blacks from the country, and their chance of success will be more flattering.

I have given a true representation of the persons connected with the aforesaid Narrative, and I respectfully submit the facts to the judgment of an impartial public.

A. C. C. THOMPSON.

No. 101 Market-st. Wilmington, Del.

Letter to William Lloyd Garrison (1846)

Frederick Douglass

Douglass seized upon A. C. C. Thompson's public questioning of the accuracy of his *Narrative* to defend himself in a letter to William Lloyd Garrison's Boston *Liberator.* Writing from his self-imposed exile in the British Isles—he was then in Scotland—Douglass rebutted Thompson's charge of not having written the *Narrative* himself and defended his indictment of the harsh conditions endured by Maryland slaves and the debased moral character of their owners. SOURCE: Frederick Douglass to William Lloyd Garrison, 27 January 1846, published in the Boston *Liberator,* 27 February 1846.

Perth, Scot. 27 Jan[uary] 1846.

To the Editor of the Liberator:
DEAR FRIEND—

For the sake of our righteous cause, I was delighted to see, by an extract copied into the Liberator of 12th Dec. 1845, from the Delaware Republican, that Mr. A. C. C. Thompson, No. 101, Market-street, Wilmington, has undertaken to invalidate my testimony against the slaveholders, whose names I have made prominent in the narrative of my experience while in slavery.

Slaveholders and slave-traders never betray greater indiscretion, than when they venture to defend themselves, or their system of plunder, in any other community than a slaveholding one. Slavery has its own standard of morality, humanity, justice, and Christianity. Tried by that standard, it is a system of the greatest kindness to the slave—sanctioned by the purest morality—in perfect agreement with justice—and, of course, not inconsistent with Christianity. But, tried by any other, it is doomed to condemnation. The naked relation of master and slave is one of those monsters of darkness, to whom the light of truth is death! The wise ones among the slaveholders know this, and they studiously avoid doing any thing, which, in their judgment, tends to elicit truth. They seem fully to understand, that their safety is in their silence. [. . .]

In replying to Mr. Thompson, I shall proceed as I usually do in preaching the slaveholder's sermon,—dividing the subject under two general heads, as follows:—

1st. The statement of Mr. Thompson, in confirmation of the truth of my narrative.

2ndly. His denials of its truthfulness.

Under the first, I beg Mr. Thompson to accept my thanks for his full, free and unsolicited testimony, in regard to my identity. There now need be no doubt on that point, however much there might have been before. Your testimony, Mr. Thompson, has settled the question forever. I give you the fullest credit for the deed, saying nothing of the motive. But for you, sir, the pro-slavery people in the North might have persisted, with some show of reason, in representing me as being an imposter—a free negro who had never been south of Mason & Dixon's line—one whom the abolitionists, acting on the jesuitical principle, that the end justifies the means, had educated and sent forth to attract attention to their faltering cause. I am greatly indebted to you, sir, for silencing those truly prejudicial insinuations. I wish I could make you understand the amount of service you have done me. You have completely tripped up the heels of your pro-slavery friends, and laid them flat at my feet. You have done a piece of anti-slavery work, which no anti-slavery man could do. Our cautious and truth-loving people in New-England would never have believed this testimony, in proof of my identity, had it been borne by an abolitionist. Not that they really think an abolitionist capable of bearing false witness intentionally, but such persons are thought fanatical, and to look at every thing through a distorted medium. They will believe you—they will believe a slaveholder. They have, some how or other, imbibed (and I confess strangely enough) the idea that persons such as yourself are dispassionate, impartial and disinterested, and therefore capable of giving a fair representation of things connected with slavery. Now, under these circumstances, your testimony is of the utmost importance. It will serve to give effect to my exposures of slavery, both at home and abroad. I hope I shall not administer to your vanity when I tell you that you seem to have been raised up for this purpose! I came to this land with the highest testimonials from some of the most intelligent and distinguished abolitionists in the United States; yet some here have entertained and expressed doubt as to whether I have ever been a slave. You may easily imagine the perplexing and embarrassing nature of my situation, and how anxious I must have been to be relieved from it. You, sir, have relieved me. I now stand before both the American and British public, endorsed by you as being just what I have ever represented myself to be—to wit, an American slave. [. . .]

Now, then, to the second part—or your denials. You are confident I did not write the book; and the reason of your confidence is, that when you knew me, I was an unlearned and rather an ordinary negro. Well, I have to admit I was rather an ordinary negro when you knew me, and I do not claim to be a very extraordinary one now. But you knew me under very unfavorable circumstances. It was when I lived with Mr. Covey, the negro-breaker, and member of the Methodist Church. I had just been living with master Thomas Auld, where I had been reduced by hunger. Master Thomas did not allow me enough to eat. Well, when I lived with Mr. Covey, I was driven so hard, and whipt so often, that my soul was crushed and my spirits broken. I was a mere wreck. The degradation to which I was then subjected, as I now look back to it, seems more like a dream than a horrible reality. I can scarcely realize how I ever passed through it, without quite losing all my moral and intellectual energies. I can easily understand that you sincerely doubt if I wrote the narrative; for if any one had told me, seven years ago, I should ever be able to write such an one, I should have doubted as strongly as you now do. You must not judge me now by what I then was—a change of circumstances has made a surprising change in me. Frederick Douglass, the freeman, is a very different person from Frederick Bailey,* the slave. I feel myself almost a new man—freedom has given me new life. I fancy you would scarcely know me. I think I have altered very much in my general appearance, and know I have in my manners. You remember when I used to meet you on the road to St. Michael's, or near Mr. Covey's lane gate, I hardly dared to lift my head, and look up at you. If I should meet you now, amid the free hills of old Scotland, where the ancient 'black Douglass' once met his foes, I presume I might summon sufficient fortitude to look you full in the face; and were you to attempt to make a slave of me, it is possible you might find me almost as disagreeable a subject, as was the Douglass to whom I have just referred. Of one thing, I am certain—you would see a great change in me!

I trust I have now explained away your reason for thinking I did not write the narrative in question.

You next deny the existence of such cruelty in Maryland as I reveal in my narrative; and ask, with truly marvellous simplicity, 'could it be possible that

*My former name.

charitable, feeling men could murder human beings with as little remorse as the narrative of this infamous libeller would make us believe; and that the laws of Maryland, which operate alike upon black and white, bond and free, could permit such foul murders to pass unnoticed?' 'No,' you say, 'it is impossible.' I am not to determine what charitable, feeling men can do; but, to show what Maryland slaveholders actually do, their charitable feeling is to be determined by their deeds, and not their deeds by their charitable feelings. The cowskin makes as deep a gash in my flesh, when wielded by a professed saint, as it does when wielded by an open sinner. [. . .]

You say that the laws of Maryland operate alike upon the white and black, the bond and free. If you mean by this, that the parties named are all equally protected by law, you perpetrate a falsehood as big as that told by President Polk in his inaugural address. It is a notorious fact, even on this side of the Atlantic, that a black man cannot testify against a white in any court in Maryland, or any other slave State. If you do not know this, you are more than ordinarily ignorant, and are to be pitied rather than censured. I will not say 'that the detection of this falsehood proves all you have said to be false'—for I wish to avail myself of your testimony, in regard to my identity,—but I will say, you have made yourself very liable to suspicion.

I will close these remarks by saying, your positive opposition to slavery is fully explained, and will be well understood by anti-slavery men, when you say the evil of the system does not fall upon the slave, but the slaveholder. This is like saying that the evil of being burnt is not felt by the person burnt, but by him who kindles up the fire about him.

FREDERICK DOUGLASS.

Scholarly Assessments

❁❁❁

The four essays excerpted here are recent scholarly examinations of Douglass's *Narrative* that discuss how his work influenced the genre of slave narrative literature. In establishing the importance of the *Narrative,* these modern literary critics examine Douglass's skillful prose and rhetorical strategies, his authority to speak for the slaves' plight, and the ways he authenticated his story for a largely white audience. The editors have reproduced these essays in the original form, except that we have omitted footnote superscripts and parenthetical page citations.

The Classic Slave Narratives: Excerpt (1987)

Henry Louis Gates, Jr.

In the introduction to his compilation of classic slave narratives, Henry Louis Gates, Jr., of the W. E. B. Du Bois Research Institute at Harvard University analyzes the wide range of rhetorical strategies that Frederick Douglass employs in his *Narrative* to make his readers aware of the inhumanity of slavery. SOURCE: From Henry Louis Gates, Jr., "Introduction," in *The Classic Slave Narratives,* ed. Henry Louis Gates, Jr. (New York: Penguin, 1987). Copyright © 1987 by Henry Louis Gates, Jr. Used by permission of New American Library, an imprint of Penguin Publishing Group, a division of Penguin Random House LLC.

The most famous [slave narrative] of them all is Frederick Douglass's 1845 *Narrative.* Classic in its elegant simplicity and its gripping readability, Douglass's compelling lucidity belies his narrative's literary complexity, a complexity that masks or disguises itself precisely because Douglass was a master rhetorician, an expert in both spoken *and* written English. Douglass tells such a good tale that his text opens itself to all classes of readers, from those who love an adventure story to those who wish to have rendered for them in fine emotional detail the facts of human bondage—what it meant to discover that one was a slave and what one proceeded to do about it, while someone else simultaneously was busy doing all manner of things to keep the slave from imagining himself or herself otherwise. Douglass's rhetorical power convinces us that he is "the" black slave, that he embodies the structures of thoughts and feelings of all black slaves, that he is the resplendent, articulate part that stands for the whole, for the collective black slave community. His superb command of several rhetorical figures—metaphor, irony, synechdoche, apostrophe, and especially chiasmus—enables him to chart with fine precision in only a few pages "how a man was made a slave," as he puts it in a chiasmus, and "how a slave was made a man."

Douglass's narrative demonstrates not only how the deprivation of the hallmarks of identity can affect the slave but also how the slaveowner's world negates and even perverts its own values. Deprivation of a birth date, a name, a family structure, and of legal rights makes of the deprived a brute, a subhuman, says Douglass, until he comes to a consciousness of these relations: through that consciousness, he comes to see that it is the human depriver who is the actual barbarian. With painstaking verisimilitude, Douglass reproduces a system of signs that we have come to call plantation culture, an ordering of the world based on a profoundly relational type of thinking. In this world, a strict barrier of difference forms the basis of a class rather than, as in other classification schemes, an ordering based on resemblances or the identity of two or more elements. Douglass's narrative strategy seems to be this: he brings together two terms in special relationships suggested by some quality that they share; then, by opposing two seemingly unrelated elements, such as the sheep, cattle, or horses on the plantation and the specimen of life known as slave, Douglass's language is made to signify the presence and absence of some quality—in this case, humanity. Douglass uses this device to explicate the slave's understanding of himself and of his relation to the world. Not only does his *Narrative* come to concern itself with two diametrically opposed notions of genesis, origins, and meaning itself, but its structure actually turns on an opposition between nature and culture as well.

"Gender-Related Difference in the Slave Narratives": Excerpt (1994)

Winifred Morgan

Just as males and females experienced slavery differently, they emphasized different themes when they recounted their lives in autobiographies. Few scholars had systematically examined such gender-role differences in the slave narrative before Winifred Morgan's article was published in 1994. A professor of English at Edgewood College in Madison, Wisconsin, Morgan notes that male slave narrators like Frederick Douglass stress the liberating impact of gaining literacy, whereas female slave narrators like Harriet Jacobs value supportive relationships with other females more than the problematic acquisition of literacy. For the slave woman, demonstrating her multiple roles as daughter, sister, mother, wife, and friend and downplaying the disempowering effects of her inherent victimization served the dual purpose of making her instantly relatable and empowered. Being able to read and write failed to prepare females for liberation in a society governed by patriarchal privilege. Instead, relationships became instrumental for self-definition and agency. Where female narrators emphasized interdependency in keeping with antebellum notions of womanliness, males, like Douglass, influenced by the dominant masculine and European culture, accentuated the importance of gaining "autonomy." SOURCE: From Winifred Morgan, "Gender-Related Difference in the Slave Narratives of Harriet Jacobs and Frederick Douglass," *American Studies* 35, no. 2 (1994): 73–94. Used by permission of *American Studies.*

As the single most widely read slave narrative, Douglass's *Narrative* has often come to represent the entire genre. Despite its impressive craft, however, it presents problems as a representative text. First of all, its implicit assumption that literacy provides the power leading to individual freedom does not characterize women's narratives. In addition, its advocacy of literacy as a major route to personal autonomy might prove misguided. Valerie Smith critiques the utility of making literacy central in a struggle for equality because literacy has often served not only as a means of access for the underprivileged but also a means by which dominant groups have controlled access to society's rewards and thus preserved their hegemony. Smith even credits Douglass's "story of his own success" as "provid[ing] counter evidence of his platform of radical change; for by demonstrating that a slave can be a man in terms of all the qualities valued by his northern middle-class reader—physical power, perseverance, literacy—he lends credence to the patriarchal structure largely responsible for his oppression." This does not necessarily mean that Douglass was wrong in his choice of language as his most important weapon for his struggle, merely that he had not examined nor critiqued that choice.

In part because of what she perceives as Douglass's limitations, Deborah McDowell also has challenged the *Narrative*'s preeminence among slave narratives and suggests that a presumably inadvertent male bias has insisted on its primacy as an Emersonian "representative" text. McDowell contends that "the literary and interpretative history of the *Narrative* has, with few exceptions, repeated with approval its salient assumptions and structural paradigms. This repetition has, in turn, created a potent and persistent critical language that positions and repositions Douglass on top, that puts him in a position of priority." Indeed, Douglass's *Narrative* has enjoyed a preeminent place among North American slave narratives. Yet [Charles T.] Davis and [Henry Louis] Gates[, Jr.,] maintain that among Douglass's contemporaries, Douglass's account may have been considered most "'representative'" because it was most "presentable." "He was most presentable because of his unqualified abilities as a rhetorical artist. Douglass achieved a form of *presence* through the manipulation of rhetorical structures within a modern language."

A number of critics, among them Elizabeth Fox-Genovese, have explored the process whereby Americans judge the significance and value of a piece of literature according to dominant male and European-derived cultural values. Reactions to Douglass's *Narrative* seem to illustrate this process because it affirms what his nineteenth-century white male audience valued. Although Douglass labels his confrontation with the slave-breaker Edward Covey *the* "turning point" in his life, most of the language and imagery of the *Narrative* emphasize Douglass's increasing fluency with and control over written language and how literacy gave him the means to make himself free and to live as a free man. With its emphasis on gaining control of language, the structure of Douglass's *Narrative* reflects accepted hierarchical values common to nineteenth-century Western culture: education leads to social uplift, and progress is good. The *Narrative* also accepts the assumptions that men are the natural heads of the family and society and that children "belong" to their father. When they found the *Narrative* "representative," Douglass's "fellows" may have responded to what felt comfortably familiar to them as male readers and writers educated in a cultural milieu that taught them to respond positively to specific paradigms.

The dominant culture values in Douglass's narrative, in turn, often reflect male values. The black women in Douglass's narrative are by nature subordinate to the men. They serve as examples of victimization, such as his aunt, or as shadowy helpmates, such as the free woman he marries. Sophia Auld may think independently as a young bride but quickly accommodates herself to her husband's preferences. The narrative assumes a hierarchy that places male prerogatives (such as the right of Hugh Auld to countermand Sophia's attempt to teach Douglass, of Douglass's father to impregnate and abandon Douglass's mother, of Douglass himself to use and ignore his wife) at the apex. If Valerie Smith and others are correct in their argument that traditionally, literacy and a literary canon have been used to support patriarchy and other powerful groups to suppress the rights of oppressed people, then women slave narrators were right to doubt the value of learning to read and write as a major strategy in achieving their freedom. Patriarchy limited their worth both before and after slavery. Women who had been slaves had reason to seek "their own independent definition of womanhood."

Douglass's use of printed language to connect with others differs considerably from the relationship-building found in the work of women writers like [Harriet] Jacobs. Female as well as male, slave narrators desired and strove for literacy. Nonetheless, being literate never saved women fugitives from the burdens of slavery, racism, or sexism and they knew it. Whether they found literacy at best a weak reed on which to lean—whether they were ultimately more cynical or perhaps more realistic in confronting the economic realities of the racist and sexist societies in which they lived—women narrators do not give central significance to the acquisition of literacy. Instead, the most significant realities in these women's lives usually derived from their personal relationships. While many nineteenth-century white women also developed significant ties among themselves, African-American women had little choice but to depend on one another in order to endure. Nineteenth-century social definitions of femininity marginalized white women but entirely excluded black women. The relationships that enabled women to survive slavery remain in their narratives like the framing timbers of a ship's hull, outlining how slave women used connections with others in their efforts to keep out the seas of oppression that threatened to overwhelm them.

To Tell a Free Story: Excerpt (1986)

William L. Andrews

William L. Andrews of the University of North Carolina at Chapel Hill examines how the antislavery pulpit, which sharpened African Americans' rhetorical skill, in conjunction with Transcendentalism, with its focus on individual self-expression, changed the perception and ultimately the function of slave narratives. These changes transformed slave narratives, and specifically Douglass's *Narrative,* from simple biographies into forms of self-liberation. SOURCE: From William L. Andrews, *To Tell a Free Story: The First Century of Afro-American Autobiography, 1760–1865* (Urbana: University of Illinois Press, 1986).

In their role as preachers from the antislavery pulpit, slave narrators gained valuable training for their literary careers. That the major slave narratives of the 1840s were produced by seasoned veterans of the abolitionist lecture circuit, not by lonely fugitives like James Williams newly arrived from the South, had much to do with their appeal to white audiences. Frederick Douglass spent more than four years on the abolitionist platform under the auspices of Garrison's American Anti-Slavery Society before that organization published his narrative in 1845. Williams Wells Brown had been employed as a lecturing agent for the Western New York Anti-Slavery Society for four years before he ventured to write his autobiography. Henry Bibb served an even longer apprenticeship in the Midwest and Middle Atlantic states before he saw his narrative into print in 1849. As these famous fugitives repeated their life stories to curious white audiences from Maine to Michigan, they had numerous chances to polish their narrative and rhetorical skills. Lionized in one town and reviled in the next, they were well schooled in the ways that their self-presentation, their modes of address, their idiom, and their tones of voice would affect whites. This preparation as oral self-historians on the abolitionist platform instilled in them a rhetorical sophistication and audience-consciousness unprecedented in the history of Afro-American autobiography.

The degree of egocentrism in black autobiography of the 1840s, when compared to the self-effacement instanced in so much of the genre before that decade, could not have appeared or have met with such public sympathy without the support and sanction of the antislavery movement. Antebellum America had never been receptive to black autobiography as an expressive mode unless it could be packaged and recommended by whites as something else—e.g., in the case of the criminal confession up through Nat Turner's work, as a warning *against* black introspection and trust in the arrogant, deluding intuition. The besetting sin in the eyes of evangelical reformers in the 1830s and 1840s was self-gratification, a charge that could easily be leveled against anyone who engaged in the egotistical act of autobiography. Yet the slave narrative of the 1840s largely escaped this censure, except from southern critics offended by notices of the celebrity of runaways among the aristocrats of Europe. Abolitionism conducted a very successful campaign of identifying the slave-holder as criminal selfishness personified, next to which the slave narrator's mere literary egoism shrank into insignificance.

Most slave narrators made the conventional modest apologies for their awkwardness and lack of personal relish or preparation for the literary task that their consciences required of them. But even when an ex-slave gloried in his triumph over his master or voiced his personal criticism of American institutions, his rebellion against authority was applauded as a demonstration of Negro nobility and his censure of the republic was welcomed as a sign of the Negro's powers of analysis and argument. Thus the abolition movement acquiesced in the self-aggrandizement that a popular slave narrative could offer its author as long as the image promulgated by the narrative did not contradict the propaganda about the essential character of the Afro-American. Although Douglass's speaking and writing sometimes led to accusations of "egotism" and "conceit," radical abolitionists in the 1840s usually defended the ex-slave's temerity as unquestionable proof of their own arguments about the natural dignity of the Negro and his unfitness for anything less than immediate freedom and citizenship. Garrison himself had taken an uncompromising stand on the question of freedom of self-expression in the denunciation of slavery. Should "the convictions of an honest soul" regarding human bondage be "gentle, and carefully selected, and cautiously expressed?" he asked the critics of his impolitic manner. "Away with such counsel," he replied; "call things by their right names and let the indignant spirit find free utterance."

As "romantic reformer" and peripheral transcendentalist, Garrison was not the only person in the antislavery movement to tap the new literary ideals of Romanticism for justification for letting the "spirit find free utterance." Slave narrators could also thank Romantic thinkers in the 1830s and 1840s for helping to prepare New England to discover value in the first-person writing of black outsiders from the South. In 1837, Ralph Waldo Emerson had informed the Phi Beta Kappa Society at Harvard that a cultural revolution, a democratization of literature, was underway; now "instead of the sublime and beautiful," "the near, the common" were to be explored. Among the new "topics of the time" was "the literature of the poor," which Emerson embraced as revelatory of "the highest spiritual cause" and law. With such a conviction he and Margaret Fuller launched *The Dial* in 1840, determined "to report life" based on resources that were "not so much the pens of practiced writers, as the discourse of the living."

One of the barriers that Emerson and his intellectual compatriots wanted most to transcend was that which separated life from the merely literary, living experience from dead, ossified language. The best of the slave narratives, as [Ephraim] Peabody and [Theodore] Parker observed, broke through these barriers and helped to restore political and literary discourse on the subject of slavery to first considerations—the tangible experience and direct perceptions of the individual. In its absence of conventional art, its rejection of elegance and classic form, its apparently spontaneous rhythms of consciousness, and its dependence on plain speech and empirical facts, the slave narrative exemplified many qualities of "living discourse" that transcendentalists believed were the grounds of true eloquence. The convergence of spiritual self-examination, romantic self-consciousness, and democratic individualism in transcendentalist writing made the self, its nature and its potential, an inescapable "topic of the time." Such an intellectual climate fostered an increasing preoccupation with selfhood and identity in the slave narrative and an expanding search for the rhetorical means by which to give them voice.

In the *Narrative of Frederick Douglass,* we see some of the first fruits of the emancipation of the black autobiographer under the influence of the cultural forces just discussed. In his preface to the *Narrative,* Garrison praised Douglass for having "very properly chosen to write his own Narrative, in his own style, . . . rather than to employ some one else." Douglass's style, the signature of his individuality more than the recitation of the facts of his past, was the most telling aspect of the ex-slave's narrative. The "most thrilling" incident in the story was not, in Garrison's view, the famous battle between the sixteen-year-old Douglass and the slave-breaker, Edward Covey. It was instead "the description DOUGLASS gives of his feelings, as he stood soliloquizing respecting his fate, and the chances of his one day being a freeman, on the banks of the Chesapeake Bay" a few months before the crucial fight with Covey. In contrast to the editor of Charles Ball's story ten years earlier, Garrison urges his reader to pay special heed to what the ex-slave reveals of himself, of his own psychological state, as he contemplated his desperate status and his ideal of freedom. Garrison directs his reader toward what Isaac Fisher shielded his reader from—a slave narrator's use of the expressive mode of speech action. Douglass's narrative is freely laced with both positive and negative expressives, utterances through which Douglass not only asserts a proposition about something but also conditions his reader's response to that assertion by couching it in an expression of his psychological state as he makes the assertion. Before the ascendency of Garrisonian radicalism, slave narratives, when they ranged beyond the assertive mode (as in the case of Moses Roper), were, in Garrison's words, "gentle" and "cautiously expressed." Douglass was the first Afro-American autobiographer to risk the negative expressive for rhetorical purposes that involved more than simply "letting the indignant spirit find free utterance." For Douglass and those who followed him, the expressive was a way to recontextualize baldly factual assertives about the past so that the reader could be shown not just the incident or what the incident signified but how to *feel* about the incident. The extensive use of the expressive in the 1840s represents an important stage in the authorizing of the narrative voice in the slave autobiography.

Douglass's *Narrative* instances an even more radical stage in the process of self-authorization that distinguished black autobiography in the 1840s. At the end of the fifth chapter of his narrative, Douglass pauses to reflect on a turning point in his life when, at the age of seven or eight, his Eastern Shore master sent him to live in Baltimore with Hugh and Sophia Auld. "Going to live at Baltimore laid the foundation, and opened the gateway, to all my subsequent prosperity," he remarks. "I have ever regarded it as the first plain manifestation of that kind providence which has ever since attended me, and marked my life with so many favors." Regarding oneself as chosen by Providence for a special destiny was not, of course, unusual among black spiritual autobiographers before Douglass. However, Douglass's special providence was not to become a minister but a rebel and later a fugitive from the law. He acknowledges his white reader's likely skepticism at his presumptuousness: "I may be deemed superstitious, and even egotistical, in regarding this event as a special interposition of divine Providence in my favor. But I should be false to the earliest sentiments of my soul, if I suppressed the opinion. I prefer to be true to myself, even at the hazard of incurring the ridicule of others, rather than to be false, and incur my own abhorrence." This is a crucial declaration in the history of black autobiography. For the first time, the black writer announces that truth to the self takes priority over what the white reader may think is either probable or politic to introduce into discourse.

What is the authority that justifies this declaration of independence in a black man's interpretation of his own life? He does not appeal to divine inspiration, nor does he appropriate from Scripture in order to empower himself with moral or prophetic authority. Instead, his authority comes from (1) the act of having claimed it; (2) his allegiance to the self rather than to the other, the reader; and (3) his definition of truth and falsehood as that which is consistent with intuitive perception and needs, not as absolute standards. In language like this Douglass and his important successors in the slave narrative implied that the writing of autobiography was itself to be understood as an act of self-liberation, part of the continuum of events narrated in the text. Instead of existing as the theme of the text, that which the slave narrative is *about,* freedom becomes the crucial property and quality *of* a text—not just *what* it refers to, but *how* it signifies. This kind of textual freedom may be read as apparent testimony to the extent to which the creator of the text has liberated himself from the authority of extratextual assumptions and conventions. Or it may be read as an index to the play of the text itself, independent of the intention of its author.

From Behind the Veil: Excerpt (1979)

Robert B. Stepto

In *From Behind the Veil,* a Yale University literary scholar, Robert B. Stepto, examines the problem that the African American slave narrators had in establishing their "authenticity" with a largely white reading audience without relying heavily on white abolitionist "guarantors." Stepto observes that more than any other slave autobiographer, Frederick Douglass used his own "narrative and authenticating strategies," rather than depending on the prefatory materials supplied by the better-known white abolitionists, William Lloyd Garrison and Wendell Phillips, to interpret his experiences in slavery to his readers. SOURCE: From Robert B. Stepto, *From Behind the Veil: A Study of Afro-American Narrative* (Urbana: University of Illinois Press, 1979).

In the [earlier] phases of slave narrative narration we observe the former slave's ultimate lack of control over his own narrative, occasioned primarily by the demands of audience and authentication. This dilemma is not unique to the authors of these narratives; indeed, many modern black writers still do not control their personal history once it assumes literary form. For this reason, Frederick Douglass's *Narrative of the Life of Frederick Douglass, an American Slave, Written by Himself* (1845) seems all the more a remarkable literary achievement. Because it contains several segregated narrative texts—a preface, a prefatory letter, the tale, an appendix—it appears to be, in terms of the narrative phases, a rather primitive slave narrative. But each ancillary text is drawn to the tale by some sort of extraordinary gravitational pull or magnetic attraction. There is, in short, a dynamic energy between the tale and each supporting text that we do not discover in the [earlier Henry] Bibb or [Solomon] Northup narratives, save perhaps in the relationship between Solomon Northup and his guarantor-become-character, Henry Northup. The Douglass narrative is an integrated narrative of a very special order. The integrating process does, in a small way, pursue the conventional path found in Northup's narrative, creating characters out of authenticating texts (William Lloyd Garrison silently enters Douglass's tale at the very end); however, its new and major thrust is the creation of that aforementioned energy which binds the supporting texts to the tale, while at the same time removing them from participation in the narrative's rhetorical and authenticating strategies. Douglass's tale dominates the narrative because it alone authenticates the narrative.

The introductory texts to the tale are two in number: a "Preface" by William Lloyd Garrison, the famous abolitionist and editor of *The Liberator;* and a "Letter from Wendell Phillips, Esq.," who was equally well known as an abolitionist, crusading lawyer, and judge. In theory, each of these introductory documents should be classic guarantees written almost exclusively for a white reading public, concerned primarily and ritualistically with the white validation of a newfound black voice, and removed from the tale in such ways that the guarantee and tale vie silently and surreptitiously for control of the narrative as a whole. But these entries are not fashioned that way. To be sure, Garrison offers a conventional guarantee when he writes, "Mr. DOUGLASS has very properly chosen to write his own Narrative, in his own style, and according to the best of his ability, rather than to employ some one else. It is, therefore, entirely his own production; and . . . it is, in my judgment, highly creditable to his head and heart." And Phillips, while addressing Douglass, most certainly offers a guarantee to "another" audience as well:

> Every one who has heard you speak has felt, and, I am confident, every one who read your book will feel, persuaded that you give them a fair specimen of the whole truth. No one-sided portrait,—no wholesale complaints,—but strict justice done, whenever individual kindliness has neutralized, for a moment, the deadly system with which it was strangely allied.

But these passages dominate neither the tone nor the substance of their respective texts.

Garrison is far more interested in writing history (specifically, that of the 1841 Nantucket Anti-Slavery Convention, and the launching of Douglass's career as a lecture agent for various antislavery societies) and recording his own place in it. His declaration, "I shall never forget his [Douglass's] first speech at the convention," is followed within a paragraph by, "*I rose,* and declared that PATRICK HENRY, of revolutionary fame, never made a speech more eloquent in the cause of liberty . . . *I reminded* the audience of the peril which surrounded this self-emancipated young man . . . *I appealed* to them, whether they would ever allow him to be carried back into slavery,—law or no law, constitution or no constitution" (italics added). His "Preface" ends, not with a reference to Douglass or his tale, but with an apostrophe very much like one he would use to exhort and arouse an antislavery assembly. With the following cry Garrison hardly guarantees Douglass's tale, but enters and reenacts his own abolitionist career instead:

> Reader! are you with the man-stealers in sympathy and purpose, or on the side of their down-trodden victims? If with the former, then you are the foe of God and man. If with the latter, what are you prepared to do and dare in their behalf? Be faithful, be vigilant, be untiring in your efforts to break every yoke, and let the oppressed go free. Come what may—cost what may—inscribe on the banner which you unfurl to the breeze, as your religious and political motto—"NO COMPROMISE WITH SLAVERY! NO UNION WITH SLAVEHOLDERS!"

In the light of this closure, and (no matter how hard we try to ignore it) the friction that developed between Garrison and Douglass in later years, we might be tempted to see Garrison's "Preface" at war with Douglass's tale for authorial control of the narrative as a whole. Certainly there is a tension, but that tension is stunted by Garrison's enthusiasm for Douglass's tale. Garrison writes:

> This *Narrative* contains many affecting incidents, many *passages* of great eloquence and power; but I think the most thrilling one of them all is the *description* DOUGLASS gives of his feelings, as he stood soliloquizing respecting his fate, and the chances of his one day being a free man. . . . Who can read that *passage,* and be insensible to its pathos and sublimity? [Italics added.]

Here Garrison does, probably subconsciously, an unusual and extraordinary thing—he becomes the first guarantor we have seen in this study who not only directs the reader to the tale, but also acknowledges the tale's singular rhetorical power. Garrison enters the tale by being at the Nantucket convention with Douglass in 1841 (the same year Solomon Northup was kidnapped) and by, in effect, authenticating the impact, rather than the facts, of the tale. He fashions his own apostrophe, but finally he remains a member of Douglass's audience far more than he assumes the posture of a competing or superior voice. In this way Garrison's "Preface" stands outside Douglass's tale but is steadfastly bound to it.

Such is the case for Wendell Phillips's "Letter" as well. As I have indicated, it contains passages which seem addressed to credulous readers in need of a "visible" authority's guarantee, but by and large the "Letter" is directed to Frederick Douglass alone. It opens with "My Dear Friend," and there are many extraliterary reasons for wondering initially if the friend is actually Frederick. Shortly thereafter, however, Phillips declares, "I am glad the time has come when the 'lions write history,'" and it becomes clear that he both addresses Douglass and writes in response to the tale. These features, plus Phillips's specific references to how Douglass acquired his "A B C" and learned "where the 'white sails' of the Chesapeake were bound," serve to integrate Phillips's "Letter" into Douglass's tale.

Above all, we must understand in what terms the "Letter" is a cultural and linguistic event. Like the Garrison document, it presents its author as a member of Douglass's audience; but the act of letter-writing, of correspondence, implies a moral and linguistic parity between a white guarantor and black author which we haven't seen before—and which we do not always see in American literary history *after* 1845. The tone and posture initiated in Garrison's "Preface" are completed and confirmed in Phillips's "Letter"; while these documents are integrated into Douglass's tale, they remain segregated outside the tale in the all-important sense that they yield Douglass sufficient narrative and rhetorical space in which to render personal history in—and as—a literary form.

Afterword

John R. McKivigan, Peter P. Hinks, and Heather L. Kaufman

In writing the introduction to the *Narrative,* John W. Blassingame undertook an unprecedented investigation of the contemporary critical reception of the *Narrative* and the broader context of antislavery activism at the time of the book's publication. He gathered possibly all of the contemporary critical reviews of the *Narrative*—not only from the North and the South of the United States but from the British Isles, Holland, Germany, and France. The number and length of the reviews attested to the singular impact Douglass's autobiography had in 1845 and thereafter upon the Atlantic community of literary critics, journalists, reformers, and activists, both proslavery and antislavery.

Blassingame's research on the *Narrative* was an important component of a sweeping scholarly reassessment of American slavery and the genre of slave autobiographies undertaken in the second half of the twentieth century. The *Narrative* was probably cited more than any other contemporary black account to confirm the conditions of slavery and to establish its author as simultaneously an exceptional and a representative slave.[1] Probably because of his resemblance to Aaron Anthony, his master and rumored father, Douglass gained opportunities not afforded most young Maryland plantation slaves. At an early age, instead of beginning work in the fields, he served as a companion for first a son of his master's employers, the wealthy Lloyd family, and then a son of an in-law, Baltimore artisan Hugh Auld. Douglass's sense of self-possession benefited from the superior treatment sometimes experienced by urban slaves. Auld's wife, Sophia, began Douglass's education, which quickly reinforced his own awareness of slavery's inhumanity. As a teenager he learned a valuable trade in the Baltimore shipyards. The Aulds then allowed him to hire out his own labor and to live independently outside their household. This high degree of personal autonomy afforded Douglass the opportunity to mingle with Baltimore's free blacks and ultimately to escape to the North. In the *Narrative,* Douglass admitted his special circumstances and acknowledged "that kind Providence . . . attended me, and marked my life with so many favors." As atypical as many of Douglass's youthful experiences had been and as exceptional as his intellectual talents proved to be, Douglass nevertheless endured many of the same physical and psychological wounds inflicted on all antebellum American slaves. In the *Narrative* Douglass consciously strove to testify for all those oppressed by the South's peculiar institution.[2] His vivid depiction and insightful analysis made his *Narrative* the enduring archetypical account of slavery.

By the 1980s scholars increasingly understood Douglass's first autobiography (he wrote two more) as less unique and more as a part of the larger slave narrative genre. Ironically, Blassingame's own pioneering anthology, *Slave Testimony* (1977), fostered this appreciation of the broader genre.[3] Scholars rediscovered the significance of numerous other slave narratives, such as those of Harriet Jacobs, Solomon Northup, Charles Ball, and William and Ellen Crafts[4] and thereby enriched their appreciation of these chronicles.[5] Occasionally scholars have argued that one or the other of these works surpassed Douglass's in either literary merit or historical value.[6] Nevertheless, many scholars, such as Marion Starling, Houston Baker, and William Andrews, continue to accord primacy in the genre to Douglass's first autobiography.[7]

The expanded examination of slave narratives has validated most of Blassingame's assertions on the significance of the *Narrative.* Since the 1990s, however, new scholarship on Douglass has built on Blassingame's work while moving beyond it. For example, Blassingame's collection of Atlantic-wide responses to the *Narrative* has spurred other scholars to further explore Douglass's relationship to transatlantic abolitionism in the late 1840s and 1850s.[8] Just as the *Narrative* revealed European religious and ideological influences upon his developing indictment of slave owning, his eloquent testimony about the abusive treatment of slaves helped revive lagging abolitionism overseas. Douglass and his *Narrative* also had an important impact on evolving racial attitudes in the British Isles of the mid-nineteenth century.[9]

Scholars' appreciation of the *Narrative*'s attention to the psychological dimension of slavery has also grown over recent decades. Douglass acutely observed the dynamics of day-to-day slave-master interactions.[10] His indictment of the Christmas "holidays" accorded slaves is frequently quoted and analyzed. Douglass recounted how masters often released slaves from labor between Christmas and New Year's Day to palliate them and mute their impulses to rebellion. He also noted that masters encouraged slaves to focus on sensual and debauched behavior at the expense of self-improvement.[11] Numerous scholars have also credited Douglass for articulating in his *Narrative* the way slave music revealed the anguish of the enslaved and their longing for freedom.[12] The cultural historian Houston Baker has woven Douglass's observations on slave music into his sweeping map of "blues geography" connecting African Americans' various forms of oral expression over the centuries to their changing material conditions.[13]

Modern feminist scholars of slave narratives argue that these works represent a genre skewed to the male perspective.[14] They pinpoint the upholding of masculinity through violent resistance to exploitation as a key element in the *Narrative*. After Douglass's epic battle with the slave breaker Edward Covey, he declares, "It rekindled the few expiring embers of freedom, and revived within me a sense of my own manhood." That battle and Douglass's epiphany are arguably the work's dramatic highpoint.[15] The unprecedented popularity of Douglass's autobiography stems largely from how well its author portrayed his early life as a quest for the (principally male) individual autonomy that the romantic culture of the antebellum North championed. Scholars have noted the irony of male slaves like Douglass acculturating to middle-class notions of a patriarchal family structure while remaining deprived of the power to exercise the prescribed roles.[16]

Most slave narratives were products of male authors and failed to emphasize the specifically female experience of enslavement. The sexually subordinate relations that slavery produced generated conflict for individuals, for slave family life, and for the community at large. Contemporary scholars have used Harriet Jacobs's 1861 autobiography, *Incidents in the Life of a Slave Girl*, to enlighten modern readers about the circumstances of the female slave experience. Though valuable, her book fails to adequately portray slave marriage and family life. Instead, it recounts Jacobs's repeated sexual victimization and her status as a single mother forced to hide for years separated from her children.[17] Jacobs struggled to reconcile her behavior with American notions of motherhood and family to win the sympathy of her primarily white readership. Consequently, some historians seeking insights about women's role in marriage and family life treat less frequently studied slave narrators such as Ellen and William Craft, Mary Price, Annie L. Burton, Mattie J. Jackson, and Henry Bibb as sources superior to Douglass or Jacobs.[18]

Recent scholars of African American religion have, however, made great use of Douglass's *Narrative.* Many of them understand his critique of "slaveholding religion" as a precursor to late twentieth-century liberation theology: both Douglass and liberation theologians have condemned various forms of exploitation as specifically contrary to Christian morality.[19] The virulence of Douglass's indictment of the slaveholders' moral hypocrisy has, in fact, led some scholars to see a veiled anti-Christian message in the *Narrative.* Others portray Douglass as struggling to reconcile Christian beliefs with an antislavery position.[20] In either interpretation, Douglass's autobiography, along with other slave narratives, is essential to understanding the roots and character of African American spirituality.[21]

Some recent scholarship has focused on the significance of literacy in Douglass's quest for freedom. The *Narrative* describes the ingenious strategies Douglass used as a boy to learn how to read in a society that outlawed slave literacy. Douglass recounts how reading works such as *The Columbian Orator* helped end his mentality of enslavement. Achieving literacy supplied Douglass with the intellectual tools to indict the oppressive system in which he lived. Houston Baker has suggested that Douglass "appropriated language in order to do battle with the masters."[22] Henry Louis Gates, Jr., agrees that literacy was the key to transforming a passive slave into an antislavery protagonist. Douglass's act of writing his own life story, Robert Stepto argues, only furthered the independence he established for himself outside of white control. The feminist scholar Winifred Morgan, however, maintains that gaining literacy did not have the same transformative power for antebellum women, free or enslaved, as it did for males like Douglass.[23] Eric J. Sundquist shifts the analysis of Douglass's literacy from its political to its psychological dimension, focusing on its impact upon his struggle for self-mastery.[24] Whatever the scholarly argument, the *Narrative*'s strong advocacy of education as a weapon to battle oppression has provided a paradigm for black liberation struggles from his time to our own.[25]

Douglass's and other slave narratives have also influenced the subsequent direction of African American writing. In particular, Douglass's influence upon later African American autobiographers has drawn much comment, not always positive.[26] The earliest African American fiction—for example, William Wells Brown's *Clotel; or, The President's Daughter* (1853), Frank Webb's *The Garies and Their Friends* (1857), Martin R. Delany's *Blake; or, The Huts of*

America (1859), and Harriet Wilson's *Our Nig; or, Sketches of the Life of a Free Black in a White House* (1859)—have been shown to draw on many of the major themes of slave autobiography.[27] Writers in a new genre of contemporary fictional autobiographies, dubbed "neo-slave narratives," including works by such well-received authors as Toni Morrison, Alice Walker, Charles Johnson, and Sue Monk Kidd, seek to understand and heal the trauma left by the legacy of slavery. They often draw on psychological insights by original slave narrators like Douglass about the dehumanizing impact of racism. The engagement of modern-day black authors with Douglass and the slave narrative genre attests to the power of those earlier writers to give voice to the oppressed.[28]

Although Frederick Douglass was only one individual and cannot represent the whole of the slave experience for the millions in bondage in America under widely varying conditions of labor and geography, his *Narrative* is nevertheless an unusually vivid and moving account of this horror in American history. Its vitality and relevance will never wane, and it will remain essential reading for all who seek to look into the depths of human exploitation and the spirit that has challenged it.

Chronology

❀❀❀

1619 Dutch traders bring African slaves to Jamestown, Virginia.

1634 Maryland is first settled by English colonists.

1642 Thirteen African slaves arrive in St. Mary's City, Maryland.

1664 Maryland's proprietor, Charles Calvert, rules that all slaves in Maryland are slaves for life.

1690 For the first time African slaves outnumber European indenture servants in the Maryland workforce.

1696 The Pennsylvania Yearly Meeting of the Society of Friends issues the first official pronouncement against the slave trade in English North America.

1729 Baltimore is founded.

1763 Fells Point is established along the Patapsco River east of Baltimore Town and quickly becomes a major shipbuilding area.

1767 Prominent Nantucket whaling merchant Joseph Rotch, Sr., resettles in New Bedford, Massachusetts, anticipating that city's future importance to the whaling industry.

1770s The town of St. Michaels in Talbot County, Maryland, is launched as a speculative development.

1774 Betsey Bailey, grandmother of Frederick, is born on the Skinner plantation, Talbot County.

1775–83 The American colonies fight and win their independence from Great Britain.

1779 Edward Lloyd V is born; he inherits Wye House plantation and his family's extensive properties in 1796.

1787 The U.S. Constitution is drafted. Slavery's legal status is left ambiguous.

1789 Antislavery advocates found the Maryland Society for Promoting the Abolition of Slavery and for Relief of Poor Negroes and Others Unlawfully Held in Bondage.

The discipline of the Methodist Episcopal Church condemns the "buying or selling of the bodies and souls of men, women and children, with an intention to enslave them."

1791 Black insurgents in St. Domingue (modern-day Haiti) rebel against their French colonial overlords. Ten years later, under Toussaint Louverture, they create the first black republic in the Americas.

1792 Harriet, mother of Frederick, is born on the Skinner plantation.

1793 The first federal fugitive slave bill is passed to direct officials in free states and western territories to assist southern owners in the rendition of slave runaways.

1796 Maryland passes a law forbidding the importation of slaves for sale and liberalizing the state's manumission laws regarding how and when slave owners can free their slaves.

1797 Aaron Anthony becomes chief overseer of the Lloyds' extensive Maryland landholdings and settles his slaves, including Betsey and Harriet Bailey, at Holme Hill Farm.

1808 The United States bans further importation of slaves from Africa.

1813 British amphibious forces conduct an extensive raid of the Chesapeake Bay region—an action in the War of 1812.

1815 Richard Allen establishes the African Methodist Episcopal Church, the first wholly African American church denomination in the United States, although African American Baptists had a presence in Boston, Savannah, and elsewhere by the late eighteenth century.

1816 The American Colonization Society is founded by white Americans who believe enslaved African Americans should be freed and settled in Africa.

1818 Frederick Augustus Washington Bailey, who later renames himself Frederick Douglass, is born sometime in February at Holme Hill Farm.

1819 Austin Woolfolk, Jr., establishes headquarters for his Atlantic-coast slave-trading firm in Baltimore.

1820 The U.S. Congress passes the Missouri Compromise admitting Missouri as a slave state and Maine as a free state and mutes the mounting national conflict over slavery.

1821 New York abolishes property requirements for white male suffrage while maintaining them for free black men.

1822 Denmark Vesey's plot for a slave insurrection in South Carolina is exposed and thwarted.

1824–30 *Genius of Universal Emancipation,* the nation's first exclusively anti-slavery newspaper, is published in Baltimore by a Quaker, Benjamin Lundy.

1824 Frederick is sent to live at the Wye House plantation home of his master, Aaron Anthony.

1826 Frederick is sent to live with Hugh Auld's family in Baltimore.

Aaron Anthony dies and Frederick is inherited by Anthony's daughter Lucretia, wife of Thomas Auld.

1827 *Freedom's Journal*, the first newspaper in the United States owned by an African American, begins publication in New York City.

The Maryland State Colonization Society is founded.

Douglass is returned to the Hugh Auld household, where Sophia Auld, Hugh's wife, begins to teach him to read.

1828 Construction begins on the nation's first railroad, the Baltimore and Ohio.

1831 Nat Turner leads a bloody slave uprising in Southampton County, Virginia.

William Lloyd Garrison begins publication in Boston of the *Liberator*, which endorses the immediate emancipation of all American slaves.

Douglass undergoes a religious conversion and joins the African Methodist Episcopal Church, and he buys his first book, *The Columbian Orator*.

1833 The American Anti-Slavery Society is launched in Philadelphia.

Douglass is sent back to St. Michaels to live with Thomas Auld.

The British Parliament passes an act to begin the gradual emancipation of slaves in its West Indies colonies.

1834 Douglass spends the year as a field hand hired out to the Talbot County "slave breaker," Edward Covey.

1835 Douglass is hired out to the white farmer William Freeland.

1836 David Ruggles, a free black, leads the formation of the New York Committee of Vigilance to aid runaway slaves.

After an unsuccessful escape attempt, Douglass is returned to Hugh Auld in Baltimore, where he begins learning the caulking trade.

1838 On September 3, Douglass leaves Baltimore and escapes to the North.

With the Reverend James W. C. Pennington, a fellow fugitive slave from Maryland presiding, Douglass marries Anna Murray in

New York City on September 15. The couple settle in New Bedford, Massachusetts. They eventually have five children.

1839 African slaves on board the schooner *Amistad* successfully revolt; legal proceedings in New Haven, Connecticut, win freedom for the rebels the following year.

Douglass begins speaking at black antislavery meetings in New Bedford.

1840 The American Anti-Slavery Society suffers a schism between the followers of Garrison and their opponents, who favor using politics and established religion to advance abolitionism.

1841 Douglass is hired as a traveling lecturer by Garrisonian abolitionists and relocates his family to Lynn, Massachusetts.

1845 Douglass publishes his first autobiography, *Narrative of the Life of Frederick Douglass, an American Slave, Written by Himself.*

In danger of being recaptured as a runaway slave, Douglass departs in August for twenty-one months in Great Britain as an abolitionist lecturer.

1846 British abolitionist admirers negotiate the purchase and manumission of Douglass from Hugh Auld.

1847 From his new home in Rochester, New York, Douglass publishes the first issue of his weekly newspaper, *North Star,* on December 3.

1848 Douglass attends the Seneca Falls Women's Rights Convention on July 19–20.

1849 The British reformer Julia Griffiths joins the staff of Douglass's newspaper as its unofficial business manager. Despite widely circulated rumors of an inappropriate personal relationship, she assists him until returning home in 1855.

1850 Congress passes a new fugitive slave act that strengthens procedures for southern owners to recapture runaway slaves already in the North and threatens Underground Railroad conductors such as Douglass with significant legal penalties.

1851 After breaking from the Garrisonian abolitionists, Douglass revamps his newspaper and publishes it as *Frederick Douglass' Paper,* a Liberty Party vehicle.

Douglass publishes his novella, "The Heroic Slave," in *Autographs for Freedom,* edited by Griffiths.

1855 Douglass's second autobiography, *My Bondage and My Freedom,* is published.

1859 Following the raid of John Brown and his co-conspirators on Harpers Ferry in October, Douglass flees first to Canada and then to Great Britain because of his prior close connection with Brown. Douglass is not able to return home until April 1860.

1861 On 12 April the first shots of the Civil War are fired at Fort Sumter, South Carolina.

1863 After recruiting black troops for the Union Army, Douglass has the first of three private interviews with President Abraham Lincoln.

1870 Douglass relocates to the District of Columbia and begins editing the *New National Era* to advance black civil rights as well as other reforms.

1874 Appointed president of the Freedman's Savings Bank in March, Douglass has to close the institution for insolvency in July.

1877 President Rutherford B. Hayes appoints Douglass the U.S. marshal of the District of Columbia.

1881 President James A. Garfield appoints Douglass recorder of the deeds for the District of Columbia.

Douglass publishes his third autobiography, *The Life and Times of Frederick Douglass.*

1882 Anna Murray Douglass dies in August.

1884 In January, Douglass marries Helen Pitts, a white woman, causing a public controversy.

1889 Douglass accepts an appointment as U.S. ambassador to Haiti in July. He resigns the post in August 1891 after clashes with Benjamin Harrison's administration over the attempted annexation of a Haitian port to serve as an American naval base.

1892 Douglass serves as commissioner of the Haitian pavilion at the World's Columbian Exposition in Chicago from October until December 1893.

1895 Douglass dies at his Cedar Hill home in Washington, D.C., on 20 February after attending a women's rights convention.

Four Maryland Families

❦❦❦

The powerful and wealthy Lloyd family, the aspiring Anthonys and Aulds, and the Bailey family that produced Frederick Douglass interacted intimately in Maryland's Talbot County in the century before the Civil War. These genealogical charts show key aspects of the close relationships between members of these families, white and slave. Family members named by Douglass in the *Narrative* have asterisks here and are identified more fully in the Historical Annotation to the *Narrative.*

Lloyd Family

Edward Lloyd I (c. 1650–95) m. Alice Crouch (unknown)

|

Edward Lloyd II (1670–1718) m. Sarah Covington (1683–1755): 3 children

|

Edward Lloyd III (1711–70) m. Ann Rousby (1721–69): 4 children

|

Edward Lloyd IV (1744–96) m. Elizabeth Tayloe (1750–1825): 7 children
Employs Aaron Anthony as a ship captain.

|

*Edward Lloyd V (1779–1834) m. Sally Scott Murray (1775–1854): 7 children
Employs both Aaron Anthony and Thomas Auld.
Douglass lives at his Wye House plantation as a companion of his youngest son, Daniel.

|

*Edward Lloyd VI (1798–1861) m. Alicia McBlair (1806–38): 4 children
m. Mary Howard (unknown): at least 1 child
m. Mary Donnell Chesley (unknown)

*Elizabeth Tayloe Lloyd (1800–1880) m. *Edward Stoughton Winder (1798–1840): 8 children

*James Murray Lloyd (1803–47) m. Elizabeth C. McBlair (b. 1818): 5 children

*Sally Scott Lloyd (1805–80) m. *Charles Lowndes (1798–1885): 7 children
The ship captained by Thomas Auld is named for her.

Ann Catherine Lloyd (1808–92) m. Franklin Buchanan (1800–1874): 5 children

*Daniel Lloyd (1811–75) m. Virginia Upshur (1812–43): 2 children
m. Catherine Henry (1818–86): 2 children
Douglass is his childhood companion.

Mary Ellen Lloyd (1814–85) m. William Tilghman Goldsborough (1808–76): 10 children

Anthony Family

(first name unknown) Anthony (unknown) m. Elinor Leonard (unknown)

|

James Anthony (d. c. 1768) m. Esther (unknown): 7 children

|

*Aaron Anthony (c. 1766–1826) m. Ann Catherine Skinner (unknown): 6 children
Works as ship captain, then head overseer, for the Lloyd family.
Owns the Bailey family, including Douglass.

|

*Andrew Skinner Anthony (1797–1833) m. Ann Wingate (unknown)
Inherits many Bailey family slaves, including Betsey Bailey, when his father dies.

|

John Planner Anthony (1830–71) m. Sarah Sharp (1838–1923): 2 children
Inherits Betsey Bailey and other Bailey family slaves when his father dies.

*Richard Lee Anthony (1800–1828)
Inherits many Bailey family slaves when his father dies.

*Lucretia Planner Anthony (1804–27) m. *Thomas Auld (1795–1880): 1 child
Inherits Douglass and other Bailey family slaves when her father dies.

James Anthony

Ann Anthony

John Anthony

Auld Family

James Auld (unknown) m. Jane Bock (unknown)

|

James Auld (1655–1721) m. Sarah Elliott (1669–1721): 6 children

|

John Auld (1700–1765) m. Mary Sherwood (b. 1704): 9 children

|

Edward Auld (1735–77) m. Sarah Haddaway (b. 1743): 7 children

|

Hugh Auld, Sr. (1767–1820) m. Zipporah Wilson (1775–1849): 9 children

|

*Thomas Auld (1795–1880) m. *Lucretia Planner Anthony (1804–27): 1 child

|

*Arianna Amanda Auld (1826–78) m.
John L. Sears (b. 1823): 3 children

m. *Rowena Hambleton (1812–42): 2 children

|

Sarah Louisa Auld (b. 1833)
Rowena Hambleton Auld (b. 1834)

m. Ann Harper (unknown)

m. Amanda E. Thompson (unknown)

Works for Lloyds as captain of the *Sally Lloyd.*
Inherits Douglass and other Bailey family slaves when his wife dies.
Sends Douglass to live with his brother Hugh in Baltimore.
Sells Douglass to Hugh in 1845.
Cares for Betsey Bailey in her old age.

Arianna Auld (1797–1849)

*Hugh Auld, Jr. (1799–1861) m. *Sophia Keithley (1797–1880): 6 children
Douglass resides with him in Baltimore, 1826–33 and 1836–39.
Buys Douglass from his brother Thomas in 1845.
Accepts funds from British abolitionists to manumit Douglass in 1846.

|

*Thomas Auld (1824–48)
Douglass is his childhood companion.

Ann Elizabeth Auld (1826–91)

Benjamin Franklin Auld (1828-98)

Hugh William Auld (1831–91)

Edward H. Auld (b. 1836)

Zipporah Frances Auld (1838–72)

Edward Auld (b. 1802)

Zipporah Auld (1804–48)

Willison Auld (b. 1806)

Washington Auld (b. 1810)

Sarah B. Auld (1811–75)

Haddaway Auld (1813–78)

Bailey Family

Baly (b. c. 1701) m. Sue (b. 1720)

|

Jenny (1745–c. 1781): c. 4 children

|

*Betsey Bailey (1774–1849) m. *Isaac (c. 1775–c. 1845): 12 children
Owned by Aaron Anthony.
Douglass resides with her until age seven.
Inherited by Andrew Skinner Anthony and then John Planner Anthony when Aaron Anthony dies.
Thomas Auld cares for her in her old age.

|

Milly Bailey (b. 1790): 7 children

|

Bill Bailey (1806–13)

Betty Bailey (b. 1811)

Margaret Bailey (b. 1812)

*Tom Bailey (1814–after 1864)
Owned by Aaron Anthony and then Thomas Auld.

*Henny Bailey (b. 1816)
Owned by Aaron Anthony and then Thomas Auld.
Thomas Auld emancipates her before 1840.

Nancy Bailey (b. 1819)

Infant (b. c. 1827)

*Harriet Bailey (1792–c. 1825): 7 children
Owned by Aaron Anthony.

|

*Perry Bailey (1813–after 1878)
Owned by Aaron Anthony and then Andrew Skinner Anthony.
Inherited by John Planner Anthony after Andrew Skinner Anthony dies.

*Sarah Bailey (1814–after 1883)
Owned by Aaron Anthony and then Andrew Skinner Anthony.
Sold to Mississippi planter Perry Cohee in 1832.

*Eliza Bailey (1816–c. 1876) m. Peter Mitchell (unknown): 9 children
Owned by Aaron Anthony and then Thomas Auld.
Married the free black Peter Mitchell, who emancipated her in 1844.

Frederick Douglass, birth name Frederick Augustus Washington Bailey (1818–95)
m. Anna Murray (c. 1813–82): 5 children

|

Rosetta Douglass (1839–1906)
Lewis Henry Douglass (1840–1908)
Frederick Douglass, Jr. (1842–92)
Charles Remond Douglass (1844–1920)
Annie Douglass (1849–60)

m. Helen Pitts (1838–1903)

Kitty Bailey (1820–after 1849)

Arianna Bailey (1822–after 1849)

Harriet Bailey II (b. c. 1825)

Jenny Bailey (b. 1799): 3 children

Betty Bailey (b. 1801): 7 children

Sarah Bailey (1804–16)

Maryann Bailey (b. 1806)

Stephen Bailey (1808–16)

*Hester Ester Bailey (b. 1810): 1 child
Owned by Aaron Anthony and then Thomas Auld.
Severely beaten by Auld in 1825 for continuing a relationship with Ned Roberts, a slave belonging to Edward Lloyd V.

Augustus Bailey (1812–16)

Cate Bailey (1815–15)

*Priscilla Bailey (b. 1816)
Owned by Aaron Anthony and then Richard Lee Anthony.

*Henry Bailey (b. 1820)
Owned by Aaron Anthony and then Richard Lee Anthony
Inherited by Thomas Auld when Richard Lee Anthony dies.
Joins with Douglass in failed 1836 escape plot.

Historical Annotation to the *Narrative*

❦❦❦

The page and line counts supplied below for the annotation of passages in the text refer to this 2016 Yale edition and the 1845 Boston edition, respectively. Chapter headings are counted as lines. All biographical entries were researched using family documents, letters, census records, city directories, and standard reference works. Readers interested in full citations of the sources can find them in the 1999 edition of the *Narrative* published by Yale University Press.

3.2/iii.2 I] The son of impoverished Nova Scotian immigrants to Massachusetts, William Lloyd Garrison (1805–79) learned the printer's trade as a youth and went on to become one of the nation's most influential reform journalists. In 1831, he brought out the first issue of the Boston *Liberator,* which endorsed immediate emancipation. Later Garrison became an advocate for temperance, women's rights, and many other causes. His uncompromising radical positions helped cause the schism in the abolitionist movement in 1840. Thereafter, until the Civil War, he served as president of the American Anti-Slavery Society and led the "Garrisonian" wing of abolitionism.

3.2–3/iii.2–3 an anti-slavery convention in Nantucket] On 10–12 August 1841, Douglass attended a special summer convention on the island of Nantucket called by the Massachusetts Anti-Slavery Society. Garrison also attended this gathering and strongly applauded Douglass's novice performance as an abolitionist orator.

3.10/iii.13 a resident in New Bedford] Douglass lived in New Bedford, Massachusetts, after his escape from slavery, staying in the city from 1838 until 1841.

3.23/iv.1–2 "gave . . . MAN,"] *Hamlet,* act 3, scene 4, line 62.

3.34–35/iv.18–19 "created . . . angels"] A paraphrase of Psalms 8:5; Hebrews 2:7.

4.8/iv.31 A beloved friend from New Bedford] In Chapter 11, Douglass identifies this individual as the Quaker William C. Coffin. Coffin (b. 1816) was a resident of New Bedford who in 1845 was an accountant for the local Mechanics Bank. An ardent abolitionist, Coffin was a good friend of William Lloyd Garrison and served as recording secretary of the Bristol County Anti-Slavery Society from the 1830s.

4.16/v.5–6 PATRICK HENRY] Patrick Henry (1736–99), a Virginia patriot, lawyer, and Revolutionary statesman, attended the First Continental Congress at Philadelphia and was governor of Virginia from 1776 to 1779.

4.19–20/v.10–11 the peril which surrounded this self-emancipated young man] The vulnerability of fugitive slaves in Massachusetts had been highlighted by the capture of George Lattimer in Boston in October 1842. After abolitionists failed to find legal means to block his return to the South, Lattimer's freedom was purchased for $400 by northern sympathizers.

4.25–26/v.19 the old Bay State] Massachusetts derived its nickname "Old Bay State" from its original name, the Massachusetts Bay Colony. Mitford M. Mathews, *A Dictionary of Americanisms on Historical Principles,* 2 vols. (New York: Grosset and Dunlap, 1965), 2:1155.

4.26/v.19–20 "YES!" shouted the whole mass] Nantucket abolitionist Anna Gardner confirms that the convention members shouted their pledge to protect Douglass from reenslavement.

4.27/v.21 Mason and Dixon's line] Disputes between Pennsylvania to the north and Maryland and Virginia to the south were resolved when the English surveyors Charles Mason and Jeremiah Dixon determined and marked the precise borders between these colonies in 1763–67.

5.3/vi.1 Massachusetts Anti-Slavery Society] In late fall 1831, William Lloyd Garrison convened a series of meetings to advance support in the Boston area for the principles of immediate emancipation. From these meetings emerged the New England Anti-Slavery Society in early 1832. As abolitionist strength grew in the region, state-level societies were formed. The group renamed itself the Massachusetts Anti-Slavery Society in 1835.

5.3/vi.2 JOHN A. COLLINS] Vermont native John Anderson Collins (1810–c. 1879) attended Middlebury College and Andover Theological Seminary before becoming a lecturer for the Massachusetts Anti-Slavery Society in the late 1830s. He broke his ties with the Garrisonian wing of the abolitionist movement in 1843 in order to devote himself to advancing the utopian philosophy of Robert Owen.

5.10–11/vi.12 American . . . Anti-Slavery Society] Inspired by the success of the British emancipation movement, a group of sixty-two American abolitionists, representing Quakers, free blacks, New York evangelicals, and New England radicals such as William Lloyd Garrison, met in Philadelphia in December 1833 and founded the American Anti-Slavery Society. Garrison drafted most of the society's original Declaration of Sentiments, which endorsed a blend of immediatist principles and moral suasion tactics. By the time Douglass became a lecturer for the American Anti-Slavery Society in the early 1840s, many abolitionists had quit in protest of Garrison's stands on women's rights, religious orthodoxy, and an independent antislavery political party.

5.20/vi.25–26 "grow . . . God,"] Garrison slightly adapts 2 Peter 3:18.

5.25–26/vi.34–35 CHARLES LENOX REMOND] Born to free black parents in Salem, Massachusetts, Charles Lenox Remond (1810–73) was an early member of the New England Anti-Slavery Society. A talented abolitionist lecturer, Remond toured the British Isles in 1840–41. He and Douglass frequently traveled together as speaking agents of the Massachusetts Anti-Slavery Society. A loyal Garrisonian, Remond denounced Douglass's embrace of political abolitionism in the 1850s.

6.4/vii.19 DANIEL O'CONNELL] An Irish lawyer and parliamentarian, Daniel O'Connell (1775–1847) was a leader of the movements to repeal the Act of Union between England and Ireland and to remove civil disabilities from Roman Catholics. An abolitionist since the 1820s, O'Connell loyally supported the Garrisonian cause even though it slashed American support for the Loyal National Repeal Association (1840), which sought the repeal of the legislation of 1800 that abolished the separate Irish parliament and merged the governments of Ireland and Great Britain.

6.7/vii.22–23 speech . . . in the Conciliation Hall, Dublin] Garrison refers to a controversial speech that Daniel O'Connell delivered in Dublin's Conciliation Hall, the headquarters for the Loyal National Repeal Association. O'Connell denounced slavery in his speech, as Garrison reported, but he also pledged Irish support for British efforts to block American expansion. The speech produced dissension in Irish nationalist circles and hostile attacks from the United States.

6.24/viii.11 iron fetters] Chains or manacles typically placed on the ankles.

6.30–31/viii.20–21 arm . . . save] A paraphrase of Isaiah 50:2: "Is my hand shortened at all, that it cannot redeem?"

6.32/viii.22–23 "in slaves and the souls of men."] Revelation 18:13.

6.36/viii.28 SLAVERY AS IT IS.] An allusion to Theodore Weld's *American Slavery as It Is: Testimony of a Thousand Witnesses* (New York: American Anti-Slavery Society, 1839).

7.22–27/ix.22–29 the description . . . spirit of freedom] Garrison alludes to a passage that appears in Chapter 10 of the *Narrative.*

7.28–29/ix.30–31 a whole Alexandrian library of thought] Founded in the third century BCE by Egyptian ruler Ptolemy I, the library at Alexandria was reputed to hold half a million literary works. Damaged in fighting when the Romans under Julius Caesar besieged Alexandria in 47 BCE, the library continued to function until the late third century CE.

8.8/x.16 scourgings] Brutal whippings.

8.15/x.26 thumb-screws] Medieval torture device still utilized in the antebellum South.

8.31–32/xi.13–14 two incidents of murderous cruelty] An allusion to Douglass's accounts of the murders of the slave Bill Demby by the overseer Austin Gore and of a second slave by the Maryland farmer John Beale Bordley (Beal Bondly) in Chapter 4 of the *Narrative.*

9.1–2/xi.22–23 The Baltimore American, of March 17, 1845] This news item from the

Baltimore *American and Commercial Daily Advertiser* of 17 April (not March) 1845 appeared in Garrison's Boston *Liberator* of 9 May 1845, the same issue that contained a copy of the preface he wrote for Douglass's *Narrative.*

9.4/xi.26 Charles county, Maryland] The site of the earliest European settlements in present-day Maryland, Charles County lies in the southern portion of the state along the Potomac River.

9.5/xi.27 a young man, named Matthews] Probably William B. Matthews of Charles County, Maryland, then seventeen years old.

9.6/xi.28–29 whose father . . . at Washington] William B. Matthews's father was John Matthews (b. c. 1783), a wealthy slave owner whose family owned property in the Middletown District of Charles County, Maryland.

9.15/xii.5 incompetent to testify against a white man] Garrison possibly relies on the compilation of slave codes by Theodore Weld showing that statutes, as well as public opinion, precluded testimony from slaves and free blacks when a white person was accused.

9.23–24/xii.17 a cloud of witnesses] Hebrews 12:1.

9.33–34/xii.31–32 " . . . NO UNION WITH SLAVEHOLDERS!"] In 1844, the American Anti-Slavery Society adopted a resolution, penned by Garrison, branding the U.S. Constitution a proslavery document and calling for a dissolution of the Union. The motto Garrison quotes later appeared on the masthead of his Boston *Liberator.*

10.2/xiii.2 WENDELL PHILLIPS] Boston born and Harvard educated, Wendell Phillips (1811–84) ranked second only to Garrison in influence in the American Anti-Slavery Society in the 1840s and 1850s. A highly gifted orator, Phillips was in demand as a lecturer even in nonabolitionist circles before and after the Civil War. Besides abolition, Phillips championed woman suffrage, prohibition, penal reform, Indian rights, and legislative protection for workers.

10.5/xiii.5–6 "The Man and the Lion,"] Phillips loosely adapts a fable by Aesop, which is also known as "The Lion and the Statue." Thomas Newbigging, *The Fables and Fabulists: Ancient and Modern* (1895; Freeport, N.Y.: Books for Libraries Press, 1972), 9.

10.13/xiii.16 half-peck of corn] A peck is the equivalent of one-quarter of a bushel.

10.16/xiii.20 the West India experiment] The Abolition Act passed by Parliament on 28 August 1833 launched the gradual emancipation of slavery in Great Britain's West Indian colonies, beginning in 1834. The legislation freed all slaves under the age of six but held the remainder to work for their former masters as apprentices until 1838. The owners were compensated £20 million for the emancipated slaves.

10.25/xiv.5–6 the "white sails" of the Chesapeake] Phillips probably alludes to the same passage in Chapter 10 of the *Narrative* as Garrison does in his preface to the *Narrative.*

10.35/xiv.19 Valley of the Shadow of Death] Psalms 23:4.

11.24/xv.19 the halter about their necks] Possibly an allusion to an 1840 claim made by the U.S. historian Jared Sparks that Benjamin Franklin had said to John Hancock while signing the Declaration of Independence: "Yes, we must indeed all hang together, or most assuredly we shall all hang separately." Carl Van Doren, *Benjamin Franklin* (Garden City, N.Y.: Garden City Publishing Co., 1941), 551–52.

11.35/xvi.12–13 "hide the outcast,"] A slight misquotation of Isaiah 16:3.

13.5/1.2 in Tuckahoe, near Hillsborough] Talbot County, on Maryland's Eastern Shore, had been an important tobacco-growing region since colonial times. In 1788 the state legislature designated Easton as the administrative center for state operations for all nine of the Eastern Shore counties. Hillsborough (or Hillsboro) is situated northeast of Easton on Tuckahoe Creek, a tributary of the Choptank River that forms part of the eastern boundary of Talbot County.

13.6–7/1.4 knowledge of my age] As nearly as can be determined, Douglass was born in February 1818. Ledgers kept by his master Aaron Anthony contain a table, "My Black People," with the notation "Frederick Augustus son of Harriott Feby 1818."

13.15–16/2.3–4 my master] Aaron Anthony (1767–1826), Frederick Douglass's first owner and possibly his father, was born at Tuckahoe Neck in present-day Caroline County, Maryland. Despite impoverished origins, Anthony acquired a rudimentary education and a small amount of property. In 1795 he became the captain of the *Sally Lloyd,* the family schooner of Edward Lloyd IV, the wealthiest planter in Talbot County. In 1797 he increased his wealth by marrying Ann Catherine Skinner, the daughter of an old and prominent Eastern Shore family, who brought with her the slave family into which Douglass was later born. Soon thereafter, Anthony became chief overseer and general manager of the Lloyd family's thirteen farms. He remained in this position for the remainder of his life, all the while accumulating land and slaves of his own. By the time of his death in 1826, Anthony had become a moderately wealthy planter in his own right, having accumulated three farms totaling 597 1/2 acres, thirty slaves worth $3,065, and other personal property. His entire estate was valued at $8,042.

13.21/2.6 Harriet Bailey] Harriet Bailey (1792–1825) was the second child of a free black man, Isaac Bailey, and his enslaved wife, Betsey. She was owned by her mother's master, Aaron Anthony. From 1808 until her death, she was hired out by Anthony to local farmers as a field hand. On Anthony's Holme Hill Farm in Tuckahoe Creek, she gave birth to Frederick Augustus Bailey, her fourth of six or seven children, in February 1818, and there she died in late 1825 or early 1826 after a long illness.

13.21/2.7 Isaac] Isaac Bailey (c. 1775–c. 1845) was a free black man and the husband of Betsey Bailey, a slave owned by Aaron Anthony, who lived with his wife on Anthony's Tuckahoe Creek farm. A sawyer, Bailey was frequently employed by both Anthony and Edward Lloyd V to provide lumber for their plantations. He also sometimes earned wages as a plowman and harvest laborer on Anthony's farms.

13.22/2.7 Betsey Bailey] Betsey Bailey (1774–1849), the maternal grandmother of Frederick Douglass, grew up a slave on the Skinner plantation in Talbot County, Maryland. In 1797 she became the property of Aaron Anthony through his marriage to Ann Skinner. Anthony moved her to his farm on Tuckahoe Creek in Talbot County, where she married Isaac Bailey and where she stayed, despite a succession of masters, until after his death. She bore nine daughters and three sons. She was also a midwife, a service for which Anthony paid her. Upon Anthony's death in 1826, Bailey was inherited by Andrew Skinner Anthony, Aaron's son; when Andrew died in 1833, she became the slave of John Planner Anthony. In 1840, Thomas Auld, John Planner Anthony's uncle, learned that Bailey was living alone in her cabin on the Tuckahoe Creek farm, destitute and going blind, and sent for her. He cared for her in his Talbot County home until her death.

14.3/2.32 Mr. Stewart] From 1817 to 1821, Perry Ward Steward (d. 1821), a tenant farmer who headed a large household, rented Holme Hill Farm from Aaron Anthony and hired the slave Harriet Bailey as a domestic servant.

14.14/3.17 Lee's Mill] Levi Lee owned a mill near Holme Hill Farm and the Tuckahoe River in 1820 with a household of eight family members and six slaves.

15.3/4.20 human flesh-mongers] Slave traders.

15.17/5.8 God cursed Ham] Douglass refers to Genesis 9:25, where Noah curses Canaan, the son of Ham, for an offense that Ham had committed against his father, Noah. The meaning of the curse, "a servant of servants shall he be unto his brethren," had evolved in Christian Europe as a justification for the enslavement of Africans, the "sons of Ham." Proslavery advocates in the American South used this argument extensively in the renewed debates of the 1840s.

15.28/5.24 Mr. Plummer] This individual is probably either James Plummer or Philemon Plummer. Both men were longtime residents of Talbot County and, at various times during Douglass's youth, worked for Aaron Anthony as overseers on his Tuckahoe farms.

15.29–30/5.26 cowskin and a heavy cudgel] A whip and a club.

16.1/6.4–5 an own aunt of mine] Hester Bailey (b. 1810) was one of twelve children born to Isaac and Betsey Bailey and owned by Aaron Anthony of Talbot County. Hester and her only child were awarded to Thomas Auld in 1827 after the death of his father-in-law Aaron Anthony.

16.20/7.1 Colonel Lloyd] Edward Lloyd V (1779–1834) of Wye House was the scion of Talbot County's first family. One of the state's largest landowners and slave owners, he was also Maryland's most successful wheat grower and cattle raiser. As a charter member of the Maryland Agricultural Society, a founder of at least two banks, and a speculator in coal lands, he became the wealthiest of a long line of Lloyds. In terms of slaves alone, his huge holdings increased from 420 in 1810 to 545 in 1830. Edward V became a Republican delegate to the state legislature as soon as he reached the age of majority in 1800. The following year he was active in securing passage of a bill removing all restrictions to white male suffrage. From 1806 to 1808 he was a U.S. congressman, voting in 1807 against a bill to end the African slave trade. For the next two years he was governor of Maryland, and from 1811 to 1816 he returned to the state legislature. In 1819 he was elected to the U.S. Senate, from which he resigned in 1826 to return to the Maryland senate, of which he was president until 1831. Edward V married Sally Scott Murray on 30 November 1797 and had seven children with her.

16.21/7.2 Ned Roberts] Ned Roberts (b. 1810) was a slave owned by Edward Lloyd V. It was 1825 when Aaron Anthony discovered that his slave Hester Bailey was continuing to see Ned Roberts.

17.15/8.11 two sons, Andrew] Andrew Skinner Anthony (1797–1833) was the eldest son of Aaron and Ann Catherine Skinner Anthony and the nephew of Edward Lloyd V. In 1823, after completing an apprenticeship as a cabinetmaker, he married Ann Wingate. When his father died three years later, he inherited a third of his estate, including eight slaves. Although he increased his estate and owned twenty slaves, Andrew suffered from alcoholism and operated a whiskey shop in his final years.

17.15/8.12 Richard] Richard Lee Anthony (1800–1828), the second eldest of six children born to Aaron and Ann Anthony, trained as a blacksmith for five years prior to inheriting land, money, and slaves after his father's death in November 1826. Douglass incorrectly asserted that Richard died before his father.

17.15–16/8.12 one daughter, Lucretia] Lucretia Planner Anthony Auld (1804–27) was the third child and eldest daughter of Aaron and Ann Anthony. In 1823, she married Thomas Auld, a boarder in her father's household and an employee of Edward Lloyd V. Lucretia subsequently moved to Hillsborough, Maryland, where she and her new husband opened a store. Following the deaths of her father and her brother Richard Lee, Lucretia and her older brother Andrew inherited their father's estate. Her portion included the young slave Frederick Douglass. She was survived by one child, Arianna Amanda Auld.

17.16/8.13 Captain Thomas Auld] Born in St. Michaels, Maryland, Thomas Auld (1795–1880) was the eldest son of Hugh and Zipporah Auld. Trained as a shipbuilder, Auld supervised the construction of the Lloyd sloop, the *Sally Lloyd*, and subsequently became its captain. In 1823, while a boarder in the Anthony home, he met and married Lucretia Planner Anthony. Shortly thereafter, in 1827, Auld became a storekeeper in Hillsborough, Maryland, and inherited Douglass along with ten other slaves from the estate of Aaron Anthony. References to Thomas Auld in Douglass's *Narrative* and public speeches are generally uncomplimentary, although Douglass disclaimed any personal hostility toward his former owner.

17.17/8.14 the home plantation of Colonel Edward Lloyd] Settled by Edward Lloyd I in 1658, Wye House, the home plantation of the Lloyds, was situated on a peninsula formed by the Wye River on the north and the Miles River on the south. By 1790, Colonel Edward Lloyd IV owned 11,884 acres in the region. The mansion house to which Douglass refers was built in 1784 and overlooks Lloyd's Cove on the Wye River. Aaron Anthony and his family lived in the Captain's House, a brick outbuilding near the mansion. Douglass lived at Anthony's home at Wye House from August 1824 to March 1826.

17.28–29/9.4–5 This sloop was named Sally Lloyd] In 1819, Edward Lloyd V ordered the construction of a sloop to replace the aging schooner *Elizabeth & Ann,* which carried his crops to markets in Baltimore and Annapolis and brought back supplies to his scattered Talbot County farms. Thomas Auld supervised the construction and then captained the replacement vessel, named the *Sally Lloyd* in honor of the colonel's daughter, Sally Scott Lloyd.

17.29/9.5 one of the colonel's daughters] Sally Scott Lloyd Lowndes, the second daughter of Edward Lloyd V, was the namesake of her mother, Sally Scott Murray Lloyd. She married Charles Lowndes, a U.S. naval officer, on 24 May 1824. Their son Lloyd Lowndes served as governor of Maryland from 1896 to 1900.

17.31/9.8–9 Peter, Isaac, Rich, and Jake] Two of the slaves who served as the crew of the *Sally Lloyd* appear in the business records of Edward Lloyd V: Peter (b. c. 1799) and Rich (b. c. 1817).

17.35/9.13–14 three to four hundred slaves] Douglass exaggerates the number of slaves owned by Edward Lloyd V. In 1824, the year Douglass arrived on the Lloyds' main plantation, there were 181 slaves at Wye House, including the fifteen owned by Aaron Anthony, who also lived there. The Lloyds owned slaves on adjoining farms as well, although their number is not available. Edward Lloyd IV owned 305 slaves in 1790, and his grandson, Edward Lloyd VI, owned an estimated 700 slaves, including those on his Mississippi Valley plantations.

18.3/9.17 Wye Town] Wye Town Farm comprised 260 acres at the confluence of the Miles and the Wye Rivers in Talbot County, next to the main Lloyd plantation, Wye House. At the urging of the Lloyds, the Maryland General Assembly had established a town here in 1683; it was later abandoned.

18.3/9.17 New Design] New Design Farm was one of several smaller plantations owned by Edward Lloyd V in Talbot County, which Lloyd used primarily for growing wheat.

18.4/9.19 Noah Willis] Aaron Anthony employed Noah Willis as an overseer in 1819.

18.5/9.20 Mr. Townsend] George Townsend probably worked for Aaron Anthony as an overseer, managing a farm that had twenty-three slaves.

18.12/9.30 Austin Woolfolk] Austin Woolfolk of Augusta, Georgia, a slave trader serving the American Southwest, expanded his business rapidly following the Battle of New Orleans in 1815. He settled in Baltimore in 1819 to avail himself of both the large surplus slave population in the state and the excellent shipping facilities its port afforded. Woolfolk's business prospered as he sent agents throughout Maryland ready to pay high prices in cash for young black males. He annually transported from 230 to 460 slaves to markets in New Orleans, many of them having been purchased from planters on the Eastern Shore. In the 1830s, however, Woolfolk's business declined due to increased competition from larger firms, a decrease in the number of slaves for sale because of manumissions and owner emigrations, and the heightened opposition of Marylanders to the interstate slave trade.

18.17/10.4 bushel of corn meal] The equivalent of eight gallons.

18.19/10.8 negro cloth] Coarse, durable, inexpensive cloth manufactured for slave clothing.

19.7/11.8–9 Mr. Severe] During the years 1809–12 and possibly thereafter, William Sevier worked for Aaron Anthony, probably as an overseer on his farms. In 1820, he was Edward Lloyd V's overseer for the more than 150 slaves at the main plantation.

19.25/12.3 Mr. Hopkins] James Hopkins briefly took the place of William Sevier as overseer of the Wye House plantation.

19.32–33/12.14 . . . cartwrighting, coopering] Wagon making and barrel making.

19.34–20.1/12.20 the *Great House Farm*] A reference to the principal plantation of Edward Lloyd V, the Wye House plantation. When Douglass visited there in June 1881, several younger members of the Lloyd family escorted him around the grounds.

21.17–18/14.29–30 "there . . . heart."] Douglass quotes line 8 from "The Time Piece" by William Cowper. *The Poems of William Cowper,* ed. J. C. Bailey (London: Methuen, 1905), 267.

21.33–34/15.19–20 the chief gardener, (Mr. M'Durmond.)] In 1824, Aaron Anthony hired William McDermott to work for Edward Lloyd V. McDermott lived and ate at Anthony's house at least through spring 1825.

22.20–21/16.24 old Barney and young Barney] Old Barney was Barnett Sampson (b. c.

1768). Both he and his son Young Barney, Barnett Bentley (b. c. 1810), were owned by Edward Lloyd V.

23.1/17.15 "... rubbed and curried, ..."] Grooming procedures for a horse.

23.12/17.31 Edward] Born in the Annapolis home of his maternal grandparents, Edward Lloyd VI (1798–1861) was the oldest child and principal heir of his father's great wealth. Educated at the Wye House plantation by tutors, he received charge of a nearby plantation, where his father built him the beautiful Wye Heights mansion upon his marriage in 1824 to Alicia McBlair, daughter of a Baltimore merchant who died in 1838 after bearing five children. After inheriting the bulk of his father's landholdings, Lloyd successfully shifted from tobacco to grain farming and weathered the agricultural depression that struck most of the Eastern Shore in the 1840s and 1850s. Lloyd also purchased cotton land in Mississippi in 1837 and later added more in Arkansas and Louisiana. He transferred some of his swelling slave population to those new plantations. Though reputedly a stern disciplinarian, he avoided separating families during relocations and sales. A lifelong Democrat, Lloyd served as a delegate to the Maryland constitutional convention of 1850 and as a state senator (1851–52).

23.12/17.31 Murray] James Murray Lloyd (1803—47) was the middle son of Edward Lloyd V and Sally Murray Scott. When he married, his father built a mansion for him called Presqu'ile, which quickly became a Talbot County showplace. In 1840, he was one of the region's richest farmers, owning 113 slaves.

23.12/17.31 Daniel] Daniel Lloyd (c. 1811) was the sixth-born child and youngest son of Edward Lloyd V. Daniel became a farmer and his wealth increased steadily, expanding the number of slaves he owned from eighteen to thirty-six between 1840 and 1850. After the death of his father, Daniel resided at the nearby Wye Heights plantation, earlier built for his brother Edward and Edward's wife. Daniel's son, Henry, was Maryland's governor in the 1880s.

23.13/17.32 Mr. Winder] Edward Stoughton Winder, son of Levin Winder, the sixteenth governor of Maryland, and Mary Sloss, married Elizabeth Tayloe Lloyd, the eldest daughter of Edward Lloyd V, in 1820. Their son, Charles Sidney Winder, became a Confederate brigadier general.

23.13/17.32 Mr. Nicholson] Joseph Nicholson was the son of Rebecca Lloyd, Edward V's sister, and her husband, Joseph Hopper Nicholson (1770–1817), a Democratic-Republican congressman from Baltimore from 1799 through 1806 and thereafter a prominent Maryland jurist. The younger Nicholson was the nephew of Edward Lloyd V, not the son-in-law, as Douglass identifies him.

23.13/17.32–18.1 Mr. Lowndes] Born in Kent County, Maryland, Charles Lowndes (1798–1885) entered the navy as a midshipman in 1815. He married Sally Scott Lloyd in the mid-1820s and by 1840 was a prosperous Talbot County farmer with thirty-five slaves.

By the start of the Civil War, he had risen to the rank of captain in the U.S. Navy. Suspected of Confederate sympathies, he was placed on the retired list in 1862.

23.15/18.3–4 William Wilkes] William Wilks (b. c. 1791) was a slave of Edward Lloyd V. Sometime in the first half of the 1830s he purchased his freedom and moved to Baltimore, where he worked as a general laborer.

23.20/18.9 the riches of Job] Douglass refers to the biblical story of Job, whose wealth is enumerated and who is described as "the greatest of all in the east." Job 1:1–3.

24.9–10/19.13–14 a still tongue makes a wise head] This saying probably had its roots in an old English epigram, "Hauyng a styll toung he had a besy head." *The Proverbs and Epigrams of John Heywood* (1562; New York: B. Franklin, 1967), 214.

24.27/20.6–7 Jacob Jepson] Jacob Gibson (1759–1818) resided at Marengo, a plantation bordering the Lloyd property. Douglass mistakenly refers to him as "Jacob Jepson." Residents remembered him because of his numerous vitriolic broadsides and newspaper essays as well as his physical assaults on his enemies. The 1810 U.S. census listed him as the owner of thirty-four slaves, whom he reputedly ruled over as a stern taskmaster. Gibson's plantation belonged to his son Fayette at the time to which Douglass refers.

25.4–5/20.25 Mr. Austin Gore] Austin Gore (1794–1871), also referred to as Orson Gore in the Lloyd family account and cash books, was the overseer of Davis's Farm plantation, where a young slave named Bill Demby died in 1822. A friend of Gore's later challenged Douglass's assertion that Gore coolly murdered Demby, insisting that he was "a respectable citizen living near St. Michaels, and . . . a worthy member of the Methodist Episcopal Church; . . . all who know him, think him anything but a murderer." Edward Lloyd V, who owned the planation, later promoted Gore to be overseer of the much larger Wye House plantation. A. C. C. Thompson, "To Tell the Public.—Falsehood Refuted," reprinted in this edition of the *Narrative*.

26.13/22.29 by the name of Demby] Bill Demby (c. 1802–22) lived with twenty-two other slaves, including his family, on Davis's Farm, one of several Talbot County plantations owned by Edward Lloyd V. Plantation records indicate that Demby, a prime field hand, died sometime during the year 1822.

27.12/24.12 Mr. Thomas Lanman] Thomas H. W. Lambdin (b. c. 1807) had labored at a number of trades by 1850: ship carpenter, schoolteacher, town bailiff for St. Michaels (1848), and miller (1850). In a rebuttal to Douglass's negative characterization, a Maryland friend described Lambdin as "too good-natured and harmless to injure any person but himself." A. C. C. Thompson, "To Tell the Public.—Falsehood Refuted," reprinted in this edition of the *Narrative*.

27.18/24.21 Mr. Giles Hicks] A Giles Hicks resided in Caroline County, Maryland, in 1820.

27.19/24.22 my wife's] Anna Murray Douglass (c. 1813–82), Frederick Douglass's first wife, was born free in Denton, Caroline County, Maryland. She was the eighth child of Bambarra Murray and his wife Mary, slaves who had been manumitted shortly before Anna's birth. At age seventeen she moved to Baltimore, where she worked as a domestic. She met Douglass at meetings of the East Baltimore Mental Improvement Society, helped finance his escape, and joined him in New York City, where they were married on 15 September 1838. During Douglass's tour of the British Isles in 1845–47 she remained in Lynn, Massachusetts, where she supported herself by binding shoes. There she gained a reputation for frugality and skillful household management—qualities that would contribute greatly to her family's financial prosperity over the years. A member of the Lynn Ladies' Anti-Slavery Society and a regular participant in the annual antislavery bazaars in Boston, she continued her antislavery activities after moving to Rochester, New York, in 1847. Unlettered, reserved, and, according to her husband, never completely at ease in white company, she seldom appeared at public functions with Douglass. She was nevertheless affectionately remembered by her husband's associates as a "warm" and "hospitable" hostess. On 9 July 1882, Anna Douglass suffered an attack of paralysis in Washington, D.C. She died there on 4 August. In January 1884 Douglass married Helen Pitts, a white woman.

28.8/25.25 Mr. Beal Bondly] John Beale Bordley (1800–1882) was the grandson of John Beale Bordley (1727–1804), a noted agriculturalist and Revolutionary War patriot from Maryland. Often called simply Beale Bordley, John Beale Bordley had a successful career as a portrait painter of prominent figures in Baltimore, Philadelphia, and elsewhere. A number of his paintings are held by the Maryland Historical Society.

28.28/26.20 cakes] Biscuits.

28.33/26.26 tow linen] Rough unbleached cloth manufactured from tow, the shortest fibers taken from flax or hemp.

29.14/27.24 Mr. Hugh Auld] Born in Talbot County, Maryland, Hugh Auld (1799–1861) moved to Baltimore as a young man. There he worked as a ship's carpenter, master shipbuilder, and shipyard foreman and occasionally served as a magistrate. Prior to moving to Baltimore, Hugh married Sophia Keithley. Between 1826 and 1833 and again between 1836 and 1838, the young Frederick Douglass lived and worked in their household, lent to them by his owner, Hugh's brother Thomas. In 1845, Hugh, incensed by Douglass's depiction of his family in the *Narrative,* bought Douglass, then on a lecture tour of Britain, from his brother Thomas. According to the *Pennsylvania Freeman,* Auld was determined to reenslave Douglass and "place him in the cotton fields of the South" if the fugitive ever returned to the United States. In 1846, two British abolitionists, Anna and Ellen Richardson, offered to buy Douglass from Auld in exchange for $711.66 (£150) raised among British reformers. Auld signed the manumission papers that made Douglass a free man.

29.18/27.29 scurf] Scales of epidermis continually being detached from the skin.

29.27/28.10 the mange] A term for parasites found on the skin of pigs that can be transferred to humans, causing rashes and itching.

29.33/28.19–20 I had two sisters] Sarah Bailey (b. 1814) was Frederick Douglass's oldest sister and the second of seven children born to Harriet Bailey. Aaron Anthony originally owned Sarah, but after his death in 1826, she became the chattel of his son, Andrew Skinner Anthony. In 1832, Andrew sold her, her son Henry, and four other slaves to Perry Cohee of Lawrence County, in south Mississippi. Douglass and Sarah remained separated until 1883, when Sarah, then living in Louisville, Kentucky, wrote to Douglass and reestablished their relationship.

29.33/28.19–20 I had two sisters] Douglass's sister Eliza Bailey (1816–c. 1876) was the third oldest of seven children born to Harriet Bailey, a slave owned by Aaron Anthony. When Anthony died in 1826, Eliza became the property of Thomas Auld, Anthony's son-in-law, and married Peter Mitchell, a free black who worked as a field hand in Talbot County, with whom she had nine children. In 1836, Mitchell bought Eliza and the two children they then had from Thomas Auld for $100. After settling on an acre of land, which they rented from Samuel and John Hambleton of Talbot County, they raised their own vegetables and meat and hired themselves out as a domestic and a field hand, respectively. On 6 June 1844, Mitchell freed Eliza and their children because state laws no longer required removal from Maryland upon manumission. Eliza and Frederick were reunited in 1865, when Douglass stopped in Baltimore while on a speaking tour.

29.33–34/28.20 and one brother] Perry Bailey (b. 1813), Douglass's brother, was the oldest of seven children born to Harriet Bailey, a slave of Aaron Anthony's. When Anthony died in 1826, Perry was inherited by Anthony's son Andrew, who died in 1833, leaving Perry, now married to a slave named Maria, to John Planner Anthony, who sold Maria to a slave owner in Brazos County, Texas. Perry followed his wife to Texas, where a post-emancipation labor shortage allowed him to earn "fifteen dollars gold wages a month." In 1867, Perry, Maria, and their four children traveled to Rochester, New York, to reunite with Frederick, who built a cottage for them on his Rochester estate. In 1869, Perry and Maria returned to Maryland's Eastern Shore, where Perry died sometime after 1878.

30.9/29.5 Cousin Tom] Tom Bailey (b. 1814), the fourth of Milly Bailey's seven children and Douglass's cousin, was a slave belonging to Aaron Anthony. When Anthony died in 1826, Bailey became the property of Thomas Auld. Auld granted Bailey his freedom in 1845. The last record of Bailey's existence is a letter to

Douglass from his own son Lewis, who visited Talbot County in 1865. During his visit, Lewis wrote, he met with Bailey, who was still living in St. Michaels.

30.18/29.18 Miles River] Originally known as the St. Michaels River, the twelve-mile-long Miles River lies entirely within Talbot County. It flows southwest for its first eight miles and then, making a right angle, flows northwest to meet the Chesapeake Bay at the town of St. Michaels.

30.18/29.18–19 on a Saturday morning] Douglass departed St. Michaels for Baltimore on a Saturday in March 1826, probably the 18th.

30.22/29.24 bows of the sloop] The forwardmost part of the deck of a single-masted sailing ship.

30.30–31/30.5 at Smith's Wharf, not far from Bowley's Wharf] Smith's Wharf and Bowley's Wharf were two sturdily built wharves below Pratt Street in Baltimore's inner harbor, the Basin, west of Fells Point. The city directory at times spelled the latter "Bowly's Wharf."

30.32–33/30.7–8 the slaughter-house of Mr. Curtis] The Baltimore city directory of 1824 lists two "victuallers": Thomas Curtain on Eden Street and James Curtain on Bond Street. Three years later the city directory lists Thomas Curtis as a "victualler." A victualler sells food provisions or perhaps runs a tavern.

30.34/30.10 my new home in Alliciana Street] Neither the 1824 nor the 1827 Baltimore directories, the only extant directories from this period, list Hugh Auld's residence. The Baltimore City Commission on Historical and Architectural Preservation has established that Hugh Auld's house was on the southeast corner of Aliceanna and Durham (formerly Happy Alley) Streets in Fells Point. Contemporary sources spelled the street "Alisanna" (1824) or "Alice Anna" (1827).

30.35/30.11 near Mr. Gardner's ship-yard] William Gardner, a ship carpenter or shipbuilder, resided on Fleet Street, Fells Point, between 1827 and 1836. The shipyard of George and William Gardner was at the "lower end of Fountain Street," on the eastern edge of the Fells Point wharf area.

30.35/30.11 on Fell's Point] Fells Point, first settled by William Fell in 1726, was an enclave east of central Baltimore that was not annexed to Baltimore until 1773. This hooked piece of land jutting into the outer harbor had been a shipbuilding site since the mid-eighteenth century. After the War of 1812 it was the construction site for the famous Baltimore clipper ships. By the time of Douglass's arrival, Fells Point was a heavily populated neighborhood whose residents worked in shipbuilding and other maritime pursuits. Shipyards and wharves for unloading cargo lined its waterfront. To reduce the frequency of yellow fever epidemics, a marshy area between Fells Point and the central city was dredged in the 1820s to form the City Dock, also called the City Block, which added to the Fells Point wharf area. A drawbridge at the entrance to the City Dock connected Block Street in Fells Point to the Basin area wharves.

30.36–31.1/30.13 their little son Thomas] Thomas Auld (1824–48), the son of Hugh and Sophia Auld and the nephew of Thomas Auld, Aaron Anthony's son-in-law, was the charge of the young slave Douglass. He died in an unsuccessful attempt by the brig *Tweed* to rescue a sinking British vessel.

31.3/30.17 Sophia Auld] Sophia Keithley Auld (1797–1880) was born in Talbot County, Maryland, to Richard and Hester Keithley. Her parents were poor, devout Methodists who held to the antislavery teachings of their church. Before marrying Hugh Auld, Jr., she worked as a weaver. Soon after their marriage, the couple moved to Baltimore, where Hugh worked as a ship's carpenter, master shipbuilder, and shipyard fireman. Between 1826 and 1833 and again in 1836–38, the young slave Frederick Douglass lived and worked in their household. Both Douglass and Sophia Auld retained enormous affection for one another long after Douglass had established himself in the North. Douglass tried to visit Sophia Auld in Baltimore during the Civil War. Years after her death, her son Benjamin told Douglass that "mother would always speak in the kindest terms of you, whenever your name was mentioned." Benjamin F. Auld to Douglass, 11 September 1891, General Correspondence File, reel 6, frame 240, Frederick Douglass Papers, Library of Congress.

32.28/33.12–13 "If you give a nigger an inch, he will take an ell"] A paraphrase of the old English proverb "For whan I gaue you an ynche, ye tooke an ell." An ell is an antiquated English unit of length equal to forty-five inches. Heywood, *Proverbs and Epigrams,* 78.

34.1/35.13 Philpot Street] Philpot Street ran east to west, parallel to the waterfront on Fells Point. The Aulds moved to Philpot Street in 1827 or 1828, soon after Hugh Auld, Jr., began working at Durgin and Bailey's shipyard.

34.1/35.13 Mr. Thomas Hamilton] Thomas Hamilton, a ship carpenter, lived at 22 Philpot Street in Baltimore from at least 1831 through 1838. In 1833 his address was listed, probably incorrectly, as 18 Philpot Street.

34.14/35.31 *gip*] Gypsy.

34.19/36.8 offal] Entrails and other animal parts generally discarded in the butchering process.

35.8/37.13–14 for every mourner that came within her reach] Possibly a loose paraphrase of Proverbs 25:20–23.

36.8/38.31–32 Durgin and Bailey's ship-yard] John Durgin and Thomas Bailey operated a shipwright business on Philpot Street in Fell's Point in the late 1820s and the 1830s. Douglass recalls carrying dinner to Auld, then employed as a carpenter at the shipyard, which was near the Auld home. Bailey continued to work as a ship carpenter in the same area into the 1830s.

36.17/39.12 "The Columbian Orator"] Boston schoolteacher and bookseller Caleb Bingham (1757–1817) edited *The Columbian Orator: Containing a Variety of Original and Selected Pieces, together with Rules; Calculated to Improve Youth and Others in the Ornamental and Useful Art of Eloquence* (1797; Boston: J. H. A. Frost, 1827), one of the first textbooks on English grammar and rhetoric published in the United States. It contained short extracts from speeches by such famous orators as William Pitt, George Washington, Charles James Fox, and Cicero, as well as plays and poems on the themes of patriotism, education, and freedom. *The Columbian Orator* remained one of the most popular textbooks of its kind in America through the 1820s. Bingham himself contributed an essay on oratorical skills, "General Directions for Speaking," whose rules Douglass followed in his early years as a public speaker.

36.18–19/39.14–15 a dialogue between a master and his slave] The anonymous "Dialogue between a Master and Slave" is a conversation between a master and slave in which the slave is caught trying to run away for the second time. Bingham, *The Columbian Orator*, 240–42.

36.28–29/39.27–28 Sheridan's mighty speeches on and in behalf of Catholic Emancipation] Although Richard Sheridan (1751–1816), the Irish orator, playwright, and politician who entered Parliament in 1780, championed Irish and other reform causes, the only speech extracted in *The Columbian Orator* is "Mr. Sheridan's Speech against Mr. Taylor," which is not on Catholic "emancipation." Douglass is probably referring to another selection in the anthology entitled "Part of Mr. O'Connor's Speech in the Irish House of Commons, in Favor of the Bill for Emancipating the Roman Catholics, 1795." Arthur O'Connor (1763–1852), a liberal Protestant member of the Irish parliament, was a strong supporter of Catholic rights, including "Catholic emancipation," or the right of Catholics to hold office and sit in Parliament. O'Connor resigned his seat after delivering this speech.

38.4/42.1–2 petitions from the north] The sending of petitions to Congress, calling for an end to the slave trade and to slavery in the District of Columbia, dated back to the early years of the federal government. In 1828, a national petition drive had helped force the House of Representatives to vote on abolishing slavery in the District of Columbia. The newly organized movement for immediate emancipation adopted the petition strategy in the 1830s and deluged Congress with antislavery memorials bearing thousands of signatures.

38.9/42.9 on the wharf of Mr. Waters] George P. Waters was a ship chandler and grocer who operated both of his businesses very near the wharf he owned at the south end of Fell Street in Fells Point.

38.10/42.10 scow] A small flat-bottomed boat used to haul heavy freight.

38.31/43.9 larboard side] The left side of a ship when looking toward the bow.

38.32/43.10 starboard side] The right side of a vessel when looking toward the bow.

39.11/43.32 copying the italics] The italic font most closely resembles handwritten letters.

39.11/44.1 Webster's Spelling Book] The first version of the spelling book *A Grammatical Institute of the English Language* (Hartford, Conn.: Hudson and Goodwin, 1783), by Noah Webster (1758–1843), a Connecticut teacher, editor, and Federalist politician, rapidly became the standard spelling and pronunciation guide in the new nation. In 1788 the title became *The American Spelling Book;* and in 1829, *The Elementary Spelling Book.*

39.16/44.7–8 the Wilk Street meeting-house] The Fifth Methodist Episcopal Church, on the corner of Wilke (Wilks) Street and Apple Alley, was about seven blocks from Auld's house on Philpot Street.

39.24/44.18 youngest son Richard died] Douglass is mistaken in believing that Richard died before his father. According to the Anthony family Bible, Richard did not die until 18 May 1828 and had shared in the division of his father's estate.

39.25/44.20 Captain Anthony, died] Aaron Anthony died on 14 November 1826, at age fifty-nine. According to his great-granddaughter Harriet Lucretia Anthony, he was buried in an unmarked grave in the family graveyard on Holme Hill Farm.

39.35/45.7 Captain Rowe] Captain Joseph H. Rowe lived in Baltimore on Market Street south of Bank Street from at least 1831 through 1836.

39.35/45.7–8 the schooner Wild Cat] The schooner *Wild Cat* was a slow, shallow-draft merchant ship designed to carry cargo up and down the tidal creeks of the Chesapeake Bay.

40.14/45.27 then came the division] Aaron Anthony's heirs, Richard Lee Anthony, Andrew Skinner Anthony, and Thomas Auld, agreed to the division of his slaves on 27 September 1827. The twenty-eight slaves, valued at $2,805, were divvied up. Frederick was among the slaves awarded to Thomas Auld, widower of Lucretia Planner Anthony Auld.

41.7/47.5–6 was sent immediately back to Baltimore] After court-appointed appraisers oversaw the assignment of Aaron Anthony's slaves to each of his heirs, Douglass returned to Baltimore, probably by November 1827 at the latest.

41.12/47.12–13 my mistress, Lucretia, died] Lucretia Planner Anthony Auld died on 6 July 1827. Douglass is mistaken in his recollection that he was awarded to Lucretia, for she had died after her father, Aaron Anthony, but before his estate was settled. County records indicate that Frederick was awarded to her husband, Thomas Auld, who was her heir.

41.13/47.13–14 one child, Amanda] Born in Hillsborough, Maryland, Arianna

Amanda Auld Sears (1826–78) was the only child of Thomas and Lucretia Planner Anthony Auld. After her mother's death in 1826 and her father's subsequent remarriage, she fell under the charge of her stepmother Rowena Hambleton Auld. In 1843 she married John L. Sears, a Philadelphia coal merchant, with whom she had four children. The Searses moved to Philadelphia, where Amanda Auld's childhood acquaintance with Frederick Douglass was reestablished in 1859, when he called upon her while on a speaking engagement. Douglass and Auld maintained a warm friendship over the years that followed. After her death, her husband, John, wrote to Douglass, "God bless you for your kindness to her." John L. Sears to Douglass, 10 January 1878, General Correspondence File, reel 3, frames 215–16, FD Papers, Library of Congress.

41.13–14/47.14–15 after her death, Master Andrew died] Andrew Skinner Anthony died in June 1833, but not before he had sold several of Douglass's Bailey relatives to a Mississippi slaveholder.

42.4/48.20–21 the slave's poet, Whittier] Born in Haverhill, Massachusetts, the Quaker poet and abolitionist John Greenleaf Whittier (1807–72) was a writer and editor for such journals as *Free Press, American Manufacturer,* the Washington (D.C.) *National Era,* and the *Atlantic Monthly.* Among Whittier's volumes of poetry are *Voices of Freedom* (1846), *The Panorama and Other Poems* (1856), and *At Sundown* (1890). Douglass often quoted Whittier's poems in his speeches.

42.16/48.33 Woe is me, my stolen daughters] Douglass quotes the first twelve lines from the 1838 poem "The Farewell of a Virginia Slave Mother to Her Daughter Sold into Southern Bondage," by John Greenleaf Whittier. *The Poetical Works of John Greenleaf Whittier,* 4 vols. (Boston: Houghton, Mifflin, 1892), 3:56.

42.34/49.25 Rowena Hamilton] Douglass got the name wrong. Rowena Hambleton Auld (1812–1842) was the eldest daughter of William Hambleton, not Hamilton, a wealthy slaveowner in Martingham, Maryland. She became the second wife of Thomas Auld on 21 May 1829.

42.35/49.26 Mr. William Hamilton] William Hambleton (b. c. 1783), not Hamilton, descended from an old Eastern Shore family and lived at Martingham, a Talbot County plantation. He was the father of Rowena Hambleton Auld and the brother of "Purser" Samuel Hambleton, who had won national fame as a hero at the Battle of Lake Erie in the War of 1812.

43.3/49.30 to live with himself at St. Michael's] Hugh Auld returned Douglass to Thomas Auld in St. Michaels in March 1833, not 1832, as Douglass erroneously believed at the time of writing the *Narrative.*

43.19–20/50.21 Captain Edward Dodson] Edward Dodson was captain of a packet ship that conveyed passengers and freight between St. Michaels and Baltimore in the early nineteenth century.

43.22/50.24 on reaching North Point] North Point is a cape at the mouth of the Patapsco River where it opens into Chesapeake Bay. To reach northern ports from Baltimore, ships rounded North Point and headed north on the bay to the Chesapeake and Delaware Canal, which opened to navigation in 1830.

43.29–30/51.4 at St. Michael's, in March, 1832] Actually March 1833.

44.14/52.4 my aunt Priscilla] Priscilla Bailey (b. 1816), the eleventh of twelve children born to Isaac and Betsey Bailey, was a slave belonging to Aaron Anthony. When Anthony died in 1826, his son Richard Lee Anthony inherited her.

44.14/52.4 Henny] Henny Bailey (b. 1816), a cousin of Frederick Douglass, was one of seven children born to Milly Bailey, a slave on one of Aaron Anthony's farms. Henny was apparently ill fitted for work: Anthony estimated her value at $50 in 1826, less than half the value he placed on her younger cousin Frederick. When Anthony died in 1826, his son-in-law Thomas Auld inherited Bailey and four other slaves. Sometime before 1840, Auld granted Bailey her freedom. The last record of Henny's existence is an entry in the 1840 U.S. Census, which identifies her as a free black, between the ages of thirty-six and fifty-five, living in St. Michaels District.

45.19/53.30–31 my master attended a Methodist camp-meeting] Douglass accompanied his master Thomas Auld to some of the services at a Methodist camp meeting held at Haddaway's Woods on what is presently known as the Tilghman Peninsula at the headwaters of Chesapeake Bay. The meeting lasted from 16 to 21 August 1833 and attracted people from as far away as Baltimore.

45.32/54.16–17 class-leader and exhorter] Recognized positions in the Methodist faith for lay preachers who assisted the minister in church services.

46.1/54.24–25 Mr. Storks] The Reverend Levi Storks was the circuit preacher of the Talbot Circuit of the Methodist Episcopal Church in 1832 and 1833. When the British invaded the Eastern Shore in 1814, Storks served as a private in a local regiment. In 1820 he was probably an overseer in Talbot County, and in 1834 he married Anne G. Nicholson.

46.1/54.25 Mr. Ewery] In 1832, William Uriey (c. 1810–1880) was a circuit preacher for the Methodist Episcopal Church's Talbot Circuit, which included St. Michaels Parish.

46.2/54.25 Mr. Humphry] Joshua Humphries (c. 1801–1879) entered the Methodist Episcopal ministry in 1829 and soon became a prominent member of that faith in Talbot County. In 1834 he was the presiding elder and circuit preacher for the church's Talbot Circuit.

46.2/54.25 Mr. Hickey] William—or possibly Thomas—Hickey was a Methodist preacher who in the 1830s rode a circuit that included St. Michaels Parish.

46.2/54.26 Mr. George Cookman] Born into a wealthy family in Hull, England,

George Grimston Cookman (1800–1841) began working in his father's merchant firm by the age of twenty. Between 1821 and 1823, he visited the United States on business and during this sojourn became convinced of his duty to preach the gospel. Despite his father's protestations, he resolved to settle permanently in America and become a Methodist minister. Soon after emigrating in 1825, Cookman became a popular figure in the Methodists' Philadelphia Conference, preaching throughout parts of Pennsylvania, New Jersey, Maryland, and the District of Columbia. His powerful sermons won him the position of chaplain to the U.S. Congress. As revivals were sweeping the Eastern Shore, Cookman became the minister of the St. Michaels Methodist Episcopal Church in the summer of 1829 and remained in that position at least through the early 1830s. He had some antislavery leanings and apparently persuaded Samuel Harrison, one of Talbot County's largest slaveholders, to emancipate all of his adult male slaves in his will.

46.4/54.29 Mr. Samuel Harrison] Samuel Harrison (d. 1837) was one of the wealthiest slaveholders in Talbot County: in 1802 he inherited a lucrative import-export business from his father, Thomas Harrison. He increased his fortune in the 1810s by lending money and supplies to those engaged in the booming shipbuilding industry of Talbot County, and by 1830 he owned eighty-four slaves. At the request of his friend and confidant the Reverend George Cookman, Harrison stipulated in his will that all adult male slaves be manumitted upon his death.

46.13/55.8 Mr. Wilson] Nathan Wilson (c. 1797–c. 1861), an unmarried Quaker about fifty years old, taught at a local school for whites in the early 1840s near Denton, in Caroline County, only a few miles from Talbot County. Although Quakerism was no longer the influential religious force on the Eastern Shore that it had been in the eighteenth century, numerous Quakers remained in the region, and some continued to argue against slavery and for teaching the slaves to read the Bible. Among other local whites interested in black education was Louisa Hambleton from the Eastern Shore's famous first family, who unsuccessfully attempted to open a Sabbath school for St. Michaels slaves in 1843.

46.15/55.11 Mr. West] Garretson West (1800–1853) was famous among Methodists in St. Michaels for his religious enthusiasm and moral zeal. Although he worked first as an oysterman and later as a teamster, West primarily devoted himself to spurring public prayer, exhorting the faithful at the Methodist classes he led, and—despite his illiteracy—conversing at length with others over the meaning of various biblical passages. In 1829, West was elected to the board of trustees of the Methodist church in St. Michaels, and he held that position until 1836.

46.15/55.12 Mr. Fairbanks] Wrightson Fairbank or Fairbanks (b. c. 1806), a resident of Talbot County, was married, had four children, and worked as a merchant. He was an active member of the Methodist Episcopal Church in St. Michaels and ran unsuccessfully for the board of trustees of the parish in September 1835.

46.23–25/55.25 beaten with many stripes] A paraphrase of Luke 12:47.

47.20/57.5–6 Edward Covey] Edward Covey (c. 1806–75), who started out renting a farm in Talbot County, Maryland, managed to accumulate $23,000 in real estate by 1850. Covey's reputation as a slave breaker enabled him to rent or even to receive the free use of field hands from local slave owners anxious to have their slaves taught "proper" discipline. Harriet Lucretia Anthony, the great-granddaughter of Aaron Anthony, remembered that "Mr. Covey was really noted for his cruelty and meanness." Dickson J. Preston, *Young Frederick Douglass: The Maryland Years* (Baltimore, Md.: Johns Hopkins University Press, 1980), 117–31.

48.11/58.15 in-hand . . . off-hand] In a team of harnessed animals, the in-hand one is directly under control of the driver.

48.16/58.22 few rods into the woods] A rod is a classic English measurement of length equivalent to 16 1/2 feet, or one-quarter the length of a standard surveyor's chain.

49.3/59.27 gum-tree] One of two varieties of medium-sized deciduous trees found along the East Coast: the Sweet Gum or the Black Gum.

49.19/60.19 saving-fodder time] The fall period for harvesting hay and straw.

52.11/65.4 ague] A fit of shaking or shivering, often accompanying a fever, usually malaria.

52.33/66.2 Bill Smith] Bill Smith (b. 1804) was a slave owned by Samuel Harrison of Rich Neck Manor and hired out as a servant to Edward Covey in 1834. Smith probably received his freedom in 1837, for Harrison's will stipulated that all adult male slaves should be freed upon his death.

52.34/66.4 fanning wheat] Exposing cut grain to the wind to have the chaff blown away.

53.10–11/66.21 treading-yard] Place where plants were walked on repeatedly to reduce them to a smaller size for storage.

54.33/69.9 large dose of salts] Probably Epsom salt, or magnesium sulfate, a popular natural remedy applied to open wounds to prevent infection and promote quick healing.

55.4/69.19 Mrs. Kemp's fields] Elizabeth Doyle Kemp (b. c. 1787) probably owned a farm adjacent to the farm Edward Covey rented from her son, John. Married to the shipbuilder Thomas Kemp in Baltimore in November 1809, Elizabeth moved with him to a 236-acre farm, Wades Point, west of the town of St. Michaels in Talbot County, in 1816. After her husband's death in March 1824, most of his property was divided between his two oldest sons, Thomas and John, but provisions were also made for Elizabeth.

55.13/69.32 Sandy Jenkins] Sandy Jenkins was a slave owned by William Groomes of Easton, Maryland, who often hired him out to farmers in Talbot County.

57.21/73.20 taken by the constable to the whipping-post] A public post where punishment is administered to a prisoner.

59.28/77.4 Mr. William Freeland] William Freeland, the son of William and Elizabeth Freeland of Talbot County, Maryland, was a farmer and slave owner near St. Michaels. The 1820 U.S. Census lists William as a young adult between sixteen and twenty-five years of age. Between 1820 and 1830, and perhaps later, he lived in a household headed by his mother. They shared their home with two white boys and six slaves. By 1830 the Freelands' household had diminished: Elizabeth and William now lived with only one young white man and four slaves.

60.17/78.9 the Rev. Daniel Weeden] Daniel Weeden (b. c. 1794) was a farmer and Methodist minister in Talbot County. Though an overseer without any of his own slaves in 1820, Weeden appears by 1830 to have become an independent farmer with two slaves and a growing family. In 1839 Weeden forced a free black man back into slavery by revealing that he had served time in a Maryland jail. He then purchased the man at a greatly reduced price.

60.18/78.10 the Rev. Rigby Hopkins] Rigby Hopkins was a Methodist minister who, in the year Douglass mentions, had long lived and farmed in Talbot County. In 1820 he owned seventeen slaves, but by 1830 he had none, possibly indicating a preference for renting black labor.

60.19/78.11–12 the Reformed Methodist Church] An agitation for greater lay authority inside the Methodist Episcopal Church resulted in the expulsion of a small number of members and some congregations from the church in the mid-1820s. Additional sympathizers withdrew, and the reformers established the Associate Methodist Church in 1828, soon thereafter renamed the Methodist Protestant Church. The controversy inspired a large majority of the members of the Sardis Chapel in St. Michaels to affiliate with the new denomination. The minority, led by the Reverend George Grimston Cookman and Garretson West, successfully retained the original church building and eventually rebuilt their congregation. In the late 1850s, the Methodist Protestant Church underwent a schism over the slavery issue, as had its parent Methodist Episcopal Church in the mid-1840s, and the Maryland conference sided with the South.

65.8/85.29 " . . . that we knew not of"] *Hamlet,* act 3, scene 1, lines 81–82.

65.10/85.31–86.1 resolved upon liberty or death] Douglass paraphrases Patrick Henry's speech made at a Virginia Revolutionary convention on 23 March 1775.

65.14/86.6 Henry Bailey] Henry Bailey (b. 1820) was the youngest of twelve children born to Douglass's maternal grandparents, Isaac and Betsey Bailey. Henry Bailey was owned by Aaron Anthony of Talbot County; when Anthony died in 1826,

Bailey became the property of Richard Lee Anthony. When Richard died in 1828, Thomas Auld, Richard's brother-in-law, became Bailey's master.

65.19/87.1 Easter holidays] Easter Sunday in 1836 fell on 3 April.

67.22–23/89.24 Tom Graham, the constable] Thomas Graham was the constable of St. Michaels Parish in 1833 and the next-door neighbor of Thomas Auld. In 1830 he was between forty and fifty, married, the father of one son, and the owner of one female slave. He appears to have died between 1840 and 1850, for he is not listed in the census for the latter year. After the publication of the *Narrative*, Graham publicly disputed Douglass's characterization of his treatment by Auld.

68.31/91.23–24 the sheriff, Mr. Joseph Graham] Joseph Graham (b. c. 1797) was the sheriff of Talbot County in 1836. Graham was still alive in 1878, when Douglass returned to visit Talbot County.

70.4/93.24–25 to my old home at Baltimore] Douglass returned to Baltimore in mid-April 1836. While Douglass makes no mention of the Aulds having moved, Benjamin Auld thought that his family had moved from Philpot Street to "Fell Street" around 1834. The Baltimore city directories list Hugh Auld as residing on Philpot Street until 1837, when he is listed as a shipwright on "Falls Street south of Thames."

70.9/93.31 calk] To calk, or caulk, is to seal the planking of a wooden ship through the application of a mixture of cotton and/or hemp fibers and tar pitch.

70.21/94.17 cant] To tilt or turn over an object.

70.25/94.22 fall] The loose end of a hoisting tackle.

70.29/94.28 *bowse*] To haul an object by means of a tackle.

70.34/95.5 apprentices] Novices learning a skill or occupation by assisting an experienced worker.

71.8–9/95.19–20 at once to put a stop to it] Most free blacks in Baltimore held jobs as laborers, draymen, and servants, although they also held such craft positions as carpenter, blacksmith, barber, and caulker. In the mid-1830s Baltimore witnessed increasing mob violence, brought on by worsening economic conditions and the failure of the Bank of Maryland in 1834. Claiming that free blacks were depriving them of jobs, white Baltimore workers unsuccessfully petitioned the Maryland legislature in the 1830s and 1840s to restrict free blacks from working in certain trades. Economic competition between the races continued, and in 1845 white labor had driven blacks out of many jobs in the Fells Point area.

71.15/95.28 journeymen] Workers who have completed an apprentice program but earn wages and are not self-employed.

71.36–72.1/96.28 death by Lynch law] The actual individual from whom the term "lynch law" derives its name has been disputed, but the expression was in common use by the early nineteenth century as a description for the punishment of individuals without due process of law. David C. Roller and Robert W. Twyman, eds., *The Encyclopedia of Southern History* (Baton Rouge: Louisiana State University Press, 1979), 762–64.

72.17–18/97.19 to Esquire Watson's, on Bond Street] William H. Watson (d. c. 1846) was a justice of the peace and prominent attorney who lived at 76 Bond Street in Baltimore's Fells Point district in the late 1830s. He joined a Baltimore volunteer battalion as a captain during the war with Mexico (1846–48). Watson quickly rose to the rank of lieutenant colonel but died in the Battle of Monterey in October 1846.

73.6/98.21 Mr. Walter Price] Walter Price, whose family had long been engaged in shipbuilding, operated a shipyard on Fell Street south of Thames Street along the waterfront in 1830s Baltimore. Like a number of other Baltimore shipbuilders, Price constructed clippers that found their way into the international slave trade. Both Hugh Auld and Douglass worked for Price during the construction of at least three ships, which Price covertly sold to Brazilian and Cuban slave traders, who prized these ships for their ability to evade the British blockade off Africa's Slave Coast. Slavery was legal in the United States, but international slave trading was not.

73.7–8/98.22 mallet and irons] Hand tools employed in caulking ships.

73.9/98.25–26 to the most experienced calkers] Blacks, both free and slave, dominated the semiskilled caulking occupation in Baltimore in the 1830s. Among the largest Baltimore slaveholders in the 1810s and 1820s were master shipbuilders who used slave caulkers in their own shipyards or hired them out to other shipbuilders. Although information on caulkers' wages in the 1830s is elusive, free black caulkers earned $1.50 per day in 1812, and during the height of wartime building they raised their daily wages to $1.67 1/4. Slave caulkers in 1812 earned $1.25 to $1.31 1/4 per day. By 1838 free blacks had formed their own organization, the Caulker's Beneficial Association. Controlling the trade through the 1850s, the black caulkers owed their power to an alliance with the white shipwrights' association to control wages and conditions in shipbuilding. Blacks' hold on the trade was shaken when clashes erupted in 1858 between black association members and white caulkers who were willing to accept lower wages. Blacks faced increasing discrimination in the 1860s, prompting black carpenters and caulkers to organize their own shipyard in 1866. In 1871 Douglass visited the Fells Point shipbuilding area and commented on the success of the black shipyard, noting that the "leading shipbuilders [of] forty years ago, are all gone, and have not even left their firms behind to perpetuate their names." Ironically, in 1836–38 some of the Fells Point shipyards where Douglass worked as a caulker built ships destined for the illegal African slave trade.

74.24/101.6 the *underground railroad*] Northern blacks, along with some sympathetic white supporters, maintained a loose, clandestine system to clothe, feed, and shelter fugitive slaves from the South. In addition, "vigilance committees" operated in many northern communities to expose the presence of slave hunters and, on occasion, to rescue fugitives being returned to their southern masters.

75.28–29/102.31–32 came to Baltimore to purchase his spring goods] This visit apparently occurred in March 1838.

75.30/103.1 allow me to hire my time] In the urban South masters commonly hired their slaves out to other employers for specified periods of time. The less common practice of allowing their slaves to seek their own employment and pay their masters a specified sum grew over time, causing public fears that it would undermine the slave system itself. The Maryland legislature periodically passed legislation to control or abolish this practice, with little result.

76.31/104.22–23 my attending a camp meeting] Douglass attended a camp meeting on the weekend of 4–5 August 1838. Revivals abounded in the South in the hot month of August; two more occurred near Baltimore the following weekend.

77.27/106.2–3 Mr. Butler, at his ship-yard] Samuel Butler, a Baltimore ship carpenter, established a shipyard in 1819 in partnership with Robert Lambdin. Apparently Lambdin moved to St. Michaels, Talbot County, in 1830 while maintaining his financial interest in the yard. Butler remained, managing the operation through the 1830s, during which time the shipyard launched the noted ship *Catherine*.

78.24/107.16–17 succeeded in reaching New York] Not until 1881 did Douglass publicly reveal the details of his escape from slavery. On 3 September 1838, he boarded a train bound from Baltimore to New York City. Douglass had borrowed the uniform and seaman's protection papers of a free black friend in Baltimore. Fortunately for Douglass, the conductor did not check the description in the papers carefully, and several white acquaintances on the train failed to recognize him.

79.32/109.16 Mr. David Ruggles] David Ruggles (1810–49), a free black man, was born and educated in Norwich, Connecticut. In 1827 he moved to New York, where he worked as a grocer. In 1834 he opened a printing and book shop that specialized in abolitionist literature. Ruggles became active in the New York antislavery movement, serving as a writer, lecturer, and traveling agent for a reform publication, *Emancipator and Journal of Public Morals*. He also was a conductor on the Underground Railroad, editor of the *Genius of Freedom* and the *Mirror of Liberty*, and secretary to the New York Vigilance Committee. His career in the antislavery movement ended abruptly in 1842, when temporary blindness, an illness that plagued him for the remainder of his life, forced him to curtail his activities and seek medical attention. At the Northampton Association of Education and Industry in Florence, Massachusetts, he underwent hydrotherapy, which temporarily relieved his blindness. Soon thereafter he began a new career as a hydrotherapist in Northampton, Massachusetts, treating such notable individuals as Sojourner Truth and William Lloyd Garrison. His reputation as a hydrotherapist gave him a prominence that rivaled his stature as an abolitionist.

80.4/109.26–27 the memorable *Darg* case] The Darg case became a celebrated example of the persecution of abolitionists by established local authorities and proslavery newspapers. In August 1838, Thomas Hughes, a slave, escaped from his owner, John P. Darg of Arkansas, while the two were in New York City. Hughes also stole approximately $8,000 from Darg. He soon sought assistance from Isaac T. Hopper, a leading Quaker abolitionist. Suspicious of Hughes, Hopper housed him for only one night and soon thereafter learned of the stolen money. While Hopper did not want to harbor a felon, he also did not want to return a man to slavery. Seeking counsel from David Ruggles and other abolitionists, Hopper learned that Darg would free Hughes and not charge him for theft if all of his money was returned, but local police officials working with Darg were intent upon convicting Hopper, Ruggles, Barney Corse, and others as accomplices to the theft. Only after sixteen months of legal hearings and the brief imprisonment of both Ruggles and Corse did the prosecution abandon its case as hopeless. The outcome for Hughes is not known.

80.17/110.13 the Rev. J. W. C. Pennington] Born into slavery as Jim Pembroke, James William Charles Pennington (1809–71) was owned by Frisbie Tilghman of Maryland's Eastern Shore until the age of twenty-one, when he fled north to the home of a Pennsylvania Quaker who taught him to read and write. Later Pennington found work on Long Island, attended night school and private tutorials, and taught black children in New York and Connecticut. After studying theology at Yale University, Pennington ministered to black congregations in Hartford, Connecticut, and New York City. Though committed to a variety of reform causes, such as temperance, missionary work, and world peace, Pennington's greatest exertions were devoted to the antislavery movement. In 1843 he traveled to England as a delegate at large to the World's Anti-Slavery Convention in London and lectured throughout Europe. Fearing recapture after the passage of the Fugitive Slave Law, Pennington again traveled abroad in 1850, remaining there until a Hartford friend, John Hooker, was able to purchase his freedom. In addition to many sermons, addresses, and regular contributions to the *Anglo-African Magazine,* Pennington wrote *A Text Book of the Origins and History, &c., &c. of the Colored People* (1841) and an autobiography. J. W. C. Pennington, *The Fugitive Blacksmith,* 3rd ed. (London: C. Gilpin, 1850).

80.17–18/110.14 Mrs. Michaels] In the late 1830s, Mrs. D. Michaels owned and operated a boardinghouse in New York City at 33–36 Lespanard Street. She was married to Joseph Michaels, who made floor mats and dealt in scrap metal, glass, and rags.

80.29/111.1–2 Mr. Shaw in Newport] George C. Shaw, who lived in Newport, Rhode Island, was in 1840 the corresponding secretary for the Newport Anti-Slavery Society, a group supporting William Lloyd Garrison's New England Anti-Slavery Society.

81.3/111.11 Joseph Ricketson] Joseph Ricketson (1771–1841) was the owner of a candle factory and oil refinery in New Bedford, Massachusetts. He served as a cashier and director of the New Bedford Commercial Bank and as a trustee of the New Bedford Lyceum and Atheneum. Ricketson, a Quaker, was committed to various reform and antislavery endeavors. Though a scrupulously honest and hard-working businessman, Ricketson's last years were spent in near poverty because of several serious business reversals.

81.4/111.11–12 William C. Taber] A descendant of one of the earliest settlers of New Bedford, Massachusetts, William C. Taber (b. 1797) operated a profitable store selling books, stationery, charts, and engravings. In the 1850s Taber led local businessmen in converting from whale oil for illumination to gas, coal oil, and kerosene and was the first president of the New Bedford Gas-Light Company. He was long active in the city's financial institutions, serving at different times as a director of both the Marine Bank and the New Bedford Institution for Savings. Taber also represented New Bedford in the Massachusetts Senate. An ardent Quaker, he held the post of first clerk at the Quakers' New Bedford Monthly Meeting for nineteen years.

81.9/111.19 Mr. and Mrs. Johnson] Owners of a confectionery shop and a thriving catering business, Nathan Johnson (d. 1880) and Mary Page Johnson (d. c. 1870) were two of the most prominent blacks in New Bedford, Massachusetts. They helped and housed black fugitives on many occasions, and Nathan was an active abolitionist, serving as a manager of the American Anti-Slavery Society at one point. In 1832, Nathan represented New Bedford at the National Negro Convention in Philadelphia, and in 1837 he was one of three local African Americans chosen to question all county political candidates as to their views on slavery and the slave trade. Johnson left New Bedford for California in 1849 and did not return until 1871, after his wife, who had remained behind, died.

81.28/112.15 the "Lady of the Lake,"] Sir Walter Scott (1771–1832) published *The Lady of the Lake* in Edinburgh in 1810. Ellen Douglas and her father, Lord James of Douglas, are the principal characters.

83.8–9/114.28 ". . . and he took me in"] Douglass paraphrases Matthew 25:35.

84.11/116.19 carry the hod] A three-sided wooden box with a long handle for carrying bricks or other construction materials.

84.15/116.25 the "Liberator."] The pioneer abolitionist William Lloyd Garrison published a weekly Boston newspaper, *Liberator,* from 1831 to 1865. The paper advocated women's rights, temperance, pacifism, and a variety of other reforms in addition to immediate emancipation.

84.29–30/117.17 an anti-slavery convention at Nantucket] A reference to the same abolitionist convention held at Atheneum Hall in Nantucket, Massachusetts, on 10–12 August 1841, that Garrison describes in his preface to the *Narrative.* Douglass spoke in favor of a resolution condemning northern white racial prejudice on 11 August. Douglass had earlier addressed antislavery meetings in New Bedford, Massachusetts.

85.24/118.26–119.1 "stealing . . . in."] Robert Pollok, *The Course of Time, a Poem* (Boston: Mussey, 1843), book 8, lines 616–18: "He was a man / Who stole the livery of the court of heaven, / To serve the Devil in."

87.4/120.13–28 Strength to the spoiler thine?] With minor punctuation changes, Douglass quotes the first four stanzas of John Greenleaf Whittier's 1835 poem "Clerical Oppressors." *Poetical Works of John Greenleaf Whittier,* 3:38–39.

87.6–26/121.1–30 "They bind . . . of hypocrisy and iniquity."] An adaptation of Jesus's denunciation of the scribes and Pharisees in Matthew 23:4–28.

88.18–19/123.4–6 "Shall I . . . a nation as this?"] Jeremiah 5:9, 29.

88.20/123.7–125.13 "A Parody] This parody of the popular hymn "Heavenly Union" is frequently attributed to Douglass himself. Yuval Taylor, ed., *I Was Born a Slave: An Anthology of Classic Slave Narratives,* 2 vols. (Chicago: Lawrence Hill Books, 1999), 1:599.

89.24/124.15 Bashan bull] A paraphrase of Psalms 22:12.

Notes

Introduction

1. John W. Blassingame et al., eds., *The Frederick Douglass Papers,* Series I: *Speeches, Debates, and Interviews,* 5 vols. (New Haven, Conn.: Yale University Press, 1979–92), 1:201.
2. Ibid.
3. The paucity of studies of nineteenth-century American criticism of autobiographies forces the interested student systematically to examine the magazines of the period and the collected essays on the literary critics active between 1800 and 1860. A brief overview of nineteenth-century English criticism of autobiographies can be found in Keith Rinehart, "The Victorian Approach to Autobiography," *Modern Philology* 51, no. 3 (1954): 177–86; and George P. Landow, ed., *Approaches to Victorian Autobiography* (Athens: Ohio University Press, 1979), 3–26, 39–63, 333–54. The most useful bibliography of works revealing the nature of autobiographies appears in James Olney, ed., *Autobiography: Essays Theoretical and Critical* (Princeton, N.J.: Princeton University Press, 1980).
4. C. Marius Barbeau, "Indian Captivities," *Proceedings of the American Philosophical Society* 94 (December 1950): 522–48; Richard Van Der Beets, "A Surfeit of Style: The Indian Captivity Narrative as Penny Dreadful," *Research Studies* 39, no. 4 (1971): 297–306; Roy Harvey Pearce, "The Significance of the Captivity Narrative," *American Literature* 19, no. 1 (1947): 1–20; Joseph Bruchac, "Black Autobiography in Africa and America," *Black Academy Review* 2, no. 2 (1971): 61–70; Mutulu K. Blasing, *The Art of Life: Studies in American Autobiographical Literature* (Austin: University of Texas Press, 1977); James Riley, *An Authentic Narrative of the Loss of the American Brig Commerce* (Hartford, Conn.: Judd, Loomis, 1836), iii–xiv; Eliza Bradley, *An Authentic Narrative of the Shipwreck and Sufferings of Mrs. Eliza Bradley* (Boston: George Clark, 1821); John W. Blassingame, *The Slave Community: Plantation Life in the Antebellum South,* rev. ed. (New York: Oxford University Press, 1979), 376–77.
5. Richard Van Der Beets, ed., *Held Captive by Indians: Selected Narratives, 1642–1836* (Knoxville: University of Tennessee Press, 1973), xi–xxxi.
6. Walter Graham, *Tory Criticism in the Quarterly Review, 1809–1853* (New York: Columbia University Press, 1921); William Charvat, *The Origins of American Critical Thought, 1810–1835* (1936; New York: A. S. Barnes, 1961), 1–26, 164–205; *Dic-*

tionary of National Biography, 21 vols. (London, 1921–22), 7:497–99; John Foster, *Essays in a Series of Letters* (New York: Robert Carter and Brothers, 1853), 66–81. The first edition of Foster's book was published in London in 1805. The American editions available to Douglass appeared in Hartford, Connecticut, 1807, 1844, 1845; Boston, 1811, 1833, 1839; Utica, New York, 1815; Andover, Massachusetts, 1826; and New York, 1835.

7. Foster, *Essays in a Series of Letters*, 69, 71–72, 73, 78.
8. Ibid., 76.
9. Ibid., 74.
10. *New York Review* 1 (October 1837): 475–76; 9 (October 1841): 531–33.
11. *New England Magazine* 5 (July 1833): 32–33; 9 (August 1835): 140–41; *New York Review* 7 (July 1840): 535–37; *North American Review* 10 (January 1820): 1–14.
12. *New York Review* 3 (October 1838): 403. See also *North American Review* 9 (June 1819): 58–59; *New York Review* 8 (January 1841): 1–50; Howard Helsinger, "Credence and Credibility: The Concern for Honesty in Victorian Autobiography," in Landow, *Approaches to Victorian Autobiography*, 39–63.
13. *North American Review* 54 (October 1844): 452–53.
14. *New England Magazine* 6 (June 1834): 497; *New York Review* 8 (January 1841): 1–50; *North American Review* 9 (June 1819): 58–59; 9 (October 1820): 341–43.
15. *New York Review* 3 (October 1838): 404.
16. *New England Magazine* 5 (July 1833): 31–33; *New York Review* 7 (July 1840): 535–37.
17. *North American Review* 7 (September 1818): 321.
18. Caleb Bingham, ed., *The Columbian Orator: Containing a Variety of Original and Selected Pieces, together with Rules; Calculated to Improve Youth and Others in the Ornamental and Useful Art of Eloquence* (1797; Boston: J. H. A. Frost, 1827), 65–68.
19. For examples of these autobiographical accounts, see John W. Blassingame, ed., *Slave Testimony: Two Centuries of Letters, Speeches, Interviews, and Autobiographies* (Baton Rouge: Louisiana State University Press, 1977), 128–64, 198–245, 690–95; Lydia Maria Child, "Charity Bowery," in *Liberty Bell* (Boston: American Anti-Slavery Society, 1839), 26–43; Isaac T. Hopper, "Story of a Fugitive," in *Liberty Bell* (Boston: Massachusetts Anti-Slavery Fair, 1843), 163–69; "Story of Anthony Gayle," in *The American Anti-Slavery Almanac, for 1838* (Boston: Isaac Knapp, 1838), 44; "The Conscientious Slave," in *The American Anti-Slavery Almanac, for 1843* (New York: American Anti-Slavery Society, 1843), 42–44; Lydia Maria Child, *Isaac T. Hopper: A True Life* (Boston: John P. Jewett, 1853).
20. *Frederick Douglass' Paper*, 29 April 1853; Blassingame et al., *Douglass Papers*, 1:42, 52, 75.
21. Theodore Dwight Weld, *American Slavery as It Is: Testimony of a Thousand Wit-*

nesses (New York: American Anti-Slavery Society, 1839), 9–10, 122; Blassingame et al., *Douglass Papers,* 1: 41, 51–52, 254, 279–81, 322, 485.

22. Weld, *American Slavery,* iv.
23. Blassingame, *Slave Testimony,* 145–50, 151–64, 213–16; Hopper, "Story of a Fugitive," 163–69.
24. Blassingame, *Slave Testimony,* 151, 158–59; *Frederick Douglass' Paper,* 25 November 1853.
25. *National Anti-Slavery Standard,* 22, 29 October, 12, 26 November, 3, 10, 24, 31 December 1840; 7 January, 4 February 1841.
26. *Liberator,* 9, 30 March 1838.
27. Richard Hildreth, ed., *Archy Moore, the White Slave; or, Memoirs of a Fugitive* (1856; New York: Negro Universities Press, 1969); Marion Wilson Starling, *The Slave Narrative: Its Place in American History* (Boston: G. K. Hall, 1981), 227–33.
28. *Liberator,* 9 March 1838. See also Starling, *Slave Narrative,* 115–17, 228–33; *Liberator,* 23 September 1838. See also *Narrative of James Williams, an American Slave, Who Was for Several Years a Driver on a Cotton Plantation in Alabama* (New York: American Anti-Slavery Society, 1838).
29. *Liberator,* 2 November 1838; *African Repository* 15 (June 1839): 161–63. See also *Narrative of the Life of Moses Grandy; Late a Slave in the United States of America,* ed. George Thompson (London: C. Gilpin, 1843), ii.
30. For a list of black autobiographies published between 1837 and 1845, see George P. Rawick, *From Sundown to Sunup: The Making of the Black Community* (Westport, Conn.: Greenwood Press, 1972), 179–89; Starling, *Slave Narrative,* 39–50. See also *The Interesting Narrative of the Life of Olaudah Equiano; or, Gustavus Vassa, the African* (1789; Dublin: Printed for the author, 1791), 1–2; Sidonie Smith, *Where I'm Bound: Patterns of Slavery and Freedom in Black American Autobiography* (Westport, Conn.: Greenwood Press, 1974), 3–27; Charles H. Nichols, *Many Thousand Gone: The Ex-Slaves' Account of Their Bondage and Freedom* (Leiden, Netherlands: E. J. Brill, 1963); Gilbert Osofsky, ed., *Puttin' on Ole Massa: The Slave Narratives of Henry Bibb, William Wells Brown, and Solomon Northup* (New York: Harper and Row, 1969), 9–44; Frances Smith Foster, *Witnessing Slavery: The Development of Ante-bellum Slave Narratives* (Westport, Conn.: Greenwood Press, 1979); Arna Bontemps, ed., *Great Slave Narratives* (Boston: Beacon Press, 1969), vii–xix; John F. Bayliss, ed., *Black Slave Narratives* (London: Collier Books, 1970), 7–21; Stephen Butterfield, *Black Autobiography in America* (Amherst: University of Massachusetts Press, 1974), 11–89; Charles H. Nichols, ed., *Black Men in Chains: Narratives by Escaped Slaves* (New York: Lawrence Hill, 1972), 9–24.
31. Stephen Clissold, *The Barbary Slaves* (London: Paul Elek, 1977); Blassingame,

Slave Community, 367–82; Riley, *Authentic Narrative*, x–xxii; Blassingame, *Slave Testimony*, xxxiv–xxxvii, 145–64.

32. *A Narrative of the Adventures and Escape of Moses Roper, from American Slavery* (Philadelphia: Merrihew and Gunn, 1838), 5, 7–8.
33. Blassingame et al., *Douglass Papers*, 1:37–38, 82, 88–89, 132–33.
34. Robert B. Stepto, *From Behind the Veil: A Study of Afro-American Narrative* (Urbana: University of Illinois Press, 1979), 4–5, 17–26.
35. Frederick Douglass, *Narrative* (Boston: American Anti-Slavery Society, 1845), iii, iv, v, vi, vii, xiv.
36. On kidnappings and renditions of fugitive slaves, see *National Anti-Slavery Standard*, 29 October 1840, 25 November 1841, 3 February, 15 August, 29 September, 13 October, 17, 24 November, 8, 15 December 1842, 2 February 1843, 9 May, 25 July, 26 September, 7 November 1844, 22 May 1845.
37. *North Star*, 7 January, 21 April, 29 September 1848; *National Anti-Slavery Standard*, 29 April 1847; *Liberator*, 20 June 6, 12, 19 September, 24, 31 October 1845, 2 January 1846, 12 November 1847, 24 May 1850. The foreign-language editions were: *Levensverhaal van Frederik Douglass, een' gewezen' slaaf (door hem zelven geschreven); Uit het Engelsch* (Rotterdam: H. A. Kramers, 1846); *Vie de Frédéric Douglass, escalve americain, écrite par lui-mème, traduite de l'anglais par S.-K. Parkes* (Paris: Pagnerre, 1848).
38. *Liberator*, 25 July 1845, 10 July 1846; Cork *Examiner*, 22 October 1845; *National Anti-Slavery Standard*, 4 December 1845; *British Friend*, 3:191 (December 1845); Bristol *Mercury*, 6 January 1846; *Anti-Slavery Bugle*, 9 January 1846; *Littell's Living Age* 9 (4 April 1846): 50; Newcastle *Guardian*, 11 July 1846.
39. Blassingame et al., *Douglass Papers*, 1:37–45, 76, 81–90, 109, 128, 132–33, 291, 399.
40. For an overview of the critical reception of books by nineteenth-century black authors, see Julian D. Mason, "The Critical Reception of American Negro Authors in American Magazines, 1800–1885" (Ph.D. diss., University of North Carolina, 1962).
41. *Liberator*, 23 May 1845; *National Anti-Slavery Standard*, 12 June 1845. See also Concord (N.H.) *Herald of Freedom*, 9 May 1845; Chicago *Western Citizen*, 19 June 1845.
42. *Liberator*, 6 June 1845; *National Anti-Slavery Standard*, 26 June 1845.
43. *Liberator*, 9, 23, 30 May 1845; *National Anti-Slavery Standard*, 5 June 1845.
44. Oberlin *Evangelist*, 29 April 1846; London *People's Journal*, 2 (1847): 302.
45. Massachusetts Anti-Slavery Society, *Fourteenth Annual Report* (Boston: Massachusetts Anti-Slavery Society, 1846), 44; *National Anti-Slavery Standard*, 12 June 1845.
46. Cork *Examiner*, 22 October 1845; *Chamber's Edinburgh Journal*, new ser., 5 (24

January 1846): 56; Newcastle *Guardian,* 11 July 1846. See also *New York Evangelist,* 26 June 1845; *Christian Freeman,* 29 May 1845.

47. Quoted in *Littell's Living Age* 8 (10 January 1846): 65.
48. *Courier* and *Transcript* quoted in Frederick Douglass, *Narrative* (Dublin: Webb and Chapman, 1846), cxxi; *Liberator,* 6 June 1845; *British Friend,* 3 (November 1845) 191. See also *Liberator,* 26 December 1845.
49. Quoted in *Liberator,* 28 November 1845; Douglass, *Narrative* (Dublin, 1846), cxxx–cxxxi. See also *British Friend* 3 (December 1845): 191.
50. *Religious Spectator,* n.d., as quoted in *Pennsylvania Freeman,* 31 July 1845; *National Anti-Slavery Standard,* 7 August 1845; New York *Tribune,* 10 June 1845.
51. Bristol *Mercury,* 6 January 1846, as quoted in *National Anti-Slavery Standard,* 5 March 1846; New York *Tribune,* 10 June 1845.
52. Quoted in *Pennsylvania Freeman,* 31 July 1845; *National Anti-Slavery Standard,* 7 August 1845. See also *New York Evangelist,* 26 June 1845.
53. Quoted in Douglass, *Narrative* (Dublin, 1846), cxxxii.
54. Quoted in *Littell's Living Age* 8 (10 January 1846): 64–65; New York *Tribune,* 6 June 1845.
55. *British Friend,* 3 (November 1845): 174; 3 (December 1845): 191; Newcastle *Guardian,* 11 July 1846. See also *Liberator,* 26 December 1845.
56. Lynn (Mass.) *Pioneer,* n.d., as quoted in *Liberator,* 30 May 1845; London *League,* n.d., as quoted in *Liberator,* 28 November 1845; Isaac Nelson, as quoted in Douglass, *Narrative* (Dublin, 1846), cxxxii; New York *Tribune,* 10 June 1845.
57. Wilson Armistead, *A Tribute for the Negro* (Manchester, Eng.: William Irwin, 1848), 455; *Liberator,* 6 June 1845. See also *National Anti-Slavery Standard,* 12 June 1845; New York *Tribune,* 10 June 1845; (London) *People's Journal* 2 (1847): 302–05.
58. Philadelphia *Elevator,* n.d., as quoted in *Liberator,* 15 August 1845.
59. Ibid., 26 September 1845, 15 May 1846.
60. Ibid., 18 May 1849.
61. Wilmington *Delaware Republican,* n.d., as quoted in *National Anti-Slavery Standard,* 25 December 1845.
62. *Liberator,* 27 February 1846.
63. Ibid., 20 February 1846.
64. *Narrative* (Dublin, 1846), ii–vi; Blassingame et al., *Douglass Papers,* 1:200–201.
65. Blassingame et al., *Douglass Papers,* 1:252.
66. *Liberator,* 15 May 1846; Benjamin Quarles, *Frederick Douglass* (Washington, D.C.: The Associated Publishers, 1948), 51.
67. *North Star,* 8 September 1848; 13 October 1848; 7 September 1849; *Liberator,* 14 September 1849; Blassingame, *Slave Testimony,* 48–57, 114–15.
68. Boston *Christian Examiner,* 47 (July 1849): 61–62.

69. Ibid., 80, 83, 93.
70. Ibid., 69–70.
71. Ibid., 74–75.
72. *North Star,* 3 August 1849.
73. Harriet Beecher Stowe, *A Key to Uncle Tom's Cabin; Presenting the Original Facts and Documents Upon Which the Story Is Founded* (Boston: John P. Jewett, 1853), 5, 16, 19.
74. *Southern Quarterly Review,* 24 (July 1853): 232–33.
75. *Graham's Magazine,* 42 (January 1853): 209–14; 42 (March 1853): 365.
76. *Frederick Douglass' Paper,* 25 February 1853; 4 March 1853.

Afterword

1. John Ernest, "Beyond Douglass and Jacobs," in *The Cambridge Companion to the African American Slave Narrative,* ed. Audrey A. Fisch (Cambridge: Cambridge University Press, 2007), 219–20.
2. An insightful examination of how students evaluate Douglass's typicality as a slave is Mark Higbee, "Frederick Douglass and the College Classroom," *Thought and Action: The NEA Higher Education Journal* 16, no. 1 (2000): 41–54.
3. John W. Blassingame, *Slave Testimony: Two Centuries of Letters, Speeches, Interviews, and Autobiographies* (Baton Rouge: Louisiana State University Press, 1977).
4. Harriet A. Jacobs, *Incidents in the Life of a Slave Girl, Written by Herself* (1861), ed. Jean Fagan Yellin (Cambridge, Mass.: Harvard University Press, 1987); Solomon Northup, *Twelve Years a Slave* (1853), ed. Sue Eakin and Joseph Logsdon (Baton Rouge: Louisiana State University Press, 1968); Charles Ball, *Fifty Years in Chains; or, The Life of an American Slave* (1859; rpt., Mineola, N.Y.: Dover, 2003); William Craft, *Running a Thousand Miles to Freedom; or, The Escape of William and Ellen Craft from Slavery* (1860), in *Great Slave Narratives,* ed. Arna Bontemps (Boston: Beacon Press, 1969).
5. For examples, see Marion Wilson Starling, *The Slave Narrative: Its Place in American History* (Boston: G. K. Hall, 1981); William L. Andrews, *To Tell a Free Story: The First Century of the African-American Autobiography, 1760–1865* (Urbana: University of Illinois Press, 1986); Charles T. Davis and Henry Louis Gates, Jr., eds., *The Slave's Narrative* (New York: Oxford University Press, 1991).
6. For example, see Rafia Zafar, "Introduction: Over-Exposed, Under-Exposed: Harriet Jacobs and *Incidents in the Life of a Slave Girl,*" in *Harriet Jacobs and "Incidents in the Life of a Slave Girl": New Critical Essays,* ed. Deborah Garfield and Rafia Zafar (Cambridge: Cambridge University Press, 1996), 4.
7. Starling, *Slave Narrative,* 249–93; Houston A. Baker, "Introduction," in *Narrative*

of the Life of Frederick Douglass, an American Slave (New York: Penguin, 1982), 15; Andrews, *To Tell a Free Story,* 138–40. Yolanda Pierce labels Douglass's first autobiography "the quintessential slave narrative." Pierce, "Redeeming Bondage: The Captivity Narrative and the Spiritual Autobiography in the African American Slave Narrative Tradition," in Fisch, *African American Slave Narrative,* 95.

8. See, among others, Audrey A. Fisch, *American Slaves in Victorian England: Abolitionist Politics in Popular Literature and Culture* (Cambridge: Cambridge University Press, 2000); Paul Giles, "Narrative Reversals and Power Exchanges: Frederick Douglass and British Culture," *American Literature* 73, no. 4 (2001): 779–810; Fionnghuala Sweeney, "The Republic of Letters: Frederick Douglass, Ireland and the Irish *Narratives,*" in *New Directions in Irish American History,* ed. Kevin Kenny (Madison: University of Wisconsin Press, 2003), 123–39.
9. Alan J. Rice and Martin Crawford, eds., *Liberating Sojourn: Frederick Douglass and Transatlantic Reform* (Athens: University of Georgia Press, 1999); Fionnghuala Sweeney, *Frederick Douglass and the Atlantic World* (Liverpool, Eng.: Liverpool University Press, 2007).
10. Historians actually follow the lead of none other than William Lloyd Garrison, who first called attention to this special attribute of Douglass's work in the preface he supplied to its original edition. William L. Andrews, ed., *The Oxford Frederick Douglass Reader* (New York: Oxford University Press, 1996), 8; Andrews, *To Tell a Free Story,* 143–44; John Stauffer, "Frederick Douglass' Self-Fashioning and the Making of a Representative American Man," in Fisch, *African American Slave Narrative,* 201–17. Scholars such as Dickson J. Preston, Henry Louis Gates, Jr., and John Stauffer have explored the *Narrative*'s accuracy to gain insight into Douglass's psychological development as the leading spokesperson for the enslaved. They view Douglass as having taken factual liberties with details in the *Narrative* in order to fashion a persona that served the antislavery movement. See Dickson J. Preston, *Young Frederick Douglass: The Maryland Years* (Baltimore, Md.: Johns Hopkins University Press, 1980), 110–11; Henry Louis Gates, Jr., *Figures in Black: Words, Signs, and the "Racial" Self* (New York: Oxford University Press, 1986), 115; Stauffer, "Frederick Douglass's Self-Fashioning," 201–17.
11. Douglass expands on the effect the "holiday" celebrations had upon slaves' psychology in Chapter 10 of his *Narrative.*
12. John W. Blassingame was one of the first scholars to pursue that line of analyzing Douglass's *Narrative;* see his book *The Slave Community: Plantation Life in the Antebellum South,* rev. ed. (1972; Baton Rouge: Louisiana State University Press, 1979), 115–26, 137–46. See also P. Sterling Stuckey, "Afterword: Frederick Douglass and W. E. B. DuBois on the Consciousness of the Enslaved," *Journal of African American History* 91, no. 1 (2006): 451–58; Jon D. Cruz, "Historicizing the Amer-

ican Cultural Turn: The Slave Narrative," *European Journal of Cultural Studies* 4, no. 3 (2001): 305–23.

13. Houston A. Baker, *Blues, Ideology, and Afro-American Literature: A Vernacular Theory* (Chicago: University of Chicago Press, 1984), 21.
14. Kimberly Drake, "Rewriting the American Self: Race, Gender, and Identity in the Autobiographies of Frederick Douglass and Harriet Jacobs," *MELUS: Multi-Ethnic Literature of the United States* 22, no. 4 (1997): 91–108; Jennifer Fleischner, *Mastering Slavery: Memory, Family, and Identity in Women's Slave Narratives* (New York: New York University Press, 1996); Fionnghuala Sweeney, "Domestic Institutions: Transatlantic Gender Politics and Economic Power in Frederick Douglass' Variant Narratives," *Slavery & Abolition* 23, no. 3 (2002): 59–72; Jean M. Humez, "Reading the Narrative of Sojourner Truth as a Collaborative Text," *Frontiers: A Journal of Women Studies* 16, no. 1 (1996): 29–52.
15. For example, see Sarah N. Roth, "'How a Slave Was Made a Man': Negotiating Black Violence and Masculinity in Antebellum Slave Narratives," *Slavery & Abolition* 28, no. 2 (2007): 255–75; Andrews, *To Tell a Free Story*, 161.
16. Winifred Morgan, "Gender-Related Differences in the Slave Narratives of Harriet Jacobs and Frederick Douglass," *American Studies* 35, no. 2 (1994): 73–94; Drake, "Rewriting the American Self," 91–108.
17. For a thorough discussion of the authenticity of Harriet Jacobs's slave narrative, see Jean Fagan Yellin's 1987 edited volume of Jacobs's *Incidents in the Life of a Slave Girl*, as well as Yellin's biography *Harriet Jacobs: A Life* (New York: Basic Civitas Books, 2004).
18. Annie L. Burton et al., *Women's Slave Narratives* (Mineola, N.Y.: Dover, 2006); William L. Andrews, ed., *Six Women's Slave Narratives* (New York: Oxford University Press, 1989); Charles J. Heglar, *Rethinking the Slave Narrative: Slave Marriage and the Narratives of Henry Bibb and William and Ellen Craft* (Westport, Conn.: Greenwood Press, 2001).
19. Reginald F. Davis, *Frederick Douglass: Precursor of Liberation Theology* (Macon, Ga.: Mercer University Press, 2005), 1–12; John Ernest, "Crisis and Faith in Douglass's Work," in *The Cambridge Companion to Frederick Douglass*, ed. Maurice S. Lee (Cambridge: Cambridge University Press, 2009), 60–72.
20. A. James Wohlpart, "Privatized Sentiment and the Institution of Christianity: Douglass's Ethical Stance in the *Narrative*," *American Transcendental Quarterly* 9, no. 3 (1995): 181–94; Thomas Peyser, "The Attack on Christianity in *Narrative of the Life of Frederick Douglass, an American Slave*," *The Explicator* 69, no. 2 (2011): 86–89; Zachary McLeod Hutchins, "Rejecting the Root: The Liberating, Anti-Christ Theology of Douglass's Narrative," *Nineteenth-Century Literature* 68, no. 3 (2014): 292–333.

21. Scott C. Williamson, *The Narrative Life: The Moral and Religious Thought of Frederick Douglass* (Macon, Ga.: Mercer University Press, 2002); Yolanda Pierce, *Hell without Fires: Slavery, Christianity, and the Antebellum Spiritual Narrative* (Gainesville: University Press of Florida, 2005): 3, 13, 39, 43–44; Pierce, "Redeeming Bondage," 98.
22. Houston A. Baker, *The Journey Back: Issues in Black Literature and Criticism* (Chicago: University of Chicago Press, 1980), 45; Lisa A. Sisco, "'Writing in the Spaces Left': Literacy as a Process of Becoming in the Narratives of Frederick Douglass," *American Transcendental Quarterly* 9, no. 3 (1995): 195–227; Daneen Wardrop, "'While I Am Writing': Webster's 1825 Spelling Book, the Ell, and Frederick Douglass's Positioning of Language," *African American Review* 32, no. 4 (1998): 649–60.
23. Gates, *Figures in Black,* 116–25; Robert B. Stepto, "Narration, Authentication, and Authorial Control in Frederick Douglass' *Narrative* of 1845," in *Afro-American Literature: The Reconstruction of Instruction,* ed. Robert B. Stepto and Dexter Fisher (New York: Modern Language Association, 1978), 178–91. Also see Robert B. Stepto, *From Behind the Veil: A Study of Afro-American Narrative* (Urbana: University of Illinois Press, 1979), 4–31; Morgan, "Gender-Related Difference in the Slave Narratives," 81–82.
24. Sundquist also set valuable directions for later scholars by connecting this theme in the *Narrative* to Douglass's other antebellum writing. Eric J. Sundquist, "Frederick Douglass: Literacy and Paternalism," *Raritan* 6, no. 2 (1986): 108–24. See also Andrews, *To Tell a Free Story,* 13–14, 102–3, 110–11.
25. For a critical assessment of the way scholars, educators, and public commentators have made use of Douglass's advocacy of literacy, see Wendy Ryden, "Conflicted Literacy: Frederick Douglass's Critical Model," *Journal of Basic Writing* 24, no. 1 (2005): 4–23.
26. The most influential statement of this position is Deborah E. McDowell, "In the First Place: Making Frederick Douglass and the Afro-American Narrative Tradition," in *African American Autobiography: A Collection of Critical Essays,* ed. William L. Andrews (Englewood, N.J.: Prentice Hall, 1993), 192–214. Also see Stepto, *From Behind the Veil,* 106.
27. Andrews, *To Tell a Free Story,* 272.
28. Elizabeth Ann Beaulieu, *Femininity Unfettered: The Emergence of the American Neo-Slave Narrative* (Chapel Hill: University of North Carolina Press, 1995); Neal A. Lester, "'Not my mother, not my sister, but it's me, O Lord, standing . . .': Alice Walker's 'The Child Who Favored Daughter' as Neo-Slave Narrative," *Studies in Short Fiction* 34, no. 3 (1997): 289–306; Cynthia S. Hamilton, "Revisions, Rememories and Exorcisms: Toni Morrison and the Slave Narrative," *Journal of Amer-*

ican Studies 30, no. 3 (1996): 429–45; Jeffrey D. Smith, *Slave Narrative Characters in Toni Morrison's "Tar Baby"* (Greensboro: University of North Carolina at Greensboro, 1997); Timothy L. Parrish, "Imagining Slavery: Toni Morrison and Charles Johnson," *Studies in American Fiction* 25, no. 1 (Spring 1997): 81–100; Lararie Smith, "Neo-Slave Narratives," in Fisch, *African American Slave Narratives,* 168–95.

Selected Bibliography

❀❀❀

Other Works by Frederick Douglass

Blassingame, John W., et al., eds. *The Frederick Douglass Papers.* 9 vols. New Haven, Conn.: Yale University Press, 1979–.

Foner, Philip S., ed. *Life and Writings of Frederick Douglass.* 5 vols. New York: International Publishers, 1950–75.

McKivigan, John R., and Heather L. Kaufman, eds. *In the Words of Frederick Douglass: Quotations from Liberty's Champion.* Ithaca, N.Y.: Cornell University Press, 2012.

Slave Narratives by Other Authors

Andrews, William L., and Henry Louis Gates, Jr., eds. *Slave Narratives.* New York: Literary Classics of the United States, 2000.

———. *Slave Narratives after Slavery.* New York: Oxford University Press, 2011.

Ball, Charles. *Slavery in the United States: A Narrative of the Life and Adventures of Charles Ball. . . .* New York: John S. Taylor, Brick Church Chapel, 1837.

———. *Fifty Years in Chains; or, The Life of an American Slave.* 1859. Reprint, Mineola, N.Y.: Dover, 2003.

Bayliss, John F., ed. *Black Slave Narratives.* London: Collier Books, 1970.

Bland, Sterling Lecater, Jr., ed. *African American Slave Narratives: An Anthology.* 3 vols. Westport, Conn.: Greenwood Press, 2001.

Blassingame, John W., ed. *Slave Testimony: Two Centuries of Letters, Speeches, Interviews, and Autobiographies.* Baton Rouge: Louisiana State University Press, 1977.

Bontemps, Arna, ed. *Great Slave Narratives.* Boston: Beacon Press, 1969.

Gates, Henry Louis, Jr., ed. *The Classic Slave Narratives.* New York: Penguin, 1987.

Grandy, Moses. *Narrative of the Life of Moses Grandy; Late a Slave in the United States of America.* Edited by George Thompson. London: C. Gilpin, 1843.

Grimes, William. *Life of William Grimes, the Runaway Slave.* Edited by William L. Andrews and Regina Mason. New York: Oxford University Press, 2008.

Jacobs, Harriet A. *Incidents in the Life of a Slave Girl, Written by Herself.* 1861. Edited by Jean Fagan Yellin. Cambridge, Mass.: Harvard University Press, 1987.

Nichols, Charles H., ed. *Black Men in Chains: Narratives by Escaped Slaves.* New York: Lawrence Hill, 1972.

Northup, Solomon. *Twelve Years a Slave.* London, 1853.

Osofsky, Gilbert, ed. *Puttin' on Ole Massa: The Slave Narratives of Henry Bibb, William Wells Brown, and Solomon Northup.* New York: Harper and Row, 1969.

Pennington, James W. C. *The Fugitive Blacksmith; or, Events in the History of James W. C. Pennington: Formerly a Slave; Pastor of a Presbyterian Church, New York; Formerly a Slave in the State of Maryland, United States.* London: Gilpin, 1850.

Roper, Moses. *A Narrative of the Adventures and Escape of Moses Roper, From American Slavery.* Philadelphia: Merrihew and Gunn, 1838.

Ward, Samuel R. *Autobiography of a Fugitive Negro: His Anti-Slavery Labours in the United States, Canada, & England.* London: J. Snow, 1855.

Scholarly Works on Douglass's *Narrative*

Brewton, Vince. "'Bold defiance took its place'—'Respect' and Self-Making in *Narrative of the Life of Frederick Douglass, an American Slave.*" *Mississippi Quarterly* 58, no. 3 (2005): 703–17.

Carson, Sharon. "Shaking the Foundation: Liberation Theology in *Narrative of the Life of Frederick Douglass.*" *Religion and Literature* 24, no. 2 (1992): 19–34.

Davis, Reginald F. *Frederick Douglass: Precursor of Liberation Theology.* Macon, Ga.: Mercer University Press, 2005.

DeLombard, Jeannine. "'Eye-Witness to the Cruelty': Southern Violence and Northern Testimony in Frederick Douglass's 1845 *Narrative.*" *American Literature* 73, no. 2 (2001): 245–75.

Dixon, Melvin. *Ride Out the Wilderness.* Chicago: University of Illinois Press, 1987.

Drake, Kimberly. "Rewriting the American Self: Race, Gender, and Identity in the Autobiographies of Frederick Douglass and Harriet Jacobs." *MELUS* 22, no. 4 (1997): 91–108.

Ferreira, Patricia J. "Frederick Douglass and the 1846 Dublin Edition of His Narrative." *New Hibernia Review* 5, no. 1 (2001): 53–67.

Giles, Paul. "Narrative Reversals and Power Exchanges: Frederick Douglass and British Culture." *American Literature* 73, no. 4 (2001): 779–810.

Hutchins, Zachary McLeod. "Rejecting the Root: The Liberating, Anti-Christ Theology of Douglass's *Narrative.*" *Nineteenth-Century Literature* 68, no. 3 (2014): 292–322.

Martin, Terry J. "'A Slave in Form . . . [But not] in Fact': Frederick Douglass and the Paradox of Transcendence." *Proteus* 12, no. 1 (1995): 1–4.

McDowell, Deborah E. "In the First Place: Making Frederick Douglass & the Afro-American Narrative Tradition." In *African American Autobiography: A Collection of Critical Essays,* edited by William L. Andrews, 192–214. Englewood, N.J.: Prentice Hall, 1993.

Morgan, Winifred. "Gender-Related Difference in the Slave Narratives of Harriet Jacobs and Frederick Douglass." *American Studies* 35, no. 2 (1994): 73–94.

Mullane, James Thomas. "The Road to 'I'dentity in *Narrative of the Life of Frederick Douglass, an American Slave.*" *CEA Critic* 57, no. 2 (1995): 26–40.

Peyser, Thomas. "The Attack on Christianity in *Narrative of the Life of Frederick Douglass, an American Slave.*" *The Explicator* 69, no. 2 (2011): 86–89.

Sisco, Lisa A. "'Writing in the Spaces Left': Literacy as a Process of Becoming in the Narratives of Frederick Douglass." *American Transcendental Quarterly* 9, no. 3 (1995): 195–227.

Sundquist, Eric, ed. *Frederick Douglass: New Literary and Historical Essays.* Cambridge: Cambridge University Press, 1991.

Sweeney, Fionnghuala. *Frederick Douglass and the Atlantic World.* Liverpool, Eng.: Liverpool University Press, 2007.

Yancy, George. "The Existential Dimensions of Frederick Douglass's Autobiographical Narrative: A Beauvoirian Examination." *Philosophy & Social Criticism* 28, no. 3 (2002): 297–320.

Scholarly Works on Other Slave Narratives

Andrews, William L. *To Tell a Free Story: The First Century of Afro-American Autobiography, 1760–1865.* Urbana: University of Illinois Press, 1986.

———. *African American Autobiography: A Collection of Critical Essays.* Englewood Cliffs, N.J.: Prentice Hall, 1993.

Baker, Houston A. *Blues, Ideology, and Afro-American Literature: A Vernacular Theory.* Chicago: University of Chicago Press, 1984.

Beaulieu, Elizabeth Ann. *Femininity Unfettered: The Emergence of the American Neo-Slave Narrative.* Chapel Hill: University of North Carolina Press, 1995.

Chaney, M. A. *Fugitive Vision: Slave Image and Black Identity in Antebellum Narrative.* Bloomington: Indiana University Press, 2008.

Cruz, Jon D. "Historicizing the American Cultural Turn: The Slave Narrative." *European Journal of Cultural Studies* 4, no. 3 (2001): 305–23.

Davis, Charles T., and Henry Louis Gates, Jr., eds. *The Slave's Narrative.* New York: Oxford University Press, 1991.

Ernest, John. *Resistance and Reformation in Nineteenth-Century African-American Literature: Brown, Wilson, Jacobs, Delany, Douglass, and Harper.* Jackson: University Press of Mississippi, 1995.

———. *Liberation Historiography: African American Writers and the Challenge of History, 1794–1861.* Chapel Hill: University of North Carolina Press, 2004.

Ferguson, Sally Ann H. "Christian Violence and the Slave Narrative." *American Literature* 68, no. 2 (1996): 297–320.

Fisch, Audrey A., ed. *The Cambridge Companion to the African American Slave Narrative.* Cambridge: Cambridge University Press, 2007.

Fleischner, Jennifer. *Mastering Slavery: Memory, Family, and Identity in Women's Slave Narratives.* New York: New York University Press. 1996.

Foster, Frances Smith. "'In Respect to Females . . . ': Differences in the Portrayals of Women by Male and Female Narrators." *Black American Literature Forum* 15, no. 2 (1981): 6–70.

———. *Witnessing Slavery: The Development of Ante-bellum Slave Narratives.* Westport, Conn.: Greenwood Press, 1979.

Fox-Genovese, Elizabeth. "My Statue, My Self: Autobiographical Writings of Afro-American Women." In *The Private Self: Theory and Practice of Women's Autobiographical Writings,* edited by Shari Benstock, 63–88. Chapel Hill: University of North Carolina Press, 1988.

Garfield, Deborah, and Refia Zabar, eds. *Harriet Jacobs and Incidents in the Life of a Slave Girl: New Critical Essays.* Cambridge: Cambridge University Press, 1996.

Gates, Henry Louis, Jr. *Figures in Black: Words, Signs, and the "Racial" Self.* New York: Oxford University Press, 1986.

Hamilton, Cynthia S. "Revisions, Rememories and Exorcisms: Toni Morrison and the Slave Narrative." *Journal of American Studies* 30, no. 3 (1996): 429–45.

Heglar, Charles J. *Rethinking the Slave Narrative: Slave Marriage and the Narratives of Henry Bibb and William and Ellen Craft.* Westport, Conn.: Greenwood Press, 2001.

Humez, Jean M., "Reading *The Narrative of Sojourner Truth* as a Collaborative Text." *Frontiers: A Journal of Women Studies* 16, no. 1 (1996): 29–52.

Johnson, Yvonne. *The Voices of African American Women: The Use of Narrative and Authorial Voice in the Works of Harriet Jacobs, Zora Neale Hurston, and Alice Walker.* New York: Peter Lang, 1998.

Kawash, Samira. *Dislocating the Color Line: Identity, Hybridity, and Singularity in African-American Narrative.* Stanford, Calif.: Stanford University Press, 1997.

Lee, Julia Sun-Yoo. *The American Slave Narrative and the Victorian Novel.* New York: Oxford University Press, 2010.

Lester, Neal A. "'Not my mother, not my sister, but it's me, O Lord, standing . . .': Alice Walker's 'The Child Who Favored Daughter' as Neo-Slave Narrative." *Studies in Short Fiction* 34, no. 3 (1997): 289–306.

Lock, Helen. "The Paradox of Slave Mutiny in Herman Melville, Charles Johnson, and Frederick Douglass." *College Literature* 30, no. 4 (2003): 54–70.

Morgenstern, Naomi. "Mother's Milk and Sister's Blood: Trauma and the Neoslave Narrative." *Differences: A Journal of Feminist Cultural Studies* 8, no. 2 (1996): 101–26.
Pierce, Yolanda. *Hell without Fires: Slavery, Christianity, and the Antebellum Spiritual Narrative.* Gainesville: University Press of Florida, 2005.
Roth, Sarah N. "'How a Slave was made a Man': Negotiating Black Violence and Masculinity in Antebellum Slave Narratives." *Slavery & Abolition* 28, no. 2 (2007): 255–75.
Sekora, John, and Darwin T. Turner, eds. *The Art of Slave Narrative: Original Essays in Criticism and Theory.* Macomb: Western Illinois University, 1982.
Smith, Valerie. *Self-Discovery and Authority in Afro-American Narrative.* Cambridge, Mass.: Harvard University Press, 1987.
Starling, Marion Wilson. *The Slave Narrative: Its Place in American History.* Boston: G. K. Hall, 1981.
Stepto, Robert B. *From Behind the Veil: A Study of Afro-American Narrative.* Urbana: University of Illinois Press, 1979.
Sterling, Dorothy, ed. *We Are Your Sister: Black Women in the Nineteenth Century.* New York: W. W. Norton, 1984.
Twagilimana, Aimable. *Race and Gender in the Making of an African American Literary Tradition.* New York: Garland, 1997.
Yellin, Jean Fagan. *Harriet Jacobs: A Life.* New York: Basic Civitas Books, 2004.

Teaching Douglass

Adisa, Opal Palmer. "Frederick Douglass & the Value of My Life." *Teachers & Writers* 27, no. 3 (1996): 5–9.
Brown, Wesley. *The Teachers & Writers Guide to Frederick Douglass.* New York: Teachers & Writers Collaborative, 1996.
Davis, Jordan, et al. "14 Writing Ideas Using Douglass' *Narrative.*" *Teachers & Writers* 27, no. 3 (1996): 3–4.
Fabian, Ann. *The Unvarnished Truth: Personal Narratives in Nineteenth-Century America.* Berkeley: University of California Press, 2000.
Hall, James C. *Approaches to Teaching "Narrative of the Life of Frederick Douglass."* New York: Modern Language Association of America, 1999.
Higbee, Mark. "Frederick Douglass and the College Classroom." *Thought and Action: The NEA Higher Education Journal* 16, no. 1 (2000): 41–54.
Kuner, Charles. "Using Douglass' *Narrative* to Inspire Student Writing." *Teachers & Writers* 27, no. 3 (1996): 1–3.
Rodriquez, Louis, and Maria Sanelli. *Teaching about Frederick Douglass: A Resource Guide for Teachers of Cultural Diversity.* New York: Peter Lang, 2012.

Ryden, Wendy. "Conflicting Literacy: Frederick Douglass's Critical Model." *Journal of Basic Writing* 24, no. 1 (2005): 4–23.

Frederick Douglass Scholarship

Andrews, William L., ed., *The Oxford Frederick Douglass Reader.* New York: Oxford University Press, 1996.

Bennett, Evelyn. *Frederick Douglass and the War against Slavery.* Brookfield, Conn.: Millbrook Press, 1993.

Blight, David W. *Frederick Douglass's Civil War: Keeping the Faith in Jubilee.* Baton Rouge: Louisiana State University Press, 1989.

Dietrich, Maria. *Love across Color Lines: Ottilie Asking & Frederick Douglass.* New York: Hill and Wang, 1999.

Foner, Philip S. *Frederick Douglass.* New York: Citadel Press, 1950.

Gregory, James M. *Frederick Douglass, the Orator.* 1893. Reprint, New York: Apollo Editions, 1971.

Huggins, Nathan Irvin. *Slave and Citizen: The Life of Frederick Douglass.* Edited by Oscar Handlin. Boston: Little, Brown, 1980.

Keenan, Sheila. *Frederick Douglass: Portrait of a Freedom Fighter.* New York: Scholastic, 1995.

Larson, Bill, and Frank Kirkland, eds. *Frederick Douglass: A Critical Reader.* New York: Wiley-Blackwell, 1999.

Lee, Maurice S., ed. *The Cambridge Companion to Frederick Douglass.* Cambridge: Cambridge University Press, 2009.

Levine, Robert S. *Martin Delany, Frederick Douglass, and the Politics of Representative Identity.* Chapel Hill: University of North Carolina Press, 1997.

Martin, Waldo E., Jr. *The Mind of Frederick Douglass.* Chapel Hill: University of North Carolina Press, 1984.

McFeely, William S. *Frederick Douglass.* New York: W. W. Norton, 1991.

McKissack, Patricia, and Fredrick McKissack. *Frederick Douglass: The Black Lion.* Chicago: Children's Press, 1987.

Myers, Peter C. *Frederick Douglass: Race and the Rebirth of American Liberalism.* Lawrence: University of Kansas Press, 2008.

Miller, Douglass T. *Frederick Douglass and the Fight for Freedom.* New York: Facts on File, 1988.

Oakes, James. *The Radical and the Republican: Frederick Douglass, Abraham Lincoln, and the Triumph of Antislavery Politics.* New York: W. W. Norton, 2007.

Preston, Dickson J. *Young Frederick Douglass: The Maryland Years.* Baltimore, Md.: Johns Hopkins University Press, 1980.

Quarles, Benjamin. *Frederick Douglass.* Washington, D.C.: The Associated Publishers, 1948.

Rice, Alan J., and Martin Crawford. *Liberating Sojourn: Frederick Douglass & Transatlantic Reform.* Athens: University of Georgia Press, 1999.

Russell, Sharman Apt. *Frederick Douglass.* New York: Chelsea House, 1988.

Stauffer, John. *Giants: The Parallel Lives of Frederick Douglass and Abraham Lincoln.* New York: Twelve Publishers, 2009.

Sweeney, Fionnghuala. *Frederick Douglass and the Atlantic World.* Liverpool, Eng.: Liverpool University Press, 2007.

Voss, Frederick S. *Majestic in His Wrath: A Pictorial Life of Frederick Douglass.* Washington, D.C.: Smithsonian Institution Press, 1995.

Washington, Booker T. *Frederick Douglass.* Philadelphia: George W. Jacobs, 1906.

Williamson, Scott C. *The Narrative Life: The Moral and Religious Thought of Frederick Douglass.* Macon, Ga.: Mercer University Press, 2002.

General Studies of Abolition

Aptheker, Herbert. *Abolitionism: A Revolutionary Movement.* Boston: Twayne, 1989.

Dillon, Merton L. *The Abolitionists: The Growth of a Dissenting Minority.* DeKalb: Northern Illinois University Press, 1974.

Dumond, Dwight Lowell. *Antislavery: The Crusade for Freedom in America.* Ann Arbor: University of Michigan Press, 1961.

Fisch, Audrey A. *American Slaves in Victorian England: Abolitionist Politics in Popular Literature and Culture.* Cambridge: Cambridge University Press, 2000.

Gara, Larry. "The Professional Fugitive in the Abolition Movement." *Wisconsin Magazine of History* 48, no. 3 (1965): 196–204.

Grover, Kathryn. *The Fugitive's Gibraltar: Escaping Slaves and Abolitionism in New Bedford, Massachusetts.* Amherst: University of Massachusetts Press, 2001.

Harold, Stanley. *American Abolitionists.* Harlow, Eng.: Longman, 2001.

Hinks, Peter P. *To Awaken My Afflicted Brethren: David Walker and the Problem of Antebellum Slave Resistance.* University Park: Pennsylvania State University Press, 1997.

Jeffrey, Julie Roy. *The Great Silent Army of Abolitionism: Ordinary Women in the Antislavery Movement.* Chapel Hill: University of North Carolina Press, 1998.

Mabee, Carleton. *Black Freedom: The Nonviolent Abolitionists from 1830 through the Civil War.* [New York]: Macmillan, 1970.

Pease, Jane H., and William H. Pease. *They Who Would Be Free: Blacks' Search for Freedom, 1830–1861.* New York: Atheneum, 1974.

Robertson, Stacey. *Hearts Beating for Liberty: Women Abolitionists in the Old Northwest.* Chapel Hill: University of North Carolina Press, 2010.

Stauffer, John. *The Black Hearts of Men: Radical Abolitionists and the Transformation of Race.* Cambridge, Mass.: Harvard University Press, 2002.

Stewart, James Brewer. *Holy Warriors: The Abolitionists and American Slavery.* New York: Hill and Wang, 1976.

Thomas, John L. "Romantic Reform in America, 1815–1865." *American Quarterly* 17, no. 4 (1965): 656–81.

General Studies of Slavery

Bay, Mia. *The White Image in the Black Mind: African American Ideas about White People, 1830–1925.* New York: Oxford University Press, 2000.

Berlin, Ira. *Generations of Captivity: A History of African-American Slaves.* Cambridge, Mass.: Belknap Press of Harvard University Press, 2004.

———. *Many Thousands Gone: The First Two Centuries of Slavery in North America.* Cambridge, Mass.: Belknap Press of Harvard University Press, 1998.

Blassingame, John W. *The Slave Community: Plantation Life in the Antebellum South.* Rev. ed. New York: Oxford University Press, 1979.

Camp, Stephanie M. H. *Closer to Freedom: Enslaved Women & Everyday Resistance in the Plantation South.* Chapel Hill: University of North Carolina Press, 2004.

Davis, David Brion. *Inhuman Bondage: The Rise and Fall of Slavery in the New World.* New York: Oxford University Press, 2006.

Fields, Barbara Jeanne. *Slavery and Freedom on the Middle Ground: Maryland during the Nineteenth Century.* New Haven, Conn.: Yale University Press, 1985.

Fogel, Robert W. *Without Consent or Contract: The Rise and Fall of American Slavery.* 2 vols. New York: W. W. Norton, 1992.

Frey, Sylvia R., and Betty Wood. *Come Shouting to Zion: African American Protestantism in the American South and the British Caribbean to 1830.* Chapel Hill: University of North Carolina Press, 1998.

Kolchin, Peter. *American Slavery, 1619–1877.* New York: Hill and Wang, 1993.

Miles, Tiya. *Ties That Bind: The Story of an Afro-Cherokee Family in Slavery and Freedom.* Berkeley: University of California Press, 2005.

Roth, Sarah N. *Gender and Race in Antebellum Popular Culture.* New York: Cambridge University Press, 2014.

Starobin, Robert S. *Industrial Slavery in the Old South.* New York: Oxford University Press, 1970.

Stevenson, Brenda E. *Life in Black and White: Family and Community in the Slave South.* New York: Oxford University Press, 1997.

Tise, Larry E. *Proslavery: A History of the Defense of Slavery in America, 1701–1840.* Athens: University of Georgia Press, 1987.

Wade, Richard C. *Slavery in the Cities: The South, 1820–1860.* New York: Oxford University Press, 1964.

White, Deborah Gray. *Ar'n't I a Woman? Female Slaves in the Plantation South.* New York: W. W. Norton, 1985.

Scholarship about Free Blacks

Alexander, Leslie M. *African or American? Black Identity and Political Activism in New York City, 1784–1861.* Urbana: University of Illinois Press, 2008.

Berlin, Ira. *Slaves without Masters: The Free Negro in the Antebellum South.* New York: Pantheon, 1974.

Blackett, R. J. M. *Building an Antislavery Wall: Black Americans in the Atlantic Abolitionist Movement, 1830–1860.* Baton Rouge: Louisiana State University Press, 1983.

Desrochers, Robert E. "'Not Fade Away': The Narrative of Venture Smith, an African American in the Early Republic." *Journal of American History* 84, no. 1 (1997): 40–66.

Foner, Eric. *Gateway to Freedom: The Hidden History of the Underground Railroad.* New York: W. W. Norton, 2015.

Fredrickson, George M. *The Black Image in the White Mind: The Debate on Afro-American Character and Destiny, 1817–1914.* New York: Harper and Row, 1971.

Horton, James O., and Lois E. Horton. *In Hope of Liberty: Culture, Community, and Protest among Northern Free Blacks, 1700–1860.* New York: Oxford University Press, 1997.

Jones, Martha S. *All Bound Up Together: The Woman Question in African American Public Culture, 1830–1900.* Chapel Hill: University of North Carolina Press, 2007.

Kantrowitz, Stephen D. *More Than Freedom: Fighting for Black Citizenship in a White Republic, 1829–1889.* New York: Penguin, 2012.

King, Wilma. *The Essence of Liberty: Free Black Women during the Slave Era.* Columbia: University of Missouri Press, 2006.

LaRoche, Cheryl J. *Free Black Communities and the Underground Railroad: The Geography of Resistance.* Urbana: University of Illinois Press, 2013.

Litwack, Leon. *North of Slavery: The Negro in the Free States, 1790–1860.* Chicago: University of Chicago Press, 1961.

Nash, Gary B. *Forging Freedom: The Formation of Philadelphia's Black Community, 1720–1840.* Cambridge, Mass: Harvard University Press, 1988.

Quarles, Benjamin. *Black Abolitionists.* New York: Oxford University Press, 1969.

Index